MEMOIRS OF
SIR MICHAEL OGDEN, QC

MEMOIRS OF SIR MICHAEL OGDEN, QC

Variety is the Spice of Legal Life

The Book Guild Ltd
Sussex, England

First published in Great Britain in 2002 by
The Book Guild Ltd
25 High Street,
Lewes, East Sussex
BN7 2LU

Typesetting in Times by
Keyboard Services, Luton, Bedfordshire

Printed in Great Britain by
Bookcraft (Bath) Ltd, Avon

A catalogue record for this book is available from
The British Library

ISBN 1 85776 608 3

To my long-suffering family

CONTENTS

INTRODUCTION

I started to write these memoirs in January 1999 just after I ceased to be Treasurer of Lincoln's Inn. The fact that it has taken between then and now to complete them is simply an indication of my folly in thinking that I would have lots of spare time once I had retired. I have found that once I have got up, had breakfast and read *The Times* it appears to be 10 or later, which does not leave an awful lot of time to deal with one's correspondence let alone to write this.

I have written it partly for my own amusement and partly because I think that it may be of interest to my children and grandchildren and it was certainly not my intention to seek to publish it generally. However, both publishers whom I approached to publish it privately encouraged me to do it more widely. I consulted an old friend, Sir Philip Otton, a retired Court of Appeal judge, and he said the same thing. Consequently, he must share the blame if general readers, if there are any, find it boring!

London, August 2001

1

THE FAMILY

I put off writing this chapter until I had written all the rest because I was confident that it would be a very boring thing to do; indeed, I am really only doing it because of having bullying middle-aged children who insist upon it. Any sensible reader will skim over it as quickly as possible and go on to Chapter Two.

What I will do is to recite in a nutshell what I understand of the history of my family.

The name Ogden is rare in the south of England but very common in the north-west. The name originated from Oakden or Oakdene, meaning a vale of oaks. The family originated in Butterworth in the Lake District. It appears to have been well off and can probably be described as country gentry, the family having allegedly been granted a coat of arms by Charles II. This needs to be treated with considerable caution, particularly since I have grave reservations about my grandmother Margaret Cannon Mordaunt, who died long before I was born but about whom I get an impression that she had a fertile imagination so far as our ancestors were concerned.

During the Industrial Revolution one of them had the good sense to move down and founded Ogden's Bank Top Mill in Oldham. About 30 years ago I saw the building still described as 'Ogdens Bank Top Mill'. How he acquired the money to do this I do not know but, plainly, it proved very well worthwhile. Edward Ogden was born in 1823 and was twice married. I know nothing of the issue, if any, of the first marriage but he married Margaret Cannon Mordaunt in 1866. The Mordaunts were a well-known family, one of whom had assisted William III when he managed to seize the English throne, for which services he was created Earl of Peterborough. The branch of the family into which

Edward Ogden married was a prominent Liverpool shipbuilding family and so the two between them were possessed of considerable assets. Very prudently, they sold the mill and the shipbuilding business and in due course moved to the Isle of Man.

I do not know at what stage the family moved down south but my father was educated at Bedford College and Heidelberg University, although I doubt whether he did very much work at the latter establishment. Thereafter he lived in London. My grandmother was called Margaret Cannon because the Mordaunts had intermarried with the Cannons at some stage and this name duly got passed on to my father.

The Parrises were an old family who appear to have originated in Essex. I know virtually nothing about them, partly, doubtless, because my mother lost both her parents when she was young and if she knew much about the family, she certainly did not pass it on to me. My overall impression is that both the Ogdens and the Parrises were old families who were moderately affluent but undistinguished. Certainly, apart from the Mordaunt who helped to bring over William III and whose ancestry can be traced back to the Normans, none of them appears to have figured in history to any significant extent.

2

EARLY YEARS

It was on 9 April 1926 that the event of world-shattering importance occurred. I was born in Hill Street, near Harrods. In 1960, when looking for a new house because the one in Elizabeth Street was too small for three children, we were sent by an estate agent to look at it. At the time, we did not realise that it was the same house because its name had been changed to Trevor Street, doubtless to avoid confusion with Hill Street in Mayfair. We learnt about this only when recounting to my mother how our search was getting on. It was just as well that I did not know, because it might have affected my judgement; it would have been unsuitable in that it was much like Elizabeth Street and parking problems would have been appalling even then.

My mother told my wife Joan that my cousin Thecla had been to look at me and remarked, 'So this is the famous Michael.' This was not an example of second sight but may well have been due to the fact that until my father married quite late in life, since my uncle Mordaunt never married – although it is thought that he lived with a mistress – she would have inherited both their estates. As can be seen from photographs of her, she was a very attractive woman and men were duly attracted to her. She married four times. Her father, Reginald Barker, was a stockbroker who was foolish enough to speculate on the Exchange and was hammered. Thecla, like her mother Adelaide, was feckless and they were always in financial difficulties. However, her fourth husband, Tyrwhitt-Drake, was a wealthy man with a large estate in Surrey, who had been an admirer since before her first marriage. By her first husband, she had a daughter, Margot, who died when a child and by her second husband, an American named Robert Pell III, who must have had money because of the III, she had a son, Anthony, whom I met only once and disliked on sight. I know nothing of her third husband, de Savitsch. If this sounds strange, it is because my mother was a very secretive woman who imparted little information about family affairs.

When I was aged three, we moved down to Hove. Number 12 Fourth Avenue, where I spent the rest of my childhood, was a large, square house with a basement and three floors above. When I looked at it in the 1980s, it had been converted into nine flats. In the basement lived the chauffeur/butler and his wife, who cleaned the steps etc, outside and kept the boiler going. On the ground floor there was a large drawing room and dining room and the kitchens together with a pantry and staff sitting room over the garage, which contained a stately bottle-green Rolls-Royce (they were comparatively cheap then!). On the first floor there were two large bedrooms and one small, and my father's study. On the top floor was a large nursery and the children's bedroom. There were two other bedrooms, one in the attic, for staff. There was a bathroom on the first floor and another on the second.

The living-in staff in my early years consisted of a cook, maid, nanny and, after my brother's birth an under-nanny. I cannot recollect how they all fitted into the available bedrooms. Of course, there were other people who came to the house for various purposes, such as a clock-winder, who came once a week, and a barber, who came to shave my father. Miss Kendall was a woman who came once a week to do mending and make things such as curtains. She was still doing so when my daughter Celia was born and made a complete set of baby clothes, which included items of a Victorian nature, such as a stomacher, which was meant to be wound round a baby's stomach. She was fully employed for the entire day when she came because garments were all repaired rather than being thrown away; for example, all socks were darned. As a result, at the time of my marriage, I was still wearing some of my father's underclothes and to this day I possess a large number of his dress shirts, which I continue to wear.

In retrospcct, thcrc was a lot of petty crime involving some of these people. The chauffeur was dismissed after he stole a large and expensive car rug. On another occasion, when the police investigated a theft, it was discovered that both the clock-winder and the window cleaner had convictions for dishonesty.

My brother John, who was born in 1929, and I lived, as was then the custom, in what was virtually a separate household with our nanny, Nurse Burchett, and the under-nanny, Kitty Delaney, who was probably no more than sixteen when she came to us from western Ireland. We ate our meals in our nursery, the food being hauled up from the basement by a lift hoist. They were good nannies and we led happy lives.

Of course, we saw far less of our parents than do children to-day. I was told by my mother that, after breakfast, I was allowed to play in my father's study while he read the paper. One day, I started to read out the letters in his paper; I must have asked nanny about them. This horrified my father, who said that I would damage my brain if I persisted. I regret his decision; I am sure that it would have helped if I had taught myself to read earlier. After that, it was time to go out. Apparently, my father would stand, watch in hand, and shout upstairs if we had not left the house by nine. This outing would be cancelled only in the direst weather. It reminds me of games at Downside; except for the two afternoons a week spent on military training, we had to play games every day. We were only let off, if that is the right expression, if the ground was so water-logged that it was feared that we might damage the playing fields. On those occasions we were sent on a cross-country run. I should add that in Somerset the rain always seemed to fall horizontally and always straight into one's face.

After lunch, we were obliged to rest in bed but, after tea, we were allowed to go down to the drawing room until bed-time. These were the days when mah-jong was the smart game and, sometimes, there might be as many as six tables of players. Doubtless, we saw more of our parents than my account seems to suggest, but that was the bare bones of our days.

In retrospect, I suspect my parents had moved to Hove because of my father's health. My mother said that he died of cancer exactly where he had fractured his back when a passenger in a car that went over a hump-backed bridge. Since both my brother and I suffer from osteoporosis, I have no doubt that he did too, hence the fracture. In those days the disease was untreatable and fatal; I doubt whether even its existence was known. But for a magic pill, I would have died years ago.

My father was a middle-aged bachelor when he married. He

never worked, which was then quite respectable. If required to state one's occupation one wrote 'of independent means', as is stated on my birth certificate. Since many men were in the same position, they had a jolly time, although it would have driven me mad, but since they had never worked they doubtless took their life style for granted. He was very good at billiards and I think was runner-up in the amateur championship. He was also very good at golf, and the house contained a number of golfing cups, clocks and medals. I have a framed drawing by the famous caricaturist, Harry Furness, who has shown himself in the drawing. It is entitled *How Ogden Won*, and my father can be seen about to hit a ball in pouring rain and smoking a pipe. It is dated 1907. When my grandson, Guillaume, was staying with us for Christmas in 1998, he drew a remarkably good sketch of this drawing, which I have had framed and put in my study under the original.

It is obvious that my father was a very jolly and popular man. I have what can best be described as a strip cartoon set at a golf club dinner. There is a throng round a bar and a newcomer says, 'Where's Oggie?' From the midst of the throng a voice from an unseen person says, 'Here I am.' The strip ends, 'And so to bed in a revolving taxi.' Since my mother used to say that 'drink is the curse of the Ogdens', I assume that he drank as much as I have always done.

As is well-known, the Victorians ate large meals and the habit of having large cooked breakfasts still existed in my father's day. Indeed, it persisted even when our children were young. Thus before they went to school Joan would provide them with orange juice, cereal and then a cooked dish such as scrambled egg, sausages, kippers, poached eggs, etc. When my father married, he told my mother, 'You don't have to worry about breakfast for me. All I have is a sole or a plaice or something like that together with a pot of coffee, followed by a steak or a chop or something like that with another pot of coffee.' My mother told Joan, 'Within two weeks I had him on Shredded Wheat.' It must have been a terrible shock for a rather late-marrying bachelor.

Of course, he knew little about domestic affairs. When the move to our house in Fourth Avenue took place, he went off to his club. He arrived at the new house in the evening. My mother, who had had an exhausting day, met him as he came up the front steps. 'Has the ice arrived, dear?' were his opening and very nearly his last words. One of my earliest 'snapshot' recollections was standing on the other side of the street looking at the house in which we were going to live, which was covered in scaffolding. John, who had just been born, was in a large stately pram, pushed by nanny.

When they went on holiday, they tended to rent a house in the country. It was a major operation. Linen and silver were taken as a matter of course and the armchair in which he used to sit travelled covered up on the top of the Rolls.

Like many men, at the time of his marriage he had friends of whom my mother disapproved. The one who particularly comes to mind was my godfather, Henry Gilbey. He was a member of the drinks family, but, since the two founders had about fourteen children, he was impecunious. Consequently, he married an heiress, who was a niece of the Duke of Alba. Unfortunately, Lola got religious mania and gave away all her money to convents and spent her life doing the rounds staying with them. Once, on the steps of Brompton Oratory after attending Mass, dressed in black stockings and an old black overcoat held together with a safety pin, she was offered sixpence, being mistaken for a pauper. Henry had led a rackety life. On one occasion, having been to a party in London, he woke up in Liverpool about a week later, wearing someone else's clothes, with no recollection of the interim. Since he also had no money, he had to go for assistance to a Gilbey's off-licence. In 1945, when I was at Sandhurst, I visited him at his bedsit in the Cromwell Road. During the war, drink other than beer was in very short supply. However, being a Gilbey, he was able to pull out a case from under his bed and, obviously unable to concentrate on both talking and pouring, he filled an enamel tooth mug, of the kind which one had at school, to the very brim with sherry; it did not do me much good.

On another occasion I visited him at the RAC Club without notice, since I knew that he was always there in the morning. As I entered, he was crossing the hall. I greeted him but he replied in a rather distant fashion. After a few moments, he suddenly interrupted me, saying, 'Good gracious, you're my godson –

thought you were my nephew. Come and have a drink.' I liked him; he was amusing and not patronising, but I can understand why my mother disapproved of him.

Another godfather was Professor Henry Spooner, a professor of engineering – not, alas, the originator of spoonerisms, e.g. 'I have boiled my icicle.' On the only occasion that I can remember meeting him, he presented me with a paperback copy of a book which he had written, entitled *Origin, Rise and Progress of the Science of Geometry and Mathematics*. Being aged thirteen, I was hardly thrilled. How he became my godfather, I do not know.

My father was well-travelled, which was unusual in those days. Not only had he been a student at Heidelberg University, but in 1911 he made a trip round the world, and I have small album of photographs, including fancy-dress parties, at which he was obviously enjoying himself.

My mother, Daisy – her only Christian name and one which she hated – had a chequered childhood. She was born in 1891, the daughter of George White Parris and Florence Habben. She was not forthcoming about many things; in retrospect, she appeared to have worked on a 'need to know' basis. There was no particular reason for this, which extended to everything, it was simply her nature. As a result, I am not well informed about much of her life. Her father died when she was young and her mother remarried – I do not know the man's name. He lived in Streatham and bred carriage horses. My mother said that he was very fond of her and it must have been a severe blow when he, too, died. She had a brother and three sisters and, at some stage, whether before or after her mother's death I do not know, the children were separated from each other. My mother went to live with her unmarried aunt, Rosa Habben. I met her on a few occasions that I can recollect and was rather in awe of her. This was because, to my childish eyes, she looked rather like a small frog wearing heavy spectacles. However, my mother always spoke of her in terms of affection.

I have the impression that they lived in rather genteel poverty or close to it. I have no idea how she came to meet my father, who lived in much more affluent circumstances. She told my wife that at a party, my father, then apparently a confirmed bachelor, had been asked by a friend some question about marriage, to which he replied, 'I'm going to marry that pretty dark-haired girl over there,' a fact which he had not at that time communicated to my mother.

Fortunately, neither John nor I had difficult relations with her at any time. She was not a demonstrative woman but very kind. She was also very charitable. Her brother Horace had been sent to sea in the Merchant Navy. He was nice but rather ineffectual. My mother paid for his two daughters to go to boarding school. I never met my aunt May, who died young. Her three other sisters were Violet, Gladys and Rita. My mother bought a house for one of them – Violet, I think – in which she and her husband lived for the rest of their lives.

At Christmas, they all came to stay with us. Gladys had two sons, Bruce and Geoffrey Tulloch, whom I remember without great enthusiasm; they were colourless characters. Horace had two daughters, Patricia and Jeanne. I can hardly remember the latter, but the former, who was about my age, is very nice and I continue to see her occasionally. All these aunts seemed to me to be very silly, Rita particularly so. She was the youngest and, when young, was unwise enough to say at a family dinner party that one was on the shelf at thirty. When she achieved that age, she received a number of appropriate birthday cards from other members of the family. Far worse for her were the consequences of a remark made at my father's table while drinking champagne. She said that she could not tell the difference between it and lemonade. According to my mother, my father arranged that on all occasions when champagne was served, she should be given lemonade. I suspect that this did not go on for ever.

I never met my uncle Frederick William, who, for some reason unknown to me, was called Mordaunt, his mother's maiden name. Long before my birth, he travelled to Liverpool to see Adelaide and Thecla off for a visit to America. He then vanished. Only the family solicitor, Sir Gregory Rowcliffe, knew of his whereabouts. However, one night at a theatre, my father said to my mother, 'Great Heavens! There's Mordaunt. I must go and speak to him.' On his return, my mother said, with pardonable eagerness, 'Well, tell me all about it.' He replied, 'All about what?' 'What he's doing and why he's disappeared.' 'Oh,' he answered, 'we didn't discuss that; we talked about the play.' Not unsurprisingly, she felt like murdering him. I suspect that my father's response may well have been a blatant lie. No more was heard of Mordaunt until his death. As was then the custom, the family solicitor attended the funeral and afterwards said, 'At least, I'm glad that the money has come back to the family, after all.' Obviously, Mordaunt had been living with a woman who could not be introduced into polite society and she had predeceased him.

At some stage, when I was about ten, Phyllis Clarke came to live with us. She was called 'cousin Phyllis' and my mother was paying for her education at Oxford. I was never told how she fitted in to the family tree and, remarkably, I never asked my mother, who, of course, did not tell me. I suspect that she was an illegitimate child, but whose, I cannot begin to guess. She was extremely nice and we got on well. She was very good at drawing and added illustrations of an amusing nature to several of my books. Unfortunately, after Oxford, she married a GP who was a Protestant, and did so in a Protestant church; as a result, my mother never spoke to her again. To modern eyes, this would seem to be an extreme reaction. However, when Joan's brother, Alan, did the same, his father would not speak to him for many years. The degree of religious intolerance in those days was remarkable. Although I exchanged a few letters with Phyllis thereafter, I never met her again, being, like many young men, far too preoccupied with my own affairs. She had a son and died shortly after.

Phyllis was the only person, save my mother, who could get near to our parrot without being bitten. Occasionally, the detestable creature would be let out of its cage in the drawing room and if John and I were present, we would climb on to a sofa for safety – it was unable to fly. It was a grey African parrot, a gift to my mother from Arthur Coles, who had got it from its mother's nest in the Gold Coast. He was employed there by Lever Brothers and, since the place was called 'the white man's grave', anyone who survived was able to retire at the age of fifty. There used to be a grisly joke that there were always three Chief Justices of the Gold Coast – one was in office, his predecessor was in a coffin on a ship back to England and his successor had been selected. The parrot was called Cuthbert until, in 1939, roughly when war broke out, it started laying eggs, which it went on to do, stopping roughly when the war ended. To the best of my recollection they tasted rather like quails' eggs. After it started laying, it was renamed Cuthbertina, but its temper did not improve. In 1958, I managed to persuade my mother that it was ridiculous to go on living in the Hove house, now occupied only by her and Bessie, who was a very indifferent cook. I found her a very nice flat in Eaton Square, very close to where both John and I were living. It was arranged that Cuthbertina should be returned to Arthur Coles. However, by another remarkable coincidence, the bird was found dead on the very morning that my mother moved.

Arthur Coles's wife, Madge, was a friend of my mother, who took her on holidays as an unpaid companion, Arthur having died not long after Cuthbertina. She was very nice, but utterly boring, as was Arthur; how my mother came to know them I do not know.

A person whom we saw every Sunday was Lord Alfred Douglas, Oscar Wilde's friend. This was because he shared a pew in church with us, the practice in those days being to rent out pews, which one was entitled to occupy if one arrived in good time before Mass – a very strange concept, which must have been copied from the Anglican practice of families having their own box-like pews. However, since there were a number of Masses on a Sunday, I do not understand how people were expected to know whether it was going to be occupied by the persons entitled to sit there for a particular Mass. My mother was always very careful to ensure that neither John nor I sat next to him. He had the appearance of a very old turtle and was a person of interest to us boys because whenever his name was mentioned, although this cannot have been very often, all the adults would purse their lips and look severely disapproving and, of course, we did not know why. He died in 1945 at the age of seventy-five and about a year before he wrote a poem for me, something which I did not often disclose. This was because some of those conscripted were sent down the mines rather than joining the armed forces. Of course, this was not what most men wanted and this was a poem which condemned this practice, about which I must have told him. Typically, public schools got round this by sending us to recruiting offices shortly before our eighteenth birthdays, where we volunteered and then went back to school until we were eighteen, at which stage we were, at least technically, members of the armed forces, albeit unpaid, and could not be sent down the mines.

He also gave me a copy of a lecture which he gave to the Poetry Society during the war, which says a great deal for his standing as a poet despite his notoriety. It is indicative of the enormous difference between young people then and now that at no time while he was alive did I know anything about the Wilde scandal or about his reputation.

Alfred's mother, the Marchioness of Queensberry, was a friend of my mother, who said that she was the only person she had met who had 'truly violet eyes'. How they came to be friends I do not know. On her death, she left to my mother the attractive Dutch cabinet which I use as a drinks cupboard. Since Queensberry was almost insane and she had to suffer the publicity about Alfred, she must have led a miserable life. My mother said that Lady Queensberry never told her anything at all about the scandal; however, since, although herself very reticent, she was extremely inquisitive, I very much doubt whether this was true.

Of course, the circles in which my mother moved in Hove, by the time that I was able to notice such things, were very different from those in which she had moved before she left London. She recounted to me the life she and my father led in London, which is inconceivable to-day. After breakfast, they would go out to 'do' something, such as buying a tie or a half Stilton, all such operations being undertaken with great care, e.g. several Stiltons would be tried, accompanied with a glass of port. After this, my father would repair to one of his clubs, the exotically named Cocoa Tree Club being a favourite. He would remain there until it was time to dress for the evening. My mother would lunch with friends and would then go home and change into a teagown or dress. Married women would hold a tea party on a particular day each month. Consequently, she would go to Mrs X on, say, the second Wednesday each month. She might attend more than one of these affairs. However, it was their evenings which were, to modern eyes, truly remarkable. They would usually attend two or three parties unless they were guests at a dinner. On what I got the impression were the rare occasions when they dined alone at home, my father would change into a dinner jacket, a practice followed by High Court judges in the lodgings on circuit until recently.

On evenings when the staff had a night off and they did not go to a party, which seems not to have happened very often, they would go to a restaurant for dinner. It was not until the early 1950s that there were any restaurants except in hotels and in

Soho. Two of the first were opened in Elizabeth Street while we lived there – Le Matelot and Bicyclette. A rash of such restaurants spread across London very quickly. At this time Elizabeth David started writing her French cookery books. These two events caused a gastronomic revolution among the upper classes. Many dishes which are now regarded as ordinary English fare would not have been found in private houses before then. Of course, this process of change took place much more slowly so far as older people were concerned, especially outside London. In my mother's house in Hove, her cook Bessie prided herself on cooking 'plain English food', an expression commonly used by cooks in those days; garlic, to her, and much of the population, was anathema, being nasty, foreign, foul-smelling stuff.

Of course, there were a few restaurants outside Soho, such as Rules near Covent Garden and the Trocadero in Regent Street, which remained a favourite of my mother, together with Veeraswamey's off Regent Street, which I think was the only decent Indian restaurant in London. If all of this gives the impression that in my childhood English fare was somewhat unimaginative and boring, that impression is correct. At boarding schools the situation was even worse in that the 'plain English food' was very badly cooked. Bread and butter pudding was frequently served and, invariably, bits of the bread would stick out, the sticking-out bits being burnt toast; I have never been able to eat it with enjoyment to this day.

Once I was old enough to do so, my mother arranged for me to attend some class every day. Thus, once a week I went to a gym class and to a music class, where I remember hitting a triangle and, I assume, other such things. I think that my mother's idea was to provide some occupation every day. The most enjoyable of such things were the riding lessons. A groom would take a group of children up to the Downs just behind Brighton. All these lessons must have stopped when I went to prep school at the age of nine. I can recollect attending, together with John, some kind of riding school in the country and riding lessons may have taken place during holidays from prep school. These somewhat sparse riding experiences proved sufficient to ensure that when my regiment arrived in Austria, I found that I was a moderately competent horseman.

3

SCHOOL

I think that I went to my first school at about the age of six. It was run by an appositely named Mademoiselle Le Maître on the ground floor of a house a few hundred yards from our home in Hove. At some stage, I was taught to read and write, but I suspect that this happened before I went to school. I have no recollection of what I was taught by this amiable French lady, save for one deplorable thing. Every day, when leaving school, we were each given a French sentence which we were expected to learn by heart and recite the following morning. However, I discovered that, if I repeated the same sentence every day, it was not noticed. Possibly, this played a part in my inability ever to acquire reasonable fluency in French.

At about the age of seven, I went to a boys' school run by Major Phillips in his house in Brighton. In those days it was common for retired Army officers to set up small day prep schools. Again, I remember nothing of what I was taught there, save for being sent out of the classroom to look at the grandfather clock in the hall and to come back and tell him the time. This was a similar exercise to that described to me by an elderly farmworker of how pupils at his school were taken outside and required to lay out a length of chain, which was actually one chain in length, being a measure of length long fallen into disuse.

Major Phillips must have been competent, as will now become obvious. In 1935 at the age of nine I was sent to boarding school. As my mother later told Joan, this was a very hard decision for her to have to make. Her view was that it was wrong for me to continue to live at home surrounded by women and no male adult. I have no doubt that our parish priests played a major part in helping her to make this decision. In those days, there was an acute shortage of English Catholic priests and many parishes were served by priests from Ireland. They were, and for years continued to be, a very mixed bunch. Not for nothing was the Irish Church called 'the mother-in-law of the Church'. In Ireland, the only question was whether they were the equivalent of the first or the second person in the Holy Trinity. Many were as arrogant as they were stupid. Of course, English parishioners were a terrible shock to them.

Fortunately, Canon Crea and Father O'Brian were different from those just described. Canon Crea was an urbane, sensible and civilised man who was well suited to be parish priest in a wealthy parish. Father O'Brian was a more simple man, but kind and sensible. My mother relied on them a lot so far as John and I were concerned and I have no doubt that their advice was crucial to her decision to send me to boarding school.

Worth was then a preparatory school, having been founded by Downside in 1933. It is now a public school as well and has been upgraded from being a priory to an abbey, independent of Downside. It was in what had been a very large country house, which included a ballroom, and was set in a large estate. It was a very good situation, commanding extensive views across country to the South Downs, with buildings ideally suited to being a school.

My mother took me to see the Headmaster, Dom Oliver Braydon, OSB (Order of Saint Benedict). I remember nothing about him, save for that interview. These days, all children, however young, seem to be required to undergo extensive tests before being admitted to any educational establishment. What happened on this occasion was very different. I was asked two questions. What was I doing in mathematics and the same for Latin; I suspect that this interview was shortly after my ninth birthday. Having answered these questions, Braydon said to my mother that he now knew which class to put me in. Since it was the top class for my year, Major Phillips had obviously done a good job.

At this point, I should make it plain that, although I was a clever boy, I never regarded myself as being in the top flight academically; at all times, I was just short of scholarship standard. Thus, I was not even entered for a scholarship to Downside and failed to obtain one when I went up to Jesus College, Cambridge and when I went to the Bar, although I was awarded the school prize for history and, rather more surprisingly, for religious instruction in my last year at Downside. My rival for the history prize, John Hull, did get a scholarship to Jesus, where he obtained a first-class degree, and went on to become Chairman of Schroeders Bank and Deputy Chairman of the City take-overs panel. It has often struck me that people who get good seconds often do better than those with firsts; this did not apply to John Hull. Often, this is because the person with a first lacks common sense and does not succeed in careers which require it, as most do. Thus, frequently, we took on as a tenant in chambers a pupil who had got a second in preference to one who had got a first. Of course, people with firsts who also have common sense tend to be world-beaters. A man who was a member of chambers when I arrived had won every academic distinction that it was possible to win. I read an opinion by him which was a remarkably erudite disquisition on the relevant law, which should have found its way into a learned legal journal; unfortunately, it was based upon a finding of fact which no judge would ever have made. He left chambers shortly after I arrived and practised in the West Country, possibly because he did not want to live in London; he had been a cavalry officer and had the distinction of having been captured twice in 1944. He never took silk but became a county court judge (later they were called circuit judges) in 1968, the year that I took silk. He did the job, which he must have liked, until 1988, when he reached the compulsory retirement age of seventy-two. If his judgements reflected the judgement shown in the opinion mentioned, I shudder to think of the judicial errors which he would have made.

'Happy is the nation that has no history!' On the basis that I cannot remember a great deal about Worth, I must have been happy; certainly, I cannot remember being unhappy. The Benedictine monks were, by and large, a kindly lot and the teaching must have been competent. I was never much good at sports, but I remember one splendid day at the cricket field. A Walls ice-cream man arrived, as he always did, riding a tricycle containing his wares. On this occasion, which happened when we were watching a first eleven match, it was announced that the father of a boy would pay for each boy to buy ice-creams to the value of sixpence. I regret that I cannot remember the name of this benefactor.

Edward Goode was in the team; he would have made an

admirable county player since he used to bat interminably, playing defensive strokes and scoring runs at the rate of one every hour. He lived in Hove and, therefore, I saw a lot of him although he was as uninteresting as his cricket. His father was dead and his mother was almost completely blind. He was an only child and it was a catastrophic disaster for his mother when he was killed at Sandhurst, where I was at the time, when he foolishly tried to pass between a stationary tank and another which was reversing. Of course, when driving a tank, one has very little view to the rear.

Scouting was an activity which I enjoyed and there was great competition to earn as many badges as possible. I got six badges but I can only remember one, which was for reading. In order to get it one had to be tested about one's recollection of a book which one had read, which does not imply a very high standard. I remember it because it was the occasion when I first met the very civilised monk Dom (short for Dominus) Hilary Steuert, who later taught me English at Downside. I went for a walk with him for the purpose of the test and, when I said that the book was *The Iliad*, he at once said that it did not qualify since the book had to be one which one was not being taught. He was very surprised when I replied that I had read it in translation for pleasure.

In retrospect, I realise that I was, even then, a person who got singled out for responsibility. On one occasion which comes to mind such trust was sadly misplaced. Archbishop Amigo of Southwark came to the school for a service of some kind and I was chosen to carry his train. He did or said something which must have annoyed me greatly, because, as we processed down the aisle, I gave a small tug on his train, rather like reining in a horse. It was not enough to pull him off balance and I am sure that he did not realise that it was intentional; nevertheless, it gave me a wicked sense of satisfaction. I felt in some measure vindicated for this disgraceful act when, in 1940, Italy declared war on Germany's side. The egregious Amigo, who was Italian, made it difficult for clergy in his diocese to volunteer as chaplains to the Forces.

In 1938 we went on a cruise and a holiday in Switzerland. That summer we went on a cruise to Gibraltar, Oran, Madeira and the

Canary Islands. In Oran, I bought a small ivory monkey, and then went on to buy a set of three, which gave me great satisfaction and I still have them in my display cabinet. There are photographs of John and me in a sled in Madeira. This was and is a tourist attraction. The sled rushes down a steep cobbled street controlled (?) by men on foot holding ropes attached to it. That Christmas we went to Wengen in Switzerland, where I learnt to ski. Of course, children can learn very quickly and I had a good sense of balance. (It came in very handy seven years later when, as a soldier, I arrived in Austria. Of course, I was one of the very few who knew how to ski and it gave me a head-start over everyone else.) It was on the way to Switzerland that I first suffered from seasickness. Before leaving London, we had lunch at the Grosvenor Hotel; it was many years before I could face eating tomato soup again.

On both these holidays we were accompanied by Miss Arthur; probably my mother wanted her as an adult companion. John had been ill and she was employed as a governess. She was timid and silly, just as all governesses were said to be in those days. I doubt whether John learnt much from her. However, she was a harmless and kind person.

In the summer of 1939 we went on another cruise. This was on the *Arandora Star*, which was sunk in the Atlantic during the war when loaded with a large number of German prisoners of war. By now, Miss Arthur had left, since John was due to go to Worth in September, and Mrs Coles came with us. In those days, fancy dress parties were very common and I have photographs of John and me in quite a large number of costumes. We visited Iceland, where there was nothing of interest, save for the volcanic pools of steaming hot water. We could not put into the Faroes because of severe gales and John and I lay in our cabin for two or three days, either prostrate with seasickness or recuperating with a supply of chicken sandwiches. Our mother then turfed us out and we discovered that in some mysterious way we had found our sea legs.

We sailed down the west coast of Norway to Copenhagen and were on our way to Stockholm when all British ships were instructed to return home because of the imminence of war. As we crossed the North Sea, a German cruiser launched a plane which flew low over us a number of times; all our lifeboats were winched out. As we crossed the Channel the scene was incredible. As far as the eye could see, the sea was covered by vessels of all sizes making their way to England. I do not know how the ports were able to cope with such an influx. As we left the ship at Southampton, painters were swarming on board to paint it grey.

We got back to Hove late that day and the following morning I was able to listen to Chamberlain's broadcast telling us that 'a state of war existed' between us and Germany because the latter had not replied to our ultimatum; rather a strange phrase to use. John and I walked the few hundred yards to the promenade, whereupon the air-raid sirens sounded. An elderly, retired major who lived next door appeared wearing a tin helmet and shouted to everyone to get indoors. It was very comic but, having seen films of German aircraft bombing in Spain during the Civil War, everyone expected the same thing to happen here at once.

It was because of the fear of bombing that John and I were packed off to Downside, to which Worth had moved, the very next day, about a week before term started. Our mother had considered sending us to Canada; had this happened, the rest of my life might have been very different.

Downside

It is difficult to portray to those who did not live through it how strange life was in wartime England. Rationing and lack of petrol soon caused an almost complete stop to social entertaining. Travel was not encouraged and, in our case, the fact that our road was so close to the sea meant that, later in the war, one could enter it only after showing one's identity card to a sentry at the top of the road. No one was allowed on to the beach or even the promenade, where there was a great deal of barbed wire. Later, in a superb piece of bureaucratic bungling, garden railings were removed. We were told that this was so that they could be used to make guns or suchlike but they were found to be wholly unsuitable and I believe that the whole project was to no useful purpose.

Until our defeat in France in 1940, no battles of any kind took place and that period was later called the 'phoney war'. Of course, shut up in the grounds of a public school in Somerset, we were even more cut off from the war. Apart from overcrowding due to having to house Worth, there were probably few changes made in the school. At some stage, we all had to go and sleep in bunk-beds on the ground floor, but I do not remember this lasting for long.

The greatest impact was upon the quality of the teachers. Those of military age had to join the Services. This meant that retired teachers had to be called in and any monk whom it was thought might be able to teach, did so. Of course, this resulted in very uneven standards. The French teacher was a bearded fool called Monsieur Moorat, who upon entering the classroom would often say 'Open the ports, boys, open the ports.' He was a harmless fellow, but I learnt little of value from him. It is fair to add that schools evinced little interest in foreign languages and I doubt whether his teaching was worse than others'. The sole emphasis was on written rather than spoken and, still less, colloquial French. Of course, because of the war, it was impossible to travel to a French-speaking country.

I had no talent for Latin either. For me, it was penitential. Of course, the school regarded it as something of major importance. Indeed, for some weird reason, when I did my Bar exams, it was still necessary to pass a paper in Roman law. Later, when as a member of the Council of Legal Eduction, I helped to get rid of it; I got it replaced by a revenue (tax) paper. In the course of one's schooling, there were two public examinations, apart from Common Entrance, which had to be passed to the school's standard before one was admitted and was taken in one's last summer at prep school. After two years, there was the School Certificate. This was of importance because, in order to be eligible to be admitted to a university, it was necessary to obtain a credit, rather than a mere pass, in five specified subjects, namely, English, English literature, a science subject, history and Latin. Unlike now, it was not the practice to take a large number of subjects. I duly obtained credits in the necessary subjects and a pass in French. Of course, we had been taught physics and chemistry, in which I had little interest, and religious knowledge.

At the start of the next school year in September 1941, being then fifteen, I found that I had been put down to take history and Latin as my main subjects for the Higher Certificate Examination, together with elementary politics and economics as my subsidiary subject. Had I been able to do so I would have wished to do history and mathematics, but the school time-table permitted one to take mathematics only if one coupled it with science subjects. I was full of admiration when my son Edward, when in a similar position, contrived to teach himself ancient history and satisfy the examiners in both O and A levels. I was horrified to find that I was due to do Latin and went to see the Headmaster, later Bishop, Christopher Butler. His response was to say, 'Don't be lazy!' However, I persisted and got my way.

My English teacher, Dom Wulstan Phillipson, was a disaster. His idea of teaching English was to read poetry with a soulful voice. As a result, to my rage and fury, two years later, I failed English by five marks and had to do the examination a second time in 1944. Fortunately, on this occasion I had been taught by Dom Hilary Steuert. He was a very able teacher and I got on well with him. As a result, on every occasion when I met him after leaving school, he reminded me that I had obtained the highest mark in the Chaucer paper ever achieved by anyone while he was teaching at Downside.

I have always been very glad that I read history and English for the Higher Cert. I have retained a keen interest in history and we seem constantly to be buying new history books. English, too, is a civilising subject. When I was Treasurer of Lincoln's Inn, Joan and I had to attend a dinner at the Royal College of Surgeons. The company was excruciatingly dull but, on my complaining about this, Joan replied that I should remember that they were just 'vile mechanicals'. There is a lot in this, in that our educational system causes a bifurcation at about the age of sixteen which, while making it impossible for me to continue with mathematics, means that doctors and scientists cease to be taught anything save scientific subjects. Moreover, apart from basic arithmetic, I have never had cause to use any mathematical knowledge beyond that stage; for example, no geometry or physics or trigonometry. The sole exception was electricity, which I needed in fire cases, of which I did a great many, since it was always necessary to exclude an electrical fault as a cause of the fire when insurers, for whom I acted in such cases, alleged that the assured had burnt down his own premises, usually because his business was in trouble, in order to claim the insurance money. However, one piece of useless knowledge remains fixed in my mind, namely the formula for arithmetical progression, which, of course, I have never had to use.

When I went to Downside, I spent a year in the Junior House, of which Brendan Lavery was Housemaster. He was an Irishman whose eccentricity was only just on the side of sanity. However, he was a nice man and quite amusing. After this year I was in Roberts House, named after St John Roberts. The Housemaster was Rudesind Brookes, OBE, MC, TD. He was an extraordinary man. He was the son of a Russian Count who was an attaché in London at the time of Rudy's birth. His mother was Swedish, and after she was divorced and remarried, he was brought up by his stepfather, whose name he was given. In 1915, at the age of seventeen, he joined the Army, where he served in France in the Irish Guards under the future Field Marshal Alexander.

After the war he served as ADC to the Governor of Malta but, in 1924, he resigned from the Army and became a monk at Downside. In many ways, he was a hopeless Housemaster, being useless at administration and having scant idea of boys' minds. For example, at house assembly one night, he said that a letter had been found and handed in which was to 'Mummy' and signed 'Michael' in which the author said that he had been chosen for some games team. When I claimed it after assembly he said, 'Of course, I realised that it was you, but I knew that you wouldn't mind.' Needless to say, I minded very much, although by that age I had learnt to command my features so that they could be wholly expressionless, a characteristic which my mother told Joan she found infuriating; consequently, I am confident that Rudy was unable to perceive my feelings, which doubtless confirmed his view that I did not mind.

It would be easy to say that he was a hopeless disciplinarian. In one sense it is true; however, he was a very charismatic figure and much liked, so that boys of a difficult and rebellious nature felt that they should behave so as not to hurt his feelings. I was too junior to get to know him well before, in 1942, he went off as a chaplain to his old regiment. I am not sure that I saw him again until Anthony Wheatley gave a dinner in his house in Wimbledon in the early nineties, shortly before Rudy's death; not surprisingly, it was obvious that he had no recollection of me at all.

He served in North Africa, where he was awarded the Military

Cross for bravery in the field, which was a most unusual distinction for a chaplain. In Italy, he was Alexander's chaplain. After the war, in 1955, Alexander, who was now Minister of Defence, extracted him from Downside to go to Malta as the Governor's chaplain. In 1956, he became Rector (Headmaster) of a public school in Malta until, for eleven years from 1966, he was Abbot Procurator (representative or ambassador) of the English Benedictines in the Vatican, before retiring, first to an English convent and then to Downside. He was a very remarkable man, known as 'Dolly' in the Army, I think because he was always dressed immaculately.

Throughout my time at Downside, the Abbot was the formidable Sigebert Trafford (it will not have escaped the reader's notice that many monks adopted the religious name of obscure mediaeval saints). He had been Headmaster until 1939. He was of the old school of headmaster, who regarded sport as being as important, if not more so, than academic work. Of course, I had no contact with him but he had a pervasive influence on the school in some undefined way.

Christopher Butler succeeded Trafford and remained Headmaster throughout my time at Downside and until becoming Abbot in 1946; he was made a bishop some years later. I asked him why he agreed to become a bishop and he replied that he enjoyed it, which surprised me. He had been an Anglican priest and, when a bishop, was in the forefront of the ecumenical movement. Like many of the other monks, he had little idea of how boys thought. I had a good relationship with him and would sometimes go and have a cup of something, not coffee, which was almost unobtainable, in his room after dinner. In my last year, I was one of those whom he would invite to his room to meet distinguished guests. He came to my wedding.

His successor was Wilfrid Passmore, a former solicitor. He was a very competent man and a very good Headmaster. Because of this, it would have been easy to think that he was not a deeply religious man; nothing could be further from the truth. In my later years in the school he was Bursar and at no time did he play any part in the affairs of the school. How I ever came to have any contact with him at all I do not know; in retrospect, it was odd. However, once or twice a term, I would make my way to his room, which was between the school and the Abbey. He would then give me a glass of sherry, which, apart from the fact that it was almost unobtainable during the war, was very remarkable – and the more so since I must still have been sixteen when this first happened. It was my view that, being a man of great curiosity about the school, he was interested to hear all the gossip, and I was certainly one of the right people to ask. When Butler became Abbot in 1946, Passmore succeeded him as Headmaster and I used to meet him when my sons were in the school. On such occasions, he punctiliously addressed me as Mr Ogden. Later still, he was a very good abbot.

School life merits little comment. Time was fully occupied, save for the period after dinner. Every afternoon, one was obliged either to play games or, twice a week, put on uniform and undergo army training in the Officers' Cadet Corps. I had not inherited my father's eye nor his strength. Although shaped rather like John and me, he must have been very broad-shouldered since he had a party trick of tearing telephone directories in half – of course, they were much slimmer then. For many years a poker bent by him was exhibited in a hotel at Keswick. Not having his gifts, I was not very good at nor did I enjoy team games very much.

The OTC was a different matter. Being a leader by nature, except for having to run about over muddy fields, which is what caused me to go into the Armoured Corps, I rather enjoyed it. The Corps was commanded by Cuthbert McCann, a monk who had been a regular officer. He was an energetic but rather stupid man, who did not like me very much but made me the second senior cadet officer.

It is difficult to remember any event of real interest during my time at Downside, save that I was nearly killed. In May 1943, a Spitfire crashed among spectators watching a cricket match, killing nine boys and the pilot. Doubtless, the passage of time makes me think that it came down nearer to me than was the case, but I am confident that it was no more than twenty yards away and a piece of it passed over my body and killed a boy who was further away. The pilot was under instruction and had been engaged in 'follow the leader'. The leader must have thought that it would be fun to 'buzz' us. There were two playing fields with a bank between them and everyone was watching a first eleven match. The dead pilot miscalculated and caught the top of the bank.

Apart from a narrow escape, two events during the aftermath stick in my mind. In those days telephones were few and there was only one public telephone for all the boys to use, and there were over two hundred of us. There was no telephone in the pavilion. Since there were plenty of adults about to look after the injured, it was obvious that ambulances should be called as soon as possible. I took a nearby bicycle and went down to the main school building, about six hundred yards away. I ran inside and up the stairs facing me where the Headmaster had his room. I ignored the red light and went in and told Butler, who, without hesitation reached for his telephone. I recount this, not because I regard what I did as exhibiting quick thinking, but because I was amazed that the thought of getting ambulances appeared to have occurred to no one else, although it is possible that someone may have gone to the village which was no closer than the school.

I went back to the cricket field but the plane's petrol tank exploded and a bit whizzed past my ear. I set about finding John to ensure that he was unharmed and then, together with another boy, I went to the village post office and sent a telegram to my mother saying that we were safe, without stating what had happened to reassure her.

The second strange incident took place at School Assembly that evening. Butler told us that we were not to tell our parents what had happened. What prompted this weird decision I do not know. It should have been obvious that there was no possibility of keeping the matter quiet. I suppose that it is possible that he had been asked to do this by 'the authorities'; during the war, the Press could be muzzled and perhaps he was told that this would be done, but it did not happen. In any case, since parents visited their sons and we were all required to write home once a week, it is inconceivable that all boys would have obeyed his instruction. After Assembly I and the boy who had come with me to send a telegram told Butler what we had done. This was just as well because, when my mother paid her next visit to the school, she told Butler how grateful she was that I had sent the telegram and not left her to read about it in the papers next day; it must have made Butler feel very foolish.

There was an inquest and, it being war-time, everything was glossed over. The instructor had been incredibly foolish and reckless and I have no doubt that in peace-time he would have been court-martialled. However, for the rest of his life, and it is possible that he is still alive, he had the frightful burden of the deaths of the boys and the pilot on his conscience.

One of the dead boys, who was my exact contemporary, was in Roberts and sat next to me at table. One day he struck a blow at me with his meat knife, resulting in my receiving a classic defence injury to my right wrist, which left a scar that is still just discernible to-day. I bore him no ill-will because I must have provoked him beyond endurance in some way which I cannot now remember.

Having passed Higher Certificate, with the gratifying result in the Chaucer paper mentioned earlier, I returned to school in September 1943. With two terms to go before joining the Army, I was now in the sixth form reading only history. My teacher was also my Housemaster, Adrian Morey, MA, FRHistS, Ph.D. In common with my contemporaries in Roberts, I disliked him. He was undoubtedly clever, had written several books of biography about obscure mediaeval men and I have no doubt that, had he not become a monk, he would have been a lecturer at Oxbridge. However, he was very smug and self-satisfied and had no understanding of boys at all. He was wholly unsuited to be a Housemaster. Since I was now a house prefect, I was obliged to be in close contact with him, which included being one of the four prefects who sat within speaking distance of him at lunch and dinner, to which dreary duty was added the fact that he was now my only teacher in a scholarship class of three, the other two members of which had the good fortune to be in other houses.

It soon became obvious that we were not getting on well and he told me that I was giving him insufficient support and would no longer be a prefect. This suited me, since, as a sixth former, I had all the privileges of a prefect but none of the boring duties. It was interesting that at least two other people thought that I ought to mind dreadfully. Dennis Agius was a Maltese monk. He looked very Maltese, having a rather sallow complexion and a face which did not look English. He had taught me at Worth and

I had always got on well with him, although not everyone did. I found him amusing and witty, with a somewhat caustic tongue. We traded gossip in a slightly malicious way, although I would not have trusted him an inch. He came to my room and said that he hoped that I would not do anything silly. I assume that he meant run away. I nearly burst out laughing and assured him that I did not mind in the least, at which he looked astonished. Perhaps it was not surprising that Butler asked me for coffee after dinner. Obviously, he expected me to raise the subject but I did not do so, and after a time he did. I think that he assumed I would complain, which I would have been entitled to do, since the other prefects had behaved in no different way from me. Of course, I did not do so, which plainly left him very puzzled.

A bonus for me was that Morey decided that he would no longer teach me, which was a sensible decision. Ostensibly, I was then taught by another monk, but by this time I was quite capable of learning on my own and only required assistance about which books to read. As recounted earlier, I failed to get a scholarship to Cambridge, but I do not believe that this episode played any part in that.

I have no doubt that many of the monks were saints in that they duly went to Heaven but one of them was the only person I have met who positively exuded saintliness and managed to do so while remaining a very nice, sensible and friendly person. This was Ralph Russell. He was truly remarkable, as the following incident will demonstrate. Someone went to Bath station to pick him up. 'Tusky', which was his nickname because of his protruding teeth, got out of the train, followed by a dirty-looking, unshaven young man, who was profusely thanking him for saying that he would answer his letters. Tusky was a doctor of canon law and it must have been he who caused me to be awarded the Gregorian Prize for Religious Knowledge. To do him justice, it must have been Adrian Morey who caused me to be awarded the same prize for history, rather than John Hull, who was the only other possible candidate.

I am conscious of having said nothing about boys, either at Worth or Downside. This is because it is uninteresting to read about people unless they did something memorable. One such person was a notable prankster. He was idle but very clever. With some misgivings that he might 'let the school down', he was allowed to sit for a scholarship at Cambridge. Of course, he walked off with a major scholarship. This was in March. Most boys would have rushed about spreading the glad tidings; not this boy. He waited until April Fool's day to tell his Housemaster, Morey, who, perhaps understandably, replied 'I thought that you could have done better than that!' The boy withdrew, looking suitably crestfallen. The school was told about it by the college some days later and Butler sent for the boy, saying that he was wrong not to have told anyone. Of course, he was able to exonerate himself – at least, in theory.

Before this, he had caused a considerable stir when a newspaper ran a piece saying that a vicar had been to a pub; in those days it was thought to be almost an improper thing to do. He wrote a letter to the paper, purporting to be from another vicar of some genuine church, saying that he frequently went to his village pub and if sometimes he had to be helped home, he considered that it was all in a good cause.

Considerable controversy had been caused by the appointment as Headmaster of a leading public school of someone who was not a teacher. My friend wrote to, I think, the *Daily Telegraph*, purporting to be Headmaster of some very minor public school, saying that he had been a successful brewer prior to his appointment, and that it was a good idea to have someone who was not conditioned by the system; for example, the abolition of the prefectorial system had greatly strengthened the link between masters and boys. On the same day another letter appeared in, I think, the *Spectator*, purporting to come from the successor to the writer of the first letter, saying that, although the latter had been very successful in various ways, some of his changes had not been a good idea; for example, the abolition of the prefectorial system had greatly weakened the link between masters and boys. These letters resulted in a letter in each publication from the school, denouncing the letters as fakes and listing the names of the existing and several previous Headmasters, all of whom had such improbable names that the letter must initially have been thought to be a hoax. I assume that to-day editors would not be so gullible, Fortunately the Downside authorities did not know about either of these events, although I suspect that some monks did.

I came across him again at Cambridge; he was unaltered. One day, he asked if he could come and stand in the bay window of my sitting room at 6 o'clock. He explained that he had put an advertisement in the *Cambridge Evening News* announcing that a limited supply of Irish whiskey was for sale, giving the address of a house opposite and the name of a boy who had been at Downside with us. Since spirits were still in short supply, no sooner had we taken up positions at the window, armed with glasses of cheap South African sherry, than a steady stream of men arrived and knocked on the unfortunate man's door. Of course, the hapless fellow got more and more infuriated with each caller and eventually resorted to putting a notice on the door.

The last escapade of which I knew required considerable ingenuity and perseverance. He and another former Downside boy invented a school. They had writing paper printed and proceeded to engage in widespread correspondence with people to whom it would never have occurred that it was not genuine. George Bernard Shaw was an obvious target because he loved writing letters in what he regarded as a witty manner; he duly obliged. So well did they conduct the affair that they persuaded two Headmasters to agree to propose the school for membership of the Headmasters' Conference. Unfortunately, they were unmasked by some miserable journal. Their college authorities had little sense of humour and I think that both of them were rusticated.

I must recount one last important incident which happened early in 1944. I went to see Butler and said to him, 'As you know, I have to join the Army in May. Please advise me about what career I should pursue if I survive the war (a prescient caveat since, as I discovered later, my regiment was earmarked to land on the mainland of Japan). My father died when I was young and I have no suitable male relative or family friend whose advice I would want to rely on.' Without a moment's hesitation he replied, 'Michael, you talk a great deal too much, you had better do a job in which you are paid to do it; go to the Bar.' 'Thank you very much, sir,' I said, and from that moment onwards that was my settled intention. It had not been in my mind before I asked him; my recollection is that I had not had anything in mind and, certainly, had discussed it with no one else. I have no doubt that it was sound advice. I would not have flourished in any occupation in which I was commanded by someone else, e.g. the Services or the civil service and most large companies, etc.

Thus ended my schooldays, which I can not complain about in any way. I was not bullied and few people, masters or boys, were ever beastly to me. Except for music and art, about which I knew almost nothing, I ended up having had a very good education.

4

THE ARMY

It was on 7 February 1944 that I visited Bath to sign on as a soldier, in order to avoid the risk of being made a miner, and returned to school. On 3 May 1944 I reported for duty at the Royal Armoured Corps Headquarters at Bovington. Joining the Army is an eventful day for anyone but, in retrospect, it was a more important day for me than for others. Had Rudolph Krefting or I joined a week later for any reason, the whole course of my life would have been different, as I will describe later.

Arriving at Bovington Station, the new recruits were marched up to Bovington Camp, issued with uniforms etc. and put into a Nissen hut. These things, which were much used by the Armed Forces during and after the war, consisted of a semi-circle of corrugated iron stuck on to a concrete foundation. For heating there was a metal stove with a metal pipe for a chimney, which stuck through the roof. We slept in two-tier bunk beds and went to a special block for our ablutions. Those of us who had come from boarding schools took it in our stride but for those who had hitherto lived at home with their parents, it was a frightful shock and for some nights there were pathetic sounds of crying.

It was a basic infantry training regiment, since it was considered that we ought to know the rudiments of being an infantryman. I have scant recollection of the training, save that it involved being taught how to use rifles and suchlike weapons, which most of us had learnt at school, and, of course, drill, together with a great deal of physical exercise. The recruits comprised all those who were considered to have the possible makings of an officer. After a month or so a number of people were weeded out and the rest of us went on to an RAC training regiment in Farnborough. We were taught how to drive tanks, put back their tracks if they came off (a ghastly task), how to fire the tank's main gun and machine-gun, how to operate the wireless and to change frequencies when it was travelling across country (not easy) and suchlike things. The part which I hated most was being taught to ride motorcycles across country, since all officers were expected to be able to do this. Army motorcycles were, of necessity, very tough and consequently very heavy. I was not very good at doing it and frequently ended up in muddy pools of water. When I managed to get the wretched machine and myself up, the engine invariably stopped and had to be kick-started, which was not easy. Often, I was the last to arrive at the end of a run, where the others were waiting and resting, whereupon we set off again.

At least, we were sleeping in wooden huts. Moreover, we seemed to have a little time off. On Sundays I went to Farnborough Abbey, where the kindly Benedictine monks would give us tea, which was very welcome and civilised. It was a community started by French monks and housed the magnificent tombs of Napoleon III and his son the Prince Imperial, who was killed in the Zulu War.

Sandhurst was a great improvement. Unlike the wretched Foot Guards, who were in a hutted encampment a few miles away, the RAC Officer Cadet Training Unit was in the splendid old buildings at the Royal Military College in Camberley. Not only were we only two to a room, but we even had the servants from prewar days as batmen. This meant that no longer did we have to polish boots etc., and it was amusing that when we went on parade in the morning, they stood looking out of the windows as we were inspected.

It was tough. The first month was used to train us to be infantry officers. We had to run up Snowdon in full battle kit, carrying our rifles, and do a ten-mile forced march. On both occasions, we were told, 'Gentlemen, the record time is X, but if you do it in less than Y, you will have to do it again next week.' We did it within the stipulated time! This was followed by more training with tank weapons and wireless and as officers commanding a troop of tanks. Of course, our drill had to be impeccable and we had Guards sergeant-majors under the Senior Regimental Sergeant-Major in the British Army. Physical training every day, including the assault course twice a week, was under the supervision of a former captain of the English football team. I have never been fitter in my life.

We were Number 8 Troop, rather surprisingly described as being of the Honourable Artillery Company Squadron. I suspect that this was to perpetuate in an unbroken fashion this London Territorial Army unit, which is of ancient standing. Passing Out Parade was quite an event. I was in command of the troop, twenty of us having survived from the date when we joined the Army. This involved marching off the parade ground up the stairs and into the building. There was a flight of steps, a landing on the right side of which stood the general taking the parade and another flight of steps. As my foot stepped on to the landing, I had to salute the general and did so until the moment that I stepped on to the upper flight. Of course, I was not allowed to glance down to ensure that my foot was properly on the step. This was daunting, since one had to avoid tripping or slipping. In this I had the interesting experience of being personally drilled by the Senior RSM. Fortunately, I did this all right, which was just as well, since my mother was among the invited spectators. Years later, she told Joan that it was amusing to see the troop being commanded by its smallest member, although Bill Warre was actually about the same size. It was quite an affair, since all the cadets in the college were on parade together, with its band under the overall command of the Adjutant, Earl Cathcart, who rode his horse up the steps and into the building immediately before us.

In the evening there was a dinner, for some forgotten reason described on the menu as being 'on the occasion of the disbanding of the HAC Company Squadron', attended by the Commandant, Adjutant and twenty-one other officers who had participated in our training. Even by peace-time standards, it was a very good eight-course menu: pâté, consommé, turbot, then cold goose, chicken, York ham, asparagus and lettuce salad, followed by venison, peach melba and egg savoury, aided by sherry, champagne, burgundy, chablis and port, assisted by the RMC band. The ability to put on such a splendid dinner was due to the fact that, apart from the small piece of ham in the cold meat and salad dish, nothing eaten was rationed; it was all fish or fowl. It exemplified the fact that country dwellers lived much better than those in urban areas and the Armed Forces best of all.

The Second Royal Gloucestershire Hussars

I passed out on 5 October 1945 and was commissioned a second lieutenant. 1RGH had been so decimated in the Western Desert that it had been disbanded and its remaining members sent to other regiments. 2RGH had been raised shortly before my arrival, it being intended that it should form part of the troops to assault the mainland of Japan. Fortunately, following the dropping of the second atom bomb on Nagasaki, Japan had surrendered in August. Its war cabinet had been divided as to whether or not to do so and it happened only on the express command of the Emperor. Since the Japanese soldiers had fought virtually to the last man as the Americans captured islands south of Japan, it seems very likely that I would not be writing these memoirs had the war not ended when it did. Credit must go to President Truman, who had no hesitation in ordering the bombs to be dropped, and the Emperor deserved to avoid being tried and executed as a war criminal for his courage in ordering the surrender. In the 1960s foolish 'do-gooders' said that it was morally wrong for us to have dropped the bombs; if this was said in my hearing, they received a very acerbic response and I said that, quite apart from people like me, there were thousands of allied prisoners of war being kept in savage, sub-human conditions by their Japanese captors who did not deserve to spend a day longer in captivity; it was not we who started the war. In 1998, as Treasurer of Lincoln's Inn, I attended a dinner of the Pakistan Society in Lincoln's Inn. On my left was a Pakistani, who must have been very eminent in their community to be sitting where he was. He said did I think that it was morally right to drop the bombs, which the Japanese regarded as a racist act. Although I gave him short shrift, he went on to ask whether I thought it was morally right to invade Germany. I was bewildered; 'Invade when?' I said. 'In 1945.' 'Did you expect us to stop at the border, leaving the Nazi State intact?' 'You could have negotiated with Goebbels or someone like that.' 'Don't you realise that we hated him almost more than Hitler?' Fortunately, his wifc, who was between us and could see that I was getting close to hitting him, said, 'Don't you think that he knows more about it than we do?' whereupon he shut up and I turned to the High Commissioner on my right and did not address another word to the wretched man. Incredible.

The regiment was in a hutted camp in Essex, but, shortly after joining it, we went by troopship to Taranto in the heel of Italy. It was the first time that I had been abroad as an adult and it was a revelation to me. Although we were in tents, in which one could find one's boots bobbing about in water when one woke up, we were just outside the town where there was an officers' club to which, of course, we went every night. I drank large quantities of marsala and kummel, and I have no doubt that this choice of sweet drink was due to my body craving for sugar, of which there had been insufficient available during the war. It was also astonishing to come from a country where the ration was one egg a week (two if pregnant) and find bowls of them on every bar counter. (Rationing continued in England until 1954 – nine years after the end of the war! Celia was born just in time to have a ration book. It was noticeable that, the moment rationing stopped, there were ample supplies of all food, which made one wonder what had been happening to it before.)

The regiment travelled by train in cattle trucks from the heel of Italy to the middle of Austria. The journey took about a week and, although the train grew ever further behind schedule, this did not deter the Army from providing us with the precise meal that we were scheduled to eat at each stop, so that we were eating dinner at breakfast time and vice versa. At one point, the train stopped for so long that an officer who spoke Italian went to the engine and found that the driver and fireman were engaged in a fierce argument as to whether the train should fork left or right. The officer in question, Nigel Knight-Bruce, had been a prisoner of war of the Italians and did not care much for them. He simply drew his revolver and ordered the crew to take the right fork, which resolved the problem at once. We were surprisingly comfortable, because our camp-beds were excellent (I still have mine, which has been used by many of the children and grandchildren.) Of course, there was nothing to do save read, talk and drink – we had taken the precaution of having a case of gin and another of vermouth, which we replenished at every stop.

We arrived in Austria shortly before Christmas and our squadron was stationed in a small village west of Graz, the capital of Styria. The RGH was a yeomanry regiment and, although newly raised, contained a number of those who had been in the peace-time regiment. Consequently, there was a very different atmosphere from that in a Regular regiment. I realised this the moment I joined it and presented to the Quartermaster, as one was required to do, the list of equipment issued to me; he simply tore it up and threw it away. There were probably no more than about forty officers, of whom three were subsequently knighted, which must be an extremely high proportion.

Of course, there was nothing to do. After the First World War everyone was demobilised as soon as possible, thereby creating massive unemployment and, very sensibly, in 1945 the Government released people in batches, according to age and length of service, which is why I did not get out until November 1947 – over two years after Japan's surrender. Fortunately, my short pre-war holiday in Wengen came in very useful. Young boys learn to ski quickly and I was one of very few in the regiment able to do so at all, which gave me an advantage over the others. After Christmas, I was able to go up into the mountains, where I was part of the regimental ski team, and I stayed there until the snow melted.

In the spring, I was lent to the Royal Army Service Corps, which, as its title implies, existed to supply the fighting troops. Their officers were relatively old and were demobilised earlier than others, so that there was suddenly a dire shortage of them. Shortly after this happened, I found myself in Leoben, in command of the supply depot for the whole of the British Army in Austria. We supplied everything – food, clothes, fuel, anything, save weapons, that soldiers need, together with sixty large three-ton lorries. It was ridiculous that, as a lieutenant aged twenty, I should have had so responsible a command; had I been older I would probably have felt daunted, but it caused me no anxiety at all. My predecessor and superior officer was a drunk. He wore dark glasses at all times, including breakfast, at which he would force a few mouthfuls of coffee down, while his cup chattered on his teeth, before having his first drink of the day. He was then able to work, after a fashion, for about two hours, after which the drink took over. It was the first time that I had come across an alcoholic at close quarters and it was frightening. While drunk, he fell over and broke his leg and I was easily able to persuade the doctor in the Army hospital that it was in everyone's interests, particularly the unfortunate drunken captain, that he should be repatriated at once and I never saw him again. I suspect that he had a short life expectancy.

It was to be expected that the senior RASC officers would have the lowest expectations of a young cavalry officer who was not intending to be a Regular officer. Accordingly, I took precautions. Running the depot was simple. All young officers are advised to do what the Sergeant-Major says, and this I did. On one occasion, when invited as a guest to the sergeants' mess, I noticed that there were large quantities of apricot brandy on offer, this being just after the Sergeant-Major had asked me to sign a document writing off a consignment of apricots as having gone bad, which made me guess that some of the load must have been salvageable and exchanged for the bottles in the mess. It caused me no anxiety; it simply reflected the real world in an occupying army which had just won a war.

I committed one act which was undoubtedly a court-martial offence. I was commanding 918 Company of the RASC, when I received a letter from Headquarters telling me that, since 918 was a war-time company, it was to become 60 Company, which was a Regular Army company. This was of no interest to me but the letter instructed me that all of 918's accounts were to be closed, the funds in them to be remitted to Headquarters, and I was to open new accounts for 60 Company. One of these accounts existed solely as a fund for the welfare of the men; I forget how it was funded, but, in effect, it was their money. I regarded this part of my orders as grossly unfair. There was no point in arguing about it, so I set about transferring all but a pittance from the old account to the new by means which could only be described as dubious. I felt no guilt about this.

There is an old Army saying, 'Bullshit baffles brains'. This can be translated as 'If everything looks as it ought to, no one will look further.' In accordance with this maxim, I bought brightly-coloured checked tablecloths for the dining tables in the men's mess, together with little flower vases, which I ensured were filled with fresh flowers. I created a team of four prisoners of war under the command of a lance-corporal. After the men went on parade in the morning, this team went round the barrack rooms, tidied the men's beds and the kit on them and generally cleared up the barrack rooms as well as all other rooms in communal use. Then they went round the camp picking up cigarette ends and other rubbish. After that, starting at the entrance to the camp, they whitewashed everything that could possibly be whitewashed and painted red anything like fire alarms; having done this all round the camp, they did it again. The intention was to create the appearance of a camp in peace-time Aldershot, which it achieved, resulting in it looking smarter than any other camp in Austria. Of course, this was possible because I held all the supplies of paint and whitewash, which others had to request and be able to justify doing so.

When the Colonel Commanding the RASC in Austria (CRASC) arrived, together with his Adjutant (a Captain), expecting to find what they expected to find with a young cavalry lieutenant in charge, they were dumbfounded. They never got round to discovering that many of the vehicles did not work; for good reasons, but I never had to give them. They left having not been able to make a single criticism and having been on the receiving end of as many complaints and suggestions that I had been able to think of.

Shortly after this, a Regular officer, a Major, arrived and took charge. Not long after, a bridge in Italy which carried the railway line from there into Austria was swept away in a storm. I was sent with about forty lorries to collect stranded troops. On my way, I encountered a checkpoint with a Corporal who had instructions to check the documents of every Army vehicle, which I think was to prevent people going on unauthorised weekends to Italy. This would have taken nearly an hour and I refused to allow him to do it, saying that my Headquarters would confirm my authority. One might have thought that whoever the Corporal reported to would have appreciated that it was hardly likely that so large a convoy was unauthorised, but a few weeks later I was sent for by CRASC (one would also have thought that he would have had more sense). He and his Adjutant were both dressed in Service dress rather than battledress, as I was. Doubtless, this was to demonstrate the seriousness of it. I explained the (obvious) reason for what I had done and ended by saying that I would act in the same way again. This completely nonplussed CRASC, who, presumably, had expected a repentant apology, which would have resulted in my being given a lecture and warning about my future conduct. As it was, there was very little that he could do about it. To court-martial me would have been wholly absurd, and I had only been lent to the RASC by my regiment. I cannot remember that he said anything; certainly nothing by way of condemnation and I went off, to the evident rage of the Adjutant, who did not like me.

I saw CRASC once again a few months later in an officers' club in Vienna. He had ceased to be CRASC having reverted to his peace-time rank of Major. He smiled at me weakly and I smiled back. I was rather sorry for him. He must have been in his late forties and at the end of a six-year world war was only a Major and probably retired as such.

16th/5th The Queen's Royal Lancers

Being a yeomanry, i.e. not a peace-time, regiment, the RGH was disembodied in the summer of 1946 and, thankfully, I was able to join the 16th/5th not very far away in Austria. It was very different from the RGH in two respects. It had landed in Tunisia and engaged in the last phase of the Desert War. It had then fought its way into Sicily and up Austria, and all its senior officers had been decorated. Being a Regular regiment, it observed rules and regulations to an extent that the RGH did not. However, it was very civilised and was very tolerant of young officers who did not intend to stay in the Army.

I cannot remember which regiment I was in when I found myself with my troop in a small market town on the eastern border of Styria in charge of a crossing point into the Russian zone. We did not have to do very much except to deal, to such extent as we could, with complaints by farmers that Russian troops had crossed the border and robbed their farmhouses. I would meet the young Russian officer who commanded their side of the crossing point and complain about it and he would deny that it had happened. Sometimes, he would give me some schnapps and sometimes I would give him whisky. He was unable to tolerate the whisky to the extent that I could the schnapps. He disappeared, and I learnt that the poor fellow had fallen from his motorcycle when crossing the bridge and had broken his leg. He seemed a nice enough chap and I hope that he survived all of Stalin's purges, which I am sure was not likely in the case of those Polish officers whom I met in Italy who returned to Poland.

I met the Polish officers when I was sent on an absurd physical training course in Venice and I went there again when I was instructed to take three prisoners of war there. Two were German Generals who were to give evidence at General Kesselring's trial (he was sentenced to death but reprieved and released seven years later). I was accompanied by two regimental policemen, who are always the stupidest men in the regiment. The Generals were working for the Americans and I accepted their parole. The third man was to be tried for shooting a British prisoner of war and I had him manacled to the side of the railway compartment throughout the overnight journey. I handed over this last man to a Sergeant in Field Intelligence, who was a small man with a large revolver. When I returned from handing over the Generals, I found that the regimental policemen had vanished, persuaded by the little Sergeant, who should never have been sent on his own, to accompany him. As the regiment was about to move to Schleswig in north Germany near the Danish border, they took about a month to get back to us. As the Adjutant flatteringly put it when I told him that the RPs had vanished, 'It would not have mattered so much if it had been you who disappeared.' Although I did not have a reserved compartment on my return journey, I was left on my own because I had bought three gorgonzolas for the mess and everyone who tried to join me was driven away by the smell.

The winter of 1946/47 was great fun. In effect, except for the Christmas period, I spent most of my time skiing. There were satisfactory ski slopes not far away and the regimental ski team also took a house in St Anton. Of course, the area was much less developed than is now the case and there was only one ski lift. However, except for week-ends, we were about the only people on the ski slopes and were able to ski down the Khandahar race course and several other routes from the top of the lift. Using skins on our skis, we were able and fit enough to walk up the mountains and ski down them through virgin snow. This was a marvellous way to earn one's pay. The penalty to be paid was having to race. Slalom races were fun but downhill races terrified me. On a race day the top of the mountain seemed much colder than on other days. Standing at the top as people hurled themselves down the near vertical start at intervals caused my heart to fall increasingly lower than my boots. Then it was my turn to stand with my skis projecting about a foot over space and the starter would say, 'Ten, five, ready, steady, go,' and with a great shove I, too, would hurl myself off the platform, after which I was far too busy trying to stay upright and get down as quickly as possible to have time to feel frightened.

The regiment won the competition for the Army in Austria (BTA) and I was selected for the BTA team to compete against British Armies elsewhere. I think that we lost, but it prolonged our skiing period until about the time that the snow melted. Amazingly, I suffered no injury, indeed, I cannot recollect falling down during a race, save for one occasion when I took off over a bump and the front of my skis went into the far side of a hole where someone had fallen earlier and which I could not see when I left the ground. Fortunately, both skis broke about a foot from the end and I merely rolled down the mountain a little way. In those days skis were made of wood and I suspect that modern skis would not break like that, but the mechanism for releasing a foot is much more effective than it was then and, of course, if the foot was not released there was a considerable risk of a leg fracture. Since I was not even the best skier in the regiment, I did not receive any personal prizes, save as a member of the regimental team. Skiing was the only sport that I was good at, although I could ride competently and had the doubtful honour of being Captain of the Third Fifteen (Rugby Football) at Downside. After I left the Army, I never took part in competitive sport – not even bridge, if one is allowed to call that a sport, which I think must be permissible since one could get a half-blue for it.

When the regiment left Klagenfurt for Schleswig, I was left behind to bring up the wives and children later. Of course, I immediately went off to ski for a couple of weeks, this being interrupted only by a message telling me that, if I did not get one of the wives out of Austria within twenty-four hours she would be arrested by the vice police. She was an Italian whom the unfortunate soldier had met as the regiment fought its way up Italy and, obviously, had resorted to her pre-marriage occupation. When I found her and persuaded her that I was not one of her clients, I discovered that she had neither a passport nor the document which was issued to such wives in lieu of a passport. I took the only sensible course and forged a document which I hoped looked rather like the real thing. It stated that it entitled her to travel from Austria to join the regiment in Germany. Technically, it was not a forgery in that I signed it in my name, writing my rank so badly that I hoped that to a casual eye it might appear that I was a Lieutenant-Colonel rather than a Lieutenant, particularly since I stamped over the rank with a smudged stamp. Of course, I was not entitled to issue such a document. I put her on to the train myself, meeting my cousin Pat, who was an Army officer, when doing so. With this document she travelled through Switzerland, into France to a Channel port, where she got on to another train and went through Belgium and Holland to Germany. I rather doubt that the marriage was successful.

When I rejoined the regiment, I found that Schleswig was a nice place in that we were in comfortable barracks on the coast of the Baltic. We were able to go yachting a great deal and had plenty of horses, together with ample time to ride them because there was no work for us to do. One day, I received a pay advice which informed me that I was an acting Captain and, shortly afterwards a temporary Captain, being the honorary rank which I was given when I left the Army. I am confident that this promotion was wholly unintentional, since I was far from being the senior lieutenant and, at those levels, promotion was by seniority. The reason for it was that I had been made Education Officer, the rank for that appointment being Captain. I am sure that neither the Colonel nor the Adjutant realised this. Of course, I did not reveal it to anyone and did not put the third pip on my uniform, but the extra pay was welcome.

I also took part in a tattoo in Berlin when the regiment put on an event invented before the war. Highwaymen, who were the best riders, were seen vaulting, peg-sticking etc. until a coach and four appeared and was held up, whereupon a troop of lancers, commanded by me, charged the highwayman. I killed their leader, who was my Squadron Sergeant-Major, in a sword fight and we rode off escorting the coach with the remaining highwaymen as our prisoners. It was put on in the evening in the Olympic Stadium. This was fun. I was in full dress and had to learn some of the old cavalry drill. I also learnt why in old prints officers are seen charging well ahead of their men. The sound of sixteen lancers riding thigh to thigh behind you with lances in the horizontal position causes one to keep well ahead! During a rehearsal, my horse, which had a hard mouth, tried to bolt. Instinctively, I brought my right hand down to grip the reins, which caused my sword to stick out horizontally and I nearly decapitated the very tall Commander-in-Chief, who had come to watch. Had I succeeded, I suspect that the penalty would have been something like boiling in oil à la *Mikado*. Fortunately, he was a 12th lancer and thought it rather funny.

I received a letter saying that I would be released from the Army in November 1947. I wrote to Jesus College reminding them that I had failed to obtain a scholarship from them in 1944 and asking if I could go up in January. In those days, there was never any question about being accepted; however, the reason why I was allowed to go up in January was that the universities were having to cope with the backlog of those who, like me, were going up late because of the war. Consequently, I was there for only five terms and did not do part one of the law degree course.

Conveniently, the regiment was posted back to England shortly before I was demobilised and, being now twenty-one, I had to embark on acquiring the necessary knowledge and qualifications to start upon the career which my Headmaster had suggested. Although at the time, I chafed at being kept in the Army for over two years after the war ended, in the long term I think that the experience was valuable to me and it was not unpleasant after I left Sandhurst.

5

CAMBRIDGE

Cambridge was in a strange state at the time in that most of the undergraduates had been in the Services and some of them, who had been through much of the war, had held quite high rank; I remember one who had been a brigadier. Also, instead of the feeling of liberation which must be experienced by someone coming straight from school, it felt absurdly restrictive. Without permission, one had to be back in college or lodgings by, I think, eleven at night. If one had not got permission it was necessary to climb walls, choosing places where there were not revolving spikes. This problem was solved for me when I met Tony Armstrong-Jones at a party and discovered that he had a key to a door in an outer wall which let one into a manually operated heavy goods lift. I had the key copied the next day.

Getting my mind to work again was also a problem. Three and a half years in the Army is not a good preparation for academic life. One of my tutors told me later that he had to keep one tutorial ahead of us. Foreseeing the problem, during my last few months in the Army, I had forced myself to learn large chunks of Shakespeare by heart, since I knew that a law degree course is largely a matter of learning the names of cases and statutes; indeed, I wonder whether it can truly be said to be something for academic study, since the amount of ratiocination is very limited and it is simply a matter of applying the law to the facts of a case, the law being the least of a barrister's problems in most cases.

Although I only did part two, it was necessary to learn some of what I would have learnt in part one. Consequently, I had to work harder than someone who had done part one. It required considerable self-discipline. Lectures and tutorials were almost a relaxation; most of my time was spent reading books and memorising cases and statutes, which is very dreary. I regard academic law as boring; it is akin to a plumber learning how to use the tools of his trade.

Throughout my life I have tried to avoid working after dinner. Getting up early was never a problem, but for me to force my mind to function after dinner has always been a real penance; I do not mind getting up as early as necessary, since, after the initial shock to the system, my mind functions far better and quicker than it does in the evening. Consequently, after dining in Hall, I would go off to a pub called The Bath (an odd name), where I would foregather with my friends, sometimes before going off to a party.

I can remember few of my tutors. There was an extraordinary Irishman, whose name escapes me, who had been obliged to resign his fellowship in a college because of drink. He was an allegedly reformed alcoholic, although it was suspected that it was not tea that he would pour out of a teapot during tutorials. He was reputed to have been President of Mexico or some similar then unstable nation for one day. However, he taught crime well and in an amusing fashion. My tutor for tort, Sir Arthur Armitage, went on to become Vice-Chancellor of Manchester University. Years later, he told me that he always relied on my advice about foreign currencies for travel purposes. How I acquired such a strange reputation in his eyes, I cannot think.

My college tutor, who also taught me contract, ended up with the most prestigious title that I know, His Excellency Sir Robert Jennings, QC. This is because he became a judge at the International Court in The Hague. He was a nice, amusing teacher and very competent. He became an Honorary Bencher of Lincoln's Inn. Not long ago, he told me that, in his view, I was the best chairman of the Jesus College Law Society because I decided that the most satisfactory use of our funds was to have a sherry party to which we invited the Jesus law dons. It would never have crossed my mind to do anything else and I cannot imagine what other chairmen might have thought was more appropriate.

I am conscious of the fact that there are no references to people who went on to achieve great things. Quite simply, I had to work so hard that, except for drinking in the evenings (in my eyes an essential relaxation), I had no time for anything else. In many ways, this was a waste of an opportunity to be at one of the best universities in the world, but I was very conscious of the need to get on as quickly as possible in competition with many others situated like me.

When I made my first appearance before a judge, it was in a moot at Cambridge. The protagonists argue a complex point of law created by stating the facts and leaving the point of law to be argued, hence the phrase a 'moot point'. In retrospect, it was an honour to be chosen to do it. I cannot remember what the point was but the judge was Tom Denning, who became Master of the Rolls and one of the most distinguished judges in the twentieth century. I do recollect that both I and my opponent had assiduously researched decisions in other common law countries as well as those in English courts. However, Tom said, 'Surely we do not need to look at foreign cases?' although it was more a statement than a question. This was quite funny, since he had a habit of seizing upon any foreign case which he thought would bolster his judgement. But he treated us very courteously, as he did when in court. It was well known that because the most difficult unrepresented litigant would feel that he was facing such a sympathetic judge, he was much briefer than would otherwise have been the case, following which Tom would dismiss his appeal with alacrity.

I appeared before him on many occasions and, when I became a Bencher in 1977, I got to know him well. It was rather a hazard to sit next to him at lunch if one was in court. The adjournment for lunch, which continued, rather quaintly, to be called 'the midday adjournment', was from one to two. One would throw one's wig and gown on to the bench and go to the Inn as quickly as possible, which took about five minutes. Although everything was organised to ensure that one was served very quickly, there was no time to waste. The fact that one was wearing one's white bands and court jacket made it obvious that one was in court. However, almost invariably, Tom would seize one's forearm in a vice-like grip, making it impossible to continue eating while he told some long tale.

He was a very nice man but, like many great men, he had his faults. His wife, who was only partially sighted, was constantly being asked to provide meals for people at virtually no notice. He had a degree of rectitude which can only be described as very excessive. Apart from his enormous ability, he had an uncanny ability to persuade usually sensible judges to agree with him in making decisions which were patently wrong. As a result I got a number of briefs in the House of Lords which I should not have done. I got the impression that he did not think much of me as a lawyer and I remember a case which involved a very recondite point of law, necessitating a great deal of research, which I won, after which he said, 'Michael, I suppose you got your junior to research the law,' which was, of course, correct up to a point, but which I thought carried an innuendo! However, I thought that it was prudent not to point out to him that I won nearly all the cases in which I had appeared before him, if not in his court, on appeal to the Lords.

He lived in Hampshire in the village in which he was born, but had a flat in the Inn. Every Monday, he would set off for London, taking with him four plastic containers which were each labelled Monday, Tuesday, etc., inside which were his dinners, which he would eat in his flat in the Inn. He was frequently asked to make after-dinner speeches, but he delivered the same speech each time. The worst instance was when he gave a speech at lunch and dinner in Sydney and, of course, gave the same speech both times; unfortunately, seventy-five per cent of the guests were the same on each occasion. At a dinner in the Mansion House, Joan was sitting next to Tommy Lund, the Secretary General of the Law Society, who had to listen to Tom so often that he knew the speech by heart. 'He will tell this one, that one and the other one, etc.,' said Tommy. During the speech, he would whisper to Joan, 'here comes number two' etc., but as it went on, he said, 'He's missed out three! No, here it comes after four.' As a result, Joan was laughing in the wrong places.

Going to London at week-ends was an interesting experience, because I stayed at the Cavendish Hotel, run by the renowned Rosa Lewis. She had been a celebrated cook, much favoured by Edward VII, to such an extent that hostesses who invited him to dinner often asked Rosa to come to their home to cook it. The hotel was, as it still is, in Jermyn Street, although the old building was demolished and it is now an ordinary large, expensive hotel. Rosa had a Crown lease, given to her by Edward; of course, it was widely rumoured that it was a reward for past favours, for which he was so notorious. It was a rambling building in a dilapidated state. I understood that there were some well-appointed suites, usually occupied by Americans. Young men stayed in rooms at the top with peeling wallpaper, and the bath – I think that there was just one for us – was covered with brown stains. There was a dining room, where people forced a cup of black coffee down at breakfast, to assist recovery from the night before. No one ate any other meal there, because the cooking was so bad. It was an ideal arrangement for all concerned. One could not stay there unless known to the management or having an introduction. We paid no more than one would have done in a doss-house, but our value to the hotel was that we were obviously upper-class, gilded youths who enhanced the raffish reputation of the place in the eyes of the Americans.

Rosa was very old when I stayed there and the place was run by an efficient woman. Rosa sat in a small sitting room just inside the hotel entrance. If you had time to kill, you walked slowly past her room and she would shout out to you to come in. Often others were already there, drinking champagne. If more of it was needed, Rosa would pull at a long bell-rope and one of the two elderly waiters would shuffle in. 'Yes Madam?' 'Champagne, Charles.' 'Whose account?' If there was an American present, he knew that it was his duty to pay. If there was no American there, Rosa would say 'Oh! That American,' and he would find it on his account. The Americans knew that this was part of the price that they had to pay in order to be allowed to stay in the hotel.

She often said to me, 'You are getting more like your father every day.' It would not have surprised me if she did know him, since I have no doubt that, as a young Edwardian bachelor, he was probably at dinners for which she cooked. However, she might well have mistaken me for someone else and I could hardly say, 'Who do you think I am?' Certainly, given my lifelong inability to remember names, I would not like it to be said to me.

In December 1948, I was a member of the Cambridge ski team and I went to Sestrière to race against Oxford. I never got my half-blue because I fractured my leg a few days before the race, albeit it was only a crack fracture. Anyone from the universities could go with us, and among those who did was Rudolf Krefting, who had joined the Army on the same day as me and had gone on to pass out at Sandhurst on the same day. He was Norwegian in origin and therefore knew how to ski. With him came his very pretty sister, Eve. So, too, did Hugh Griffiths, later a Law Lord. I had not met him before and he was there because he hoped to persuade Eve to marry him, which she did.

Meeting him was one of those accidents which determined the course of my life. He was a pupil of Ronald Armstrong-Jones, father of Tony, who married Princess Margaret. Late one night as we were drinking coarse red wine which made rivulets in the tongue, in the cheapest bar in the hotel, he asked me if I had arranged a pupillage. I told him that I had not; indeed, it had not occurred to me that I ought to do so, nor would I have known how to set about doing it. He asked me if I would like him to make the arrangements. Of course, I said yes, and a few weeks after we got back to England, I received a letter from him saying that I should arrange to see Patrick O'Connor. This I duly did. In those days it was not difficult to obtain a pupillage, whereas now my old chambers receives about 350 applications for the three pupillages offered. Patrick sat in a chaotic-looking room surrounded by heaps of papers. We had a few minutes' conversation, which enabled him to see that I was not drunk, mad, etc., and it might have helped that he was an old Downside boy; he then asked me when I would like to start. I said that I would quite like to help a candidate at the forthcoming General Election and we agreed that I should start at the beginning of the Easter term, 1950. But for meeting Hugh Griffiths, I would doubtless have ended up in different chambers, possibly doing a different kind of work. Furthermore, since it was extremely difficult to find a seat in chambers at the end of pupillage, I might have had to abandon the Bar and take up entirely different work.

In preparation for the Bar, I thought it would be useful to become used to speaking in public before an intelligent, critical and vocal audience, and the Cambridge Union was the obvious solution. I had done a great deal of debating at school and had been Chairman of the Debating Society and now I spoke at the Union quite often, and on one occasion was a 'paper speaker', i.e. listed as one of the two proponents or opponents of a motion. However, I resisted suggestions that I should become more closely involved in either the Union or the University Conservative Association: it seemed to me that I had quite enough to do.

In the summer of 1949, I duly got my degree, a 2:1, and went off with friends for a holiday to Paris. Because I had not done part one of the law degree, I had to pass two intermediate Bar exams in Roman law and constitutional law in September, before taking my finals in December. This speedy process was due to two things: first, that the Bar exams were absurdly simple, and second, the incredible law tutors, Gibson and Weldon. It was an amazing place. They were crammers. One attended their lectures in Chancery Lane and learnt by heart what was dictated to one. Of course, it was boring beyond belief, but it did the trick. The most memorable of the teachers was a man called Padley. He was a drunk. Widgery, who went on to be Chief Justice, had been a teacher there. He told me that on one occasion, never repeated, he accompanied Padley to Waterloo Station. Padley stopped at the nearest public house, which was close to Gibson's, where they had a drink. Padley then stopped and had a drink at every pub on the way to Waterloo. However, in the morning, Padley was sober and, if one simply memorised what he dictated, it was impossible to fail. I suspect that, since it must have been infinitely more boring for Padley to teach in this fashion than it was to listen, it was only tolerable when sustained by whisky in large quantities.

I was called to the Bar in January 1950, exactly two years after I started at Cambridge. After the Call Ceremony, all the newly called barristers were invited to drink port with the Benchers. I sat next to an elderly Chancery junior called Stamp. He was Treasury Counsel, his practice being confined to doing tax work for the Crown, which he had done for many years. He duly advised me that all I needed to do to succeed at the Bar was to learn the tax statutes by heart. Armed with this helpful advice, I went off to a jolly party, where I met a girl called Joan Brodrick, whom I had met first at a Christmas party a few weeks before and whom I was later to persuade to marry me, which has been one of the most sensible things that I have ever done. I cannot recall what I did between my call and the General Election in the spring, but I then went off to help John Lowe, who fought as Conservative candidate for Gravesend, which was a safe Labour seat. I found it very exciting and enjoyed it immensely, even being allowed to harangue a meeting myself – in retrospect, I suspect not very well. So, I was now all set to embark upon the daunting task of becoming a successful barrister.

6

THE BAR

In 1950, the profession was very different from what it is to-day. There were about two thousand practising barristers; to-day there are about ten thousand. As a result, everyone at the Common Law Bar in London knew everyone else. At the end of my pupillage year, I knew every Queen's Bench judge and their idiosyncrasies, of which there seemed to be a great many. Within about three years, I could say the same about every London Metropolitan stipendiary magistrate and every County Court judge who sat within fifty miles of London.

The level of competence of High Court judges was about the same as to-day, although, the Press being uncritical, the standard of conduct was much lower. County Court judges varied from competent to utterly inept. Most stipendiary magistrates were inept and the conduct of some of them was appalling. Over twenty-five per cent of the Bar was of less than five years' call, because, except for those unfit for military service, we had come to the Bar after we were released from the Services, so that, in 1950, everyone who had reached the age of eighteen after about September 1939 had started in practice after about October 1945. To these, for practical purposes, were added those who had been called a year or so before war began and had to start again from scratch. Of course, able people learnt fast by observing, as opponents, those who had not been in any form of national service, e.g. Irishmen, and some who had worked in the Judge Advocate General's Department, and their equivalents in the other forces, who had conducted courts martial. The standard of QCs was particularly low, and quite often when in court, I would think that, in all my inexperience, I could do the case better; such people would never get silk to-day.

Patrick O'Connor had the largest junior practice in Ronald Armstrong-Jones's chambers at 5 Essex Court in the Temple. It was, and is, a gloomy building, which at that time was wholly as it had been built in Victorian times – for example, the heating consisted of inadequate gas fires so that on a Monday the stalactites were not melted until about noon.

Ronnie was a strange man. Married three times, which posed problems when Tony married Princess Margaret, he had immense charm, and when meeting someone, especially a woman, he contrived to convey the impression that one was the person whom he had most wanted to meet that day. He was very kind and I remember that when Joan was still in bed after the birth of a child, he appeared with a car boot full of flowers which he had picked at his home in Wales and driven to London. He was very competent, albeit within strictly confined limits. Towards the end of his career at the Bar, he would only accept briefs in road traffic cases and those in which people fell downstairs, tripped, etc., and then only if no point of law was involved, and he would not conduct any case in the Court of Appeal, even if he had conducted it at trial. This was because he was completely lacking in confidence. When he started a speech or cross-examination, his voice would quaver for a few moments. He wrote a letter of condolence to the Lord Chancellor following a death of a relation. This was misfiled in the file of applications for silk. In those days, the selection process was extremely simple, and a Civil Servant simply collected the names at the end of the letters in the file and they were put before the Lord Chancellor, doubtless after the list had been circulated to senior judges for comment. As a result, to his complete astonishment, Ronnie was given silk without applying for it. Since his practice was good enough to warrant it, a person of a different nature would simply have accepted it; not Ronnie, and a letter of correction was published in *The Times*. Of course, it meant that when he did apply a year or so later, there could be no doubt about him getting it.

However, he was a very competent cross-examiner. He led me in a case before Lord Goddard, the Lord Chief Justice, who was sitting as a trial judge – something which would be unthinkable to-day, unless the LCJ was visiting a newly opened court. The plaintiff was a pedestrian who was crossing from Hyde Park to Park Lane when he was knocked down by our client's car. The first questions that a witness would be asked were to state his name and address and the plaintiff gave an address north of the park. Ronnie began his cross-examination by asking where the plaintiff had been going and received the reply that he had been going home; obviously, he had not expected the question. Ronnie looked and sounded puzzled about why the plaintiff had been going east when his home lay north. 'Were other people crossing in the same direction at the time?' 'Yes.' 'Were you walking in company with them?' 'No.' Ronnie continued to profess himself to be wholly puzzled and asked questions about the route home which the plaintiff had intended to take. As we knew, the truth was that the plaintiff had picked up a prostitute in Hyde Park, which was infested with them in those days, and was on his way back to her flat with her. Goddard was no fool; indeed, contrary to the way in which he was portrayed by his enemies because he was a very tough judge, he was a very clever man and very astute. He understood the position very quickly without Ronnie having to state it. Since Goddard was a very moral person in the Victorian mould, although he had to decide that our client was to blame, I have no doubt that this coloured his attitude to the plaintiff. The size of the award made to him was less than would otherwise have been the case, and his share of the blame more, and although I am sure that it was not a deliberate decision, like it or not, it is difficult to feel as benevolently disposed to someone of whom one disapproves as to others.

Goddard was the right Chief Justice for his day. After the war, inevitably, servicemen who had been encouraged to be murderous towards the enemy and who had been fully occupied and paid for being so, found themselves in civilian life where such qualities were criminal, and many of them were wholly unable to settle down in respectable employment. This also applied to officers, many of whom found it impossible to obtain jobs which were commensurate with their rank in the Services. Whereas the latter simply became disgruntled and resentful (Kipling's post-First World War poem 'Tommy' was absolutely correct), some of the former were an easy prey to temptation. Lead on church roofs was valuable and easily stolen and an epidemic of such cases was stopped only when Goddard handed out some very deterrent sentences.

He had a curious habit of staring towards counsels' entrance to his court, and for a young barrister who wandered into his court to be met by his terrifying face apparently staring directly at him was unnerving. He was extremely tough and neither wasted time himself nor allowed anyone else to do so; 'What is your best point?' he would say to counsel for an appellant. 'Well, I don't think much of it.' One way or the other, appeals before him did not take long. I put it like that because, although tough, he had a fierce sense of justice; 'He was a beast, but a just beast,' (Kipling again). Of course, he was a hate figure in the eyes of the egalitarian-minded post-war Left. (Joan has the distinction of having danced with him at an Inns of Court regimental ball.)

In one room in chambers there were good examples of how quite junior barristers had held senior ranks. Predictably, they were called 'the three old colonels'. None took silk; one, who looked like a stereotype of a colonel, save for the absence of a moustache, became Chief Metropolitan Magistrate and was knighted, as was then the custom. The second also became a 'stipe', while the third did have a fairly senior judicial office as Chairman of London Sessions. I should add that moustaches do not really look good under wigs, although two people who wore them became respectively Lord Chief Justice (Widgery) and a Lord of Appeal in Ordinary (Goff); but, obviously, they were outstanding lawyers.

One of the most remarkable members of chambers was Niall MacDermot. He had had great difficulty in deciding whether to support the extreme Left or the extreme Right. He became a colonel in the Intelligence Corps and told the story of a filing clerk who said, 'Here's a file with the same name as Major MacDermot – Oh, it is Major MacDermot!' He had been a fascist, or close to it. When I came into chambers he was very left wing but became a Labour MP of a moderate persuasion. He continued to practise as a QC until he became a minister and in 1968 was Minister of Housing. His wife was a very nice eastern European named Ludmilla. MI5 suspected her of being a Russian spy and this effectively ended his political career and he became Secretary-General of the International Commission of Jurists in Geneva. (I am confident that she was not a spy in the true sense, if anything, she merely passed on gossip.)

There were other members of chambers who decided that the Bar was not the career for them, or that they would lead a less strenuous life in chambers outside London; and one who became Chairman of London Transport.

It is daunting being a pupil. It is a very different world from that of a university and far removed from learning about the law in the academic sense. Everyone senior to me seemed to be very competent; a view which altered as I learnt more! The challenge for me was worse than for others because I did not realise for a considerable time that I was surrounded by some people of exceptional ability. Ted Eveleigh became a Lord Justice, Hugh Griffiths became a Law Lord and Patrick O'Connor became a Lord Justice. In addition, my successor as Patrick's pupil, Raymond Kidwell, was academically extremely able and had won four prizes in addition to firsts in his BA and BCL.

Patrick had a very large practice and on my first day did what was probably his last county court case, which was a road accident case against Ronnie Armstrong-Jones in front of a county court judge named Hodgson. Subsequently, I conducted many cases before Hodgson, who was a decent fellow but suffered from the distinct disadvantage that he could not drive, and nearly all my cases arose out of road accidents. Not surprisingly, he sometimes became infuriated by his inability to understand elementary points and he would sit shaking his head from side to side as if surrounded by a swarm of bees.

Patrick had an enormous capacity for alcohol only matched by mine; I am not sure which of us suffered most because of being able to match each other, although I think that his speed of recovery was better than mine. Hugh Griffiths had an extremely poor head for alcohol, which must have saved him a great deal of money over the years. Of course, in those days there was no law against driving after drinking a substantial amount; the only relevant offence was driving under the influence of drink. Someone had to be seriously drunk before a conviction could be obtained. Because sensible people did not get into this state, or their friends stopped them from driving if they did, it was possible to have several glasses of whisky after work before driving home. Consequently, many people in chambers would foregather in El Vino's, the renowned Fleet Street bar, which was patronised by barristers and the Press. I learnt a great deal about legal problems on these occasions because all the talk was about cases which people had done that day or were to do next day, or problems with cases about which they were advising. I do not recollect any of us having an accident on the way home.

Being a pupil is like being a plumber's apprentice. The pupil spends all day with his pupil-master, in court and in conferences, and writes opinions etc. which are due to be done by the pupil-master, who reads them, makes comments about them or simply does his own drafts, which the pupil reads before they are signed. Obviously some pupil-masters are more conscientious and some more able than others. I was very fortunate in having someone who was both very able and very conscientious. Of course, a competent pupil will be asked to do research, but any help that he is able to give is heavily outweighed by the value of the training which he receives. In particular, the most important training comes from simply being in court watching and listening. During the first six months of pupillage, a pupil is not allowed to appear in court himself, but in the remaining six months he is able to start to try to be a successful barrister and at once realises that it is not as easy as it appeared when watching his pupil-master and other experienced counsel.

My opportunities to demonstrate my ability were infinitesimal. I appeared on four occasions in the financial year ending 5 April 1951, the first being on 24 October 1950. In all I made £27, before expenses. Ten guineas of that was for a case before the London County Council's Licensing Committee. Theatrical and other agents of that kind had to be licensed, and a disgruntled client unsuccessfully attempted to prevent renewal of our client's licence. I was led by an unsuccessful QC, who must have been paid fifteen guineas; a junior's fee was two-thirds that of his leader. I was instructed by Hans Beer, who was then an employee. Hans was a remarkable man to whom I owed a great deal. He was an Austrian Jew, who had wisely left Austria in 1938. He was extremely clever but had recognised that, having a very thick guttural accent, being a solicitor was the sensible option rather than the Bar. He had a wife named Gretl, so they really were Hansel and Gretl. She was an excellent cook – she went on to be the *Daily Telegraph*'s cookery writer and had several cookery books published. At this time she was employed at the famous agency S.H. Benson, where Joan was an advertising copywriter. Hans said to Joan, 'I must send some work to this excellent young man of yours,' and was as good as his word. The Senior

Clerk in chambers, Harold Standring, was far too stupid to realise that Hans was more intelligent than probably all the other solicitors who came to chambers in those days. He thought that Hans's accent was very funny and called him Herr Lager almost to his face. Effectively, he discouraged Hans from instructing me for several years. Happily, Hans eventually tried again, to my considerable advantage, as will appear.

In those days barristers' clerks wielded enormous power of patronage in that they were able to steer work towards members of chambers whom they thought would prosper best. The Senior Clerk's remuneration was based on clerks' fees, which operated on a sliding scale. Thus a brief fee of two guineas resulted in payment of £2 4s 7d. Clerks also received the shillings in the guineas, so that a two-guinea brief fee would result in the clerk receiving 4s 7d. In the case for which I received £10, the brief fee was 11 guineas and Harold would have got about 15s. In Victorian times, each barrister had his own clerk but by 1950, our chambers being about sixteen strong, Harold must have earned about as much as the barrister who was about halfway down in order of earnings, because he also received ten per cent of all earnings. Even then this was ludicrously too much but it was many years before the system was changed, since it could only be done when a Senior Clerk retired. At that time, we had three clerks, the other two being paid salaries, although the second had a small bonus based on the overall earnings of chambers. Precise arrangements differed from one set of chambers to another. Like all clerks that I can remember, ours came from the East End of London and educational attainments were minimal. When I ran chambers, I remember interviewing young boys for the post of Junior Clerk. William, the then Senior Clerk, asked each of them to write his name and address, this seeming to be the only educational requirement.

In April 1951, my pupillage ended and I became a 'squatter', i.e. I was allowed to use chambers without being a member of it. This was common at that time; the idea being that one tried to find a set of chambers which would take one on or left the Bar. Of course, this was a very insecure situation which should have caused me considerable anxiety, but I cannot recollect that it did so, in spite of the fact that it was plain that Harold did not appear to like me and, certainly, did not believe that I would be successful. I suspect that my lack of concern was partly due to the fact that I had no financial problems. My mother had given me an allowance of £1,000 a year and bought me a small house in Putney, which cost about £1,500. It was cheaper than would otherwise have been the case because the first floor, which had a kitchen and two other rooms, was occupied by a couple who had security of tenure under the Rent Acts, for which they paid a rent of £1 a week. On the ground floor, I had a sitting room, bedroom, dining room and a small kitchen. The bathroom was on the first floor and this I shared with the tenants. There was a large room on the second floor, which was occupied by a friend from my Cambridge days, who paid me a small rent. These weird arrangements were made odder by the fact that the tenants also had a large built-in cupboard in the room on the second floor. This type of situation was not uncommon in the post-war years.

It was a Victorian terraced house of a kind common in the outer London suburbs. My neighbours were working-class people, who regarded me and my friends as people from another world. Of course, we used to have parties and it was extraordinary to find that groups of neighbours would stand outside watching our guests arrive. However, everyone was very tolerant about our eccentricities. Being bachelors, we tended to have parties at the week-ends which went on into the small hours, or we came back from nights out at similar hours, which resulted in us getting up late and feeling the need for a glass of beer to revive us. There was a large Victorian pub a few hundred yards away, whose landlord was quite happy for us to arrive at opening time dressed in pyjamas and dressing gowns; I think that he regarded us as bringing some colour to the place. I had a cleaning lady, who came in while I was at work and therefore we seldom met. I would leave messages for her in a notebook, asking her to buy me food etc. She did her job to a bachelor's standard and would leave notes for me in the book; these always started 'Dear Mr Ogden', but while she always put down all the letters in my name, they were never in the right order and one began 'Dear Mr Gedon'.

Of course, barristers have to be married out of term time if they want to go away on honeymoon immediately afterwards. This is why Joan and I were married on 21 December 1951, the last day of the Michaelmas term. The amount of work that a bridegroom has to do in preparation for a wedding is extremely limited. We decided that we would be married in Spanish Place and we had a reception in a building in Piccadilly which now houses the National Farmers' Union but at that time was owned by a firm of caterers, which still exists, called Searcy Tansey. Having helped to arrange that, and found a best man and some ushers, that was about all I had to do in terms of preparation although, of course, poor Joan had to rush round doing all the things that brides have to do on these occasions.

The wedding service went ahead without any difficulty, notwithstanding the fact that the altar appeared to be thronged with priests. Canon Crea officiated and there was some bishop of whom I had never heard who appeared as well, doubtless recruited by Canon Crea, and, of course, Father O'Brien was present. Bishop Butler was also present, but not at the altar. The reception went well too, but we then spent a dire night at a ghastly hotel called either the Rembrandt or the Rubens near Victoria Station, whose principal activity appeared to be juggling crockery in the early hours of the morning or hoovering outside the bedroom door. We stayed in this abominable place because we had to catch an early train and it was near Victoria Station. Next morning we crossed the Channel and boarded the Arlberg Express, which proceeded at a stately pace through France and Switzerland, but then went on very slowly until it reached our destination, Kitzbühel, in the early hours of the following morning. It was strange to find ourselves being taken to our hotel in a sleigh drawn by horses and, upon our arrival, to be greeted by the hotelier with a little woollen nightcap with a bobble on top.

Of course, we spent the time skiing, until Joan succumbed to a stomach problem caused by the food which we were given being far richer than that we were used to in England. To add to this, while skiing, I fell over and dislocated my right shoulder. Thus, the honeymoon could be said to have been fairly typical of those of which one has heard. Nevertheless, we had a very pleasant time, sitting about drinking this and that and not doing anything, and Joan had been flattered by American friends of hers who, because she had never skied before and fell down frequently, remarked upon the fact that she fell 'so fluidly'. Of course, for Joan, who had never been to Austria before, many of the sights were extremely interesting. We were subjected to the local habits such as men dressed in lederhosen slapping their thighs vigorously whilst singing loudly and dancing, and, of course, she was particularly enchanted by the ride in the sled through the snow with all the bells on the horses tinkling as they went along.

After this, we returned to England, where I was greeted by the very welcome information that I was to be kept on as a tenant in chambers, and I therefore had to start putting my practice together in earnest.

Between 6 April 1951 and 20 December 1951, I did thirty-eight cases, eighteen of them being in November and up to the day before my wedding. I think that the fact that I was by then doing quite a lot of work, which, of course, I obtained only if there was no tenant available and acceptable to the solicitor or when a solicitor specifically asked for me, may have caused Harold to revise his views about me. However, I have no doubt that I was offered a tenancy when I got back from my honeymoon because of Patrick and, I suspect, his wife Mary, who liked me. Harold, whose attitude towards me altered the moment that he was told that I was to be made this offer, took me into Ronnie's room. Typically, when making me the offer, Ronnie rather plaintively remarked, 'I don't know where it will all end!' Since, at the time of writing this, chambers is about to amalgamate with another set and will be seventy-three strong, I hate to think what he would have said about that.

Joan's arrival in my house had a sensational effect both on the tenants and the cleaning lady. However, once they had overcome their shock, things settled down and we continued to live there until 1954. I regarded it as a great compliment that, when the tenants learnt that we were leaving, they asked if they could come too.

Once I had been made a tenant, the clerks started to try to get work for me and very soon I found myself being very busy. In the year ending April 1952, I made about £250 and in the two following years, £750 and £1,000. Most of this work consisted of defending drivers in magistrates' courts or in coroners' courts, the paymaster being insurance companies. As a young officer in Austria and Germany, there had been little on which I had needed to spend money and at Cambridge my Government grant covered my expenses, so I had been able to buy a small car. This was essential because I had to go to courts up to about sixty miles from London. Traffic was much lighter than now and there were no difficulties about parking; indeed, until I got an Inner Temple parking licence, I was often able to leave the car all day in the Strand opposite the Law Courts. Quite often, I appeared in two or more courts on the same day. On one occasion I was at Kingston Coroner's Court at 9.30, Kingston County Court in the same building at 10.30, and I then travelled a few hundred yards to Surrey Quarter Sessions, also in Kingston, where I did two cases in which there were pleas of guilty. At 1.30 I was at Tower Bridge Juvenile Court and at 3.15 I did a contested case at Clerkenwell Magistrates' Court. This would be impossible to-day because of traffic congestion, parking problems and, not least, because court officials now are far less helpful than in those days. They would fit cases in to assist one, and lawyers were happy to assist by allowing each other to take precedence if someone had to go on to another court.

It was a very hectic life but, in some ways, more fun than the later stages in my career in that every day I had a new case, rather than having to spend days or weeks preparing for a long one. While the cases were simple, they were excellent training in advocacy and, particularly, cross-examination. After I had been a QC for a few years, my practice broadened and I found myself against very clever commercial silks. To my pleasure, I discovered that, by my standards, many were very poor cross-examiners. They had not gone into court as often as I had and, when they did so, they had been sitting behind a silk, who had done the cross-examining.

Some judges in the Commercial Court almost regarded hostile cross-examination as verging on the vulgar. In the late 1980s I had a reinsurance case before such a judge. A salmon fishery in a Norwegian fjord had been destroyed in a storm. It was a condition of the policy that a record should be kept of the number of fish in each cage, which consisted of nets suspended from wooden booms. How one managed to count such fish I do not know, but all involved agreed that it could be done. Breach of this condition would result in the claim failing. A witness said that there had been such a record kept in a hut at the fishery and he produced a large chart which had lists of the number of fish in each cage, which he said had been on the wall of the hut. While he was giving evidence, I got the usher to bring the chart to me. When I cross-examined, I asked where the chart was in the hut. 'On the wall.' 'On the wall? But how was it fixed to the wall?' 'By drawing pins, of course!' (said rather contemptuously). 'Show me the holes!' Of course, there were none; it was to discover this and anything else of interest that I had examined the chart. He then tried to pretend that it was only a copy of the original, but this was a hopeless lie. What was interesting was the judge's expression of utter distaste that such Old Bailey type of cross-examination should have taken place in the Commercial Court. Nevertheless, he disbelieved the witness.

In my early days, I appeared before far more extraordinary people. The coroner for the City of London had only one arm. He wrote down the evidence with something that looked like a quill pen. He wrote on sheets of paper using a dog's small gravestone as a paperweight. When he finished a page, he would put the pen in his mouth, pick up the gravestone, remove the sheet and replace the gravestone on the blank sheets. Of course, this all took time, but the proceedings were interminable because he called wholly unnecessary witnesses. 'You were the driver of the second ambulance to arrive at the scene of the accident...' On one occasion, I wanted to go to what was going to be a very good party. Time wore on and my chances of getting to the party started to look remote. Eventually, all the relevant evidence having been given, I could stand no more. I told him that I had a personal engagement that evening which I was anxious to keep. 'Oh dear, well I won't call the last four witnesses.' It was very kind of him, but all very weird. At least, the jury looked at me very gratefully.

A good stipendiary magistrate is better than the best lay bench because he needs no advice about the law from a clerk, as lay justices do, and, having no one to consult, is able to take short cuts because he does not have to consult before doing so. As a Recorder, I was very pleased when I became allowed to sit at the Central Criminal Court (the Old Bailey) and did not have to have justices sitting with me whom I had to consult about sentence. On my own, having read the papers beforehand, it was possible to say to defending counsel when he got up to mitigate, 'I do not intend to pass a sentence of imprisonment', or, if probation was mentioned, 'As far as I am concerned, it has to be a custodial sentence', meaning, 'You will have to go to the Court of Appeal to try to get that.' I did not regard myself as a severe sentencer and I am sure that I did not have that reputation, and I was only upset on appeal once, when a sentence was reduced.

A bad stipendiary magistrate is worse than any bench of justices because there is no one to temper his behaviour, whereas a Chairman of the Bench is no more than a first among equals. The only excuse is that I regard it as one of the worst jobs imaginable. True, it was three days' work a week, because there are two magistrates to each court, but each day's work is but a repetition of the previous day. Pleas of guilty all morning are followed by trials of a monotonously repetitive nature.

There were several stipendiary magistrates before whom it was virtually impossible to obtain a Not Guilty verdict and, if the nature of the case allowed it, I would always advise going to trial by jury. One such sat in South London. The only mitigating thing about him was that he was as beastly to the police as he was to everyone else. There was one occasion when a message was given to him that his car had been stolen. This produced a tirade of fury against the competence of the police, which was replaced by lavish praise when a further message came that it had been recovered. Unfortunately, there was a third message that it had been damaged when it was being brought back, which resulted in a scene more appropriate to an opera. On another occasion he got so angry with a police inspector that he threw a book at him. This was unwise because the inspector immediately went into the court next door asking for an arrest warrant for assault, since to throw something at someone is an assault, even if it misses the person that it is thrown at. This resulted in both courts having to adjourn while a very senior officer came from Scotland Yard to the court, which was in Balham, to persuade the inspector to withdraw his application.

Another stipendiary magistrate was verging on insanity. Once, during my cross-examination, when I got an answer which destroyed the prosecution case, he bounced up and down in his seat while making a two-fingered V sign to me. Another time, when I applied for bail pending trial, he turned to the police officer in charge of the case and asked what he had done with co-defendants previously committed for trial. On being told that he had remanded them in custody, he immediately said, 'Remanded in custody', without giving me a chance to say another word. Before the hearing, the officer had agreed with me that he would not oppose bail. I was so incensed that I told the officer that I intended to apply for bail to a High Court judge at the Law Courts in the Strand, which I did at 2 p.m., the decision by the Magistrate having been made at 11. As soon as the police officer confirmed that he did not oppose bail, the judge granted it so that the solicitor's clerk was waiting at the remand centre with the judge's order for release when the prison van arrived.

In a rather different mould was a kindly man who sat in South London. He spent his time either sketching the defendant or anyone else in court, or examining his stamp collection. If doing the latter, whenever he turned a page while one was addressing him he would courteously turn his head and nod at one. He was such a pleasant fellow that it was difficult to be vexed with him when he convicted, as he always did. He was not the only person to sketch while on the bench. County court judges were required to provide a copy of their notes to the Court of Appeal because there was no shorthand note taken. On one occasion the judge's note consisted only of a sketch of a villainous face entitled 'The Defendant'.

Another endearing character, named Wilson, sat at Marlborough Street. Wilson was a kindly fellow who regarded having driven fire engines etc., during the war as a very important mitigating factor in driving cases. Therefore, one would hear advocates saying things such as, 'I would ask you take into account the fact that my client drove an ambulance during the war, in the Shetlands,' or somewhere else where war made no difference at all to driving emergency vehicles save that there was no street lighting, made up for by the fact that there was very little traffic. His usual fine in such cases was five shillings, which, even then, was a paltry sum.

In Dartford there was a notorious lay magistrates' court. Only police officers were ever acquitted of driving cases in that court. Of course, all these courts which convicted everyone generated a great deal of unnecessary appeals with consequent expense.

Magistrates' courts in rural areas tended never to doubt the evidence of a police officer. A member of chambers, tells the story of a chairman of the bench who said, 'In this county we always accept the evidence of our police officers.' It would be difficult to imagine a greater inducement to perjury.

In 1952, Hans Beer instructed me to defend Bernard Gabriel Grealy at the Central Criminal Court (the 'Old Bailey'). From Grealy's perspective the incident must have been as terrifying as it was amazing. He was buying cigarettes in a tobacconist's shop when he heard a boy say, 'That's him!', whereupon he was promptly arrested for blackmail. The case against him was strong. Two other boys had picked him out at identification parades as the man who had promised them a small sum of money if they would go into a South London Underground station and collect a parcel from a man who would be holding a copy of the *Sporting Times*, a newspaper which, being pink in colour, was readily identifiable. When they did so, police officers pounced on them and each went with an officer to try to find the man, leading to Grealy's arrest. The victim, who had had the courage to go to the police, was being blackmailed for visiting a prostitute.

Grealy had only two things going for him. First, he was a very unintelligent Irish labourer and it was difficult to envisage him doing what was alleged. Second, his parish priest, who had been a member of the Baltic Exchange and believed in Grealy's innocence, persuaded his former colleagues to put up the money to have him privately represented, not only by Ogden, by now nearly a year out of pupillage, but by Gerald Howard, QC, until shortly before Senior Treasury Counsel at the Old Bailey, i.e. retained by the Director of Public Prosecutions.

In the event, neither of us had to do anything because the case was won by Beer. He discovered that the victim had driven to the prostitute's flat. He asked the AA and the RAC whether any enquiries had been made as to ownership of the vehicle. The RAC replied that there had been a routine enquiry by Dutch customs. This was untrue and resulted in the home of the clerk at the RAC who was responsible for the request having his home raided, where papers were found relating to this and other vehicles. He was arrested about two days before Grealy's trial was due to start and was later sentenced to four years' imprisonment.

I disliked Howard. He was very lazy and when later appointed a judge, he was very cold-hearted and unsympathetic. These days an acquitted defendant is automatically awarded his costs, unless he had done something to bring the prosecution on himself; in those days it was entirely discretionary. It had never occurred to me that Howard would not ask for costs. When he showed no sign of doing so, I leant forward and suggested it, but he would not. Since there was nothing to be lost by doing so, I can only think that it was because he was one of those prosecutors who feel that any defendant, proven innocent, as in this case, was very lucky. Certainly, it would have fitted in with his character as I found it when on the Bench. Had I been more senior, I would have raised my voice and spoken to Beer, who was in the row in front of Howard, and asked if I could make the application. After what Grealy had been through, it was monstrous not even to ask. Howard was also an MP, and I understood that he was equally unsatisfactory in that capacity.

I managed to put together a claim for damages against the RAC. It was based on somewhat uncertain ground in law, but the RAC did not want the publicity and we managed to get quite a reasonable sum in compensation. This horrifying case persuaded me at an early age of the dangers of convicting solely on identification evidence if the period of observation was short, although in this case there was a suggestion that the boys who picked him out at the identity parades had seen Grealy in the police station beforehand. In 1977, because of the number of wrongful convictions in such cases, the Court of Appeal laid down special guidelines for judges when summing-up in such cases. However, when I was the Assessor of compensation for all miscarriage of justice cases between 1978 and 1989, I dealt with a significant number of such cases.

In 1953, we moved to Elizabeth Street off Eaton Square. It was a pleasant Regency terraced house on four floors and therefore became increasingly impracticable as we had children, starting with Celia in 1954. However, it had the tremendous advantage of being only fifteen minutes' drive from the Temple. I had no wish to spend up to two hours every day in a metal box, whether car or train, and for the rest of my career I was never more than twenty minutes from chambers.

By this time, I was beginning to have more civil actions in county courts than motoring cases in magistrates' courts, which were more interesting and better paid. There seemed to be an even larger number of weird county court judges than there were weird stipendiary magistrates. In part, I think that many in both jobs were affected by the war. In the Army, I had noticed that many people who had spent some time as prisoners of war were odd to varying degrees and this applied no less to judges. The appalling conduct of the Japanese is well known. Apart from the SS divisions, the Germans and also the Italians observed the Geneva Convention; the Japanese were not signatories and their conduct was truly barbarous. As a result, I have never been able to feel at ease with them and I have doubts about whether their character has changed much.

One County Court Judge had been a Japanese POW. Doubtless, in his private life he was a very different person from what he was when sitting as a judge. In short, the word patience was unknown to him. Occasionally, this could be an advantage. I acted for an insurance company which was facing quite a small claim under a personal accident policy, whereby, if someone were off work due to an accident, there arose a claim for compensation under the policy. The plaintiff had hit upon quite an ingenious fraud. He would take out such a policy with an insurer, make a claim for a modest amount and then repeat the process with another insurer. His downfall occurred because he made a claim on an insurer which had recently amalgamated with another. His claim arrived on the desk of someone who had dealt with another of his claims when working for the other insurer, and it was noticed that the circumstances of the alleged accident were similar. Enquiries were made of all other accident insurers, as a result of which I was able to draw up a schedule listing a large number of claims, from which it was plain that the unfortunate man had a habit of being injured in the kitchen and when getting on and off buses. The court was full of representatives of insurers clutching files, and a whole day had been set aside. As soon as the judge sat down, he said to the plaintiff, who was representing himself, 'Are the details set out in this list (the schedule) correct?' 'I don't see what that's got to do with it.' 'If you don't answer the question I will dismiss your case.' 'I still don't see...' 'Case dismissed,' and we all went home.

Sussex had a particularly bad run of judges. When I first went to Brighton, the judge was lazy and had devised a very effective scheme for ensuring that cases were likely to proceed quickly. First, he would try cases in which both sides were represented by barristers, then those in which a barrister was on one side, followed by those in which both sides were represented by solicitors, those with solicitors on one side and, finally, cases in which there were no lawyers. Solicitors soon learnt that if their cases were not to be held back, the solution was to instruct counsel, i.e. a barrister.

He was succeeded by a very unpleasant man and after him another. On the first occasion that the latter sat at Petworth, I had to make a speech of welcome. After hearing a few summonses, I was in the only trial listed. Having just started my opening speech and given him a bundle of letters, he snarled at me, 'My page twenty-five has been transposed with page twenty-six. Why can't solicitors do a simple job like this properly?' What made it worse was that he had been a solicitor before he was called to the Bar. I thought to myself, If he's like this the first time that he sits, what will he be like towards the end of the fifteen years necessary to get a pension? Of course, I was right, but I had long before then stopped doing county court cases. What was pathetic was that he told Roy Lankaster, the Clerk of Assize on the South-Eastern Circuit, that he knew that he behaved badly but was unable to stop himself.

Two county court judges were authors who wrote detective stories. They could not have been more different. Gordon Clarke, who wrote under the name Cyril Hare, was the judge for Surrey and also sat as Chairman of the Bench at Guildford. He was sensible, pleasant and competent. Harry Leon, who wrote under the name Henry Cecil, was the more successful of the two as authors but an impossible judge. He was not unpleasant but very difficult. If he could find a problem, he would, and if he could not, he would manufacture one. It was said that he took the job in order to devote more time to his wife, who was dying. The general view was that he thought, almost certainly wrongly, that, had he been able to wait, he would have been appointed a High Court judge and was doing his best to show how clever he was in order to obtain promotion. On one occasion, when I arrived at court, I was told that a few minutes earlier the defendant had paid into court the sum claimed. Of course, I asked for an order that the defendant should pay the costs of the action. This should have been ordered without demur but Leon professed himself in doubt about it and adjourned the case until I was able to put before him the relevant statutory provision. I asked the clerk from the solicitors who had instructed me to work out the maximum costs that we could possibly ask for and also what she considered was the figure which should be allowed, while I was looking for what Leon wanted, which did not take long. We went back into court and I showed Leon what he had asked for and, as I suspected might happen, he asked what costs we were asking for. I told him that, before the taxing officer, we would ask for the higher figure but that, in the circumstances, which I did not specify, we would ask only for the lower. At this, Leon rounded on the defendant, ordering him to pay the figure for which I had asked and telling him how fortunate he was that we had been so kind to him. After his wife's death, he decided to remarry and brought a number of unfortunate women to court, presumably so that they could be suitably impressed by him. I do not know what transpired. He did not like having to try undefended divorces, which, in front of most judges, would last no more than ten minutes. He made so many difficulties in these cases that he only decided about three a day and, eventually, he was no longer required to try them, which, no doubt, is what he had intended.

In 1953, I had a piece of good fortune. Mellersh and Lovelace was an old-fashioned firm of solicitors in Godalming, and none of the partners wanted to appear in court if it could be avoided. Consequently, all their litigation was conducted by a managing clerk, Charles Cork, a former Mayor of Godalming, and his assistant Bunty. When I joined chambers all their work was done by a member of chambers, who appeared to know little about civil litigation or the law relating to it, to such an extent that I later discovered he had drafted a form of Notice to Quit to be served on tenants which was almost bound to be defective. When he became a stipendiary magistrate, they instructed another member of chambers who was no better. After I retired, I once said to Bunty Lorenz, who had married a Polish exile who became a farmer, 'I suspect that until you found me, you must have thought that there was no such thing as a competent barrister!' 'Yes,' she said. I have noticed that one can acquire a client as a result of losing a case which one has conducted efficiently and gone down with all guns blazing, and thus it was with Alderman Cork. I lost one of my first High Court cases, instructed by Cork, and thereafter, said Bunty, he said, 'It must always be Ogden.'

I went down almost weekly to Guildford County Court and was able to learn the whole range of litigation conducted by country solicitors, which was extremely useful knowledge; also the money involved was helpful since I often had several cases on the same day. Cork and Bunty were agreeable people to work with and I enjoyed going, not only to Guildford, but to all the other county courts in Surrey, where I became quite well known to judges and, more importantly, to solicitors, who then sent me work – but never against Mellersh and Lovelace!

In 1954 chambers moved from the Victorian building in Essex Court to 2 Crown Office Row, also in the Temple, where I spent the rest of my professional life. This was an enormous improvement; it was a new building which replaced one destroyed in the war, probably on the same night that the Inner Temple's hall and library in the adjacent building were destroyed. The Middle Temple lost its library but was able to restore its beautiful hall. Gray's Inn lost both hall and library as well as its chapel. Lincoln's was extremely fortunate; we are the only Inn to have two halls, both of which were undamaged, as was our library, which someone described as the most beautiful law library in the world. Our chapel was fortunate in that a bomb dropped in the 1914–18 war merely left pock-marks on the exterior.

In COR we took two floors, and the resultant accommodation seemed enormously spacious. Previously I had shared a room with Hugh Griffiths and later Raymond Kidwell. I had my back to one wall and the other occupant his back against the opposite wall and I could touch the walls on both sides of me and the other person's hand across the table which we shared. It was heated by an electric fire fixed to a wall and turned on by a switch at the door. On a Monday morning, the room would be icy cold and the fire would not warm it until about noon. One day, I rushed in, switched on the fire and rushed out to get a book, without noticing that Raymond had left his bag containing his robes leaning against the fire. When I returned I found his bag and the robe inside, smouldering. I beat out the incipient fire and placed the bag against the wall with the burnt bit out of view. When Raymond came in I said, 'I've got a very interesting case. A schoolmaster left his bag in the common room...' and described what had happened. 'Who do you think was to blame?' He thought for a bit and said, 'Well, I'm inclined to think it was the fault of the master who switched on the fire.' 'Very interesting, because that's exactly what happened to your bag half an hour ago.' He picked up his bag and turned it, and his jaw literally fell open. 'Just as well that my household insurance covers me for negligence,' I said. When we moved, we shared a larger room, which also had decent heating. There were about sixteen of us when we made our move and, thereafter, the number steadily increased.

That year also saw the arrival of Celia, who promptly nearly died. Although by now I was earning only £1,000 a year, before expenses, and Joan rather more, together with my mother's allowance of £1,000 we were able to live in our pleasant house in Elizabeth Street, just off Eaton Square, and afford a daily help and, after about two years, an au pair. The appalling rise in house prices in the 1980s now means that very few young people can afford to live in Central London, which is very sad.

Also in 1954, Frank Cassels was appointed a deputy chairman at London Sessions. He had had an entirely criminal practice centred in Surrey. Of course, there were cases which he could not do because another trial had overrun or was listed on the same date. On such occasions, I was suggested by the clerks, and the solicitors who instructed me found me to be a satisfactory substitute. Consequently, when he went on the bench, I inherited most of his work.

Also in Surrey, P. J. McNamara Ryan ran a sole practitioner practice. He was competent and an able advocate in magistrates' courts. His practice grew, to my advantage. The Police Authority was not very happy with the work of Wontners, who had conducted prosecution work for the whole of Surrey for many years, so Mac was offered all the work for two police divisions, which he accepted on terms that he would 'send all his work to Ogden or, if he could not do it, to someone else in his chambers.' This was very valuable in monetary terms but also because it got me a large volume of all kinds of criminal work and helped my standing and prestige, thus bringing me other solicitors.

I now had solidly established practices in both criminal and the general run of civil work. However, my main line of practice was insurance law. Insurers who had sent me work appearing for drivers in coroners' and magistrates' courts began to send me cases in county courts and it was a happy day when Harold, my Senior Clerk, and I were able to agree that I should no longer accept briefs at ordinary fees in coroners' and magistrates' courts.

In those days, it was common for county court judges to sit as chairmen of quarter sessions. One such was Tudor Rees, who sat at Brentford County Court and as Chairman of Surrey Quarter Sessions at Kingston. In the former capacity he was an appalling judge, because he felt himself unable to decide a case in favour of an insurance company or a landlord – it was incredible. He had a registrar – registrars have been upgraded in nomenclature, like rat-catchers becoming rodent operatives, and are now called district judges. They had power to try trivial cases and, with the consent of the parties, other cases ordinarily tried by a judge. Lists were often congested, sometimes to such an extent that they could not be heard by the judge on the date for which they were listed. This registrar liked to try cases and after lunch would go around touting for work. The trouble was that he was invariably the worse for drink after lunch. However, since it was impossible to win for an insurer in front of the judge, unless there was another insurer on the other side, I would rather that the case was tried by this registrar than by the judge; of course, some of the decisions were bizarre but at least the case was tried.

However, as Chairman of Quarter Sessions, Tudor Rees was very good. He had no inhibitions of the kind mentioned and his only quirk was an admiration for dogs, resulting in eulogies in cases in which police dogs were involved. The full extent of his naughtiness as a county court judge can be gauged by what I discovered after he had retired. In damages cases, e.g., as a result of a car accident, the defendant could pay into court a sum of money which he asserted was sufficient. If the claimant chose not to accept the money and continued the action but was awarded no more than the amount in court, he had to pay the defendant's costs from the date of payment in. Of course, the judge was not meant to know whether or not there was money in court, still less how much. The first time that I went to Brentford after Tudor Rees retired, I asked his clerk what the new judge was like. 'Oh, sir, he's very strange. Do you know that on his first day here, when I told him how much money there was in court, he was angry!'

Euan Montague, QC, who was Chairman of Middlesex Quarter Sessions, which sat in Parliament Square, was generally regarded as the very worst criminal judge in London and the South-East. He seemed to regard it as his duty to try to get every defendant convicted, although, if and when he achieved this, he was not a savage sentencer.

Sir Harold Cassell, Bart, was the son of Edward VII's financial adviser. He was standing counsel to the Metropolitan Police at Middlesex Quarter Sessions, i.e. he conducted all their cases. He disliked Montague and used to bait him. This was particularly annoying to Montague, who viewed prosecuting counsel as his natural ally. It was fun to watch.

Montague had a car accident in the Cromwell Road. He was either stationary or moving very slowly when he suddenly and without warning turned to his right to do a U-turn. The car which was about to pass him managed to stop but the next car did not and pushed the first car into Montague's, and a third car collided with the back of the second. Montague attempted to drive away and was prevented only by one of the other drivers, an excitable German, who flung himself across the bonnet of Montague's car. Montague was very lucky not to have been prosecuted.

The claims manager of a very decent insurance company came to see me and said, 'We are always very anxious to avoid bad publicity for and litigation with judges, but Montague has refused to accept our offer of three-quarters of his damages and I really don't feel able to offer any more.' 'Great Heavens,' I said, 'if you had come to me earlier, I would have advised you that he was solely to blame and should be paid nothing. However, now that you have made the offer, we will pay it into court and counter-claim.'

A firm of solicitors in Brentford sent me a great deal of work at Middlesex Quarter Sessions, so I went to see the Clerk of the Peace and told him about the litigation and said that it was obviously impossible for me to appear before Montague while it was outstanding. He agreed to list all my cases before the deputy chairman, Harold Williams, a nice man before whom I had often appeared when he had been part-time Chairman of Surrey Quarter Sessions. As a result I obtained acquittals in thirteen successive cases of driving under the influence of drink. By the time that Montague accepted the money in court, doubtless as a result of very firm advice, my practice had improved sufficiently to enable me to stop doing that kind of case.

As is the case with others who have the strange idea that a judge should do his best to secure a conviction, I was told that Montague was a pleasant man when not on the Bench, difficult as it was to believe. During the war, he was involved in a very strange incident, which he wrote up as a book. It was turned into a very good film, *The Man Who Never Was.* He was in Naval Intelligence, and engaged in attempting to deceive the Germans into thinking that, rather than sending the Eighth Army from North Africa on to Sicily, which we did and which was the obvious thing for us to do, we were going to land in Greece. Our Naval Intelligence hit upon the idea of putting into the sea off the coast of Spain a dead body, dressed as a British Army officer, having attached to its wrist a chain with a briefcase at the end. The brief-case contained a genuine letter, which was signed by the Vice Chief of General Staff, addressed to General Alexander, the Commander in the Middle East, giving information about such a plan. The Germans were to be led to suppose that the officer had died in an air accident. This was not as easy as it sounds. It worked, and substantial numbers of German troops were redeployed to defend the areas where the landings were said to be going to take place. For his part in this, Montague was awarded a CBE.

It is interesting that, although the Germans were badly caught out on this occasion, they were caught out even worse in 1944. The deception plan persuaded them that the crossing on D-Day would be to the Pas de Calais and it was several days before they realised that the landings in Normandy were not a feint. As a result, the bulk of their armoured forces did not arrive in Normandy until after the beachhead had been firmly established and the allied forces had begun to move inland.

* * *

Colonel Hackett, late of the Indian Army, lived in a flat in a pleasant thatched manor house in Hampshire. He was plagued by birds which nested under the eaves. Being the resourceful military man that he was, he decided to deal with the problem himself. He got a long stick, to which he attached an oily rag. He set fire to it and attempted to smoke out the birds. Thirty minutes later there was one country house the less in Hampshire. I consider that this provides an indication of why, initially, the Indian Army did not do well in the war in Burma.

The details of the ensuing litigation will be of no interest to the reader but it involved O'Connor leading Ogden on behalf of a Lloyds syndicate against Marven Everett, QC, who represented an insurance company. Marven was a large, imposing figure who had served in the London Fire Brigade during the Blitz; he had a loud bullying voice which went well with his physique. The judge decided in our favour and was barely out of the court-room when in a booming voice Marven said, 'Well, O'Connor and Ogden, you have done more harm to the reputation of Lloyds in the past three days than has been done in the last three hundred years.' This was very gratifying. In the Court of Appeal, Marven won 2–1. Two judges having decided for each party usually indicates a 'your guess is as good as mine' situation when it comes to the House of Lords. Unfortunately, at this stage, our insurers discovered that they were reinsuring the insurers on the other side and were, therefore in large part fighting against themselves. Consequently, in a mean-spirited way and showing a distressing lack of interest in the point of law involved or counsels' fees, they settled the case, thereby depriving all counsel concerned of their brief fees in the Lords.

Marven was an able advocate and had a very large practice. However, as this story indicates, he was very irascible. On another occasion, a meeting was arranged in the basement room in his chambers, attended by O'Connor, who was again leading me, together with our respective solicitors, in order to see whether a case could be settled. The discussion did not go well and Marven got perceptibly angry. The greater his anger became, the more I became amused and, regrettably, did little to conceal it. Eventually, Marven completely lost his temper and threw his papers up in the air and they fluttered to the floor. We took this as an indication that the meeting was over. At the top of the basement steps, Patrick said to the solicitor who was instructing Marven, 'I could do with a drink, let's go to El Vino's.' This we did, and Patrick and the solicitor settled the case over a drink. Fortunately, Marven never discovered this; he would have been furious.

Another barrister, Monty Berryman, was an undistinguished QC who did personal injuries work. Consequently, when a junior, I saw him quite frequently; he was a very nice fellow. Towards the end of his career, he developed the habit of speaking his thoughts aloud. Thus, on one occasion, when a judge asked him a question during his final speech, he replied in a clearly audible voice, 'Bloody fool!' and continued 'My Lord, in our respectful submission...' Of course, since it was obvious that Monty had not intended to say 'bloody fool' out loud, there was nothing that the judge could say or do about it and he had to pretend that he had not heard it. When this story got about, which it did at great speed, no other judge dared to say a word to him, which speeded up proceedings. He retired not long afterwards; I suspect that a friend had had a word with him.

Only once was I involved in a case which concerned a hunt. It was at Guildford County Court and I acted for the insurers of the Chiddingfold Farmers' Foxhounds. The case was brought against the hunt by the insurers of a car. Doubtless, the law has changed, but in those days it was lawful for a pack of hounds to go in pursuit of a fox across a main road. The hunt had found close to the main road between London and Portsmouth, which was one of the busiest main roads in the country (the A3). In view of the chance that the fox might go over the main road, a man was stationed at the roadside at the nearest point. The fox duly scuttled across the road, pursued by the hunt, without incident.

Unfortunately, the fox doubled back but, very inconsiderately, chose to cross the road at a point a little distance away from where the man was stationed. As the driver of the car put it, 'Suddenly the 'ole road was full of dawgs,' with which he collided, without fault on his part. Godfrey, a favourite hound, was knocked unconscious but then came to, having suffered no significant injury. As is so often the case when cars collide with animals, the tiny car, an Austin 7, was sufficiently damaged for the insurers to sue.

The issue was whether the hunt had been negligent. The going had been heavy and there was no question of the huntsman being able to whip off the hounds, not that I think that he would have tried. Although it was a wholly irrelevant question, I could not resist asking the huntsman what action he took as he approached the road. 'I sounded my horn.' Predictably, everyone laughed. (The huntsman had sounded his horn to indicate to his whip and the hunt followers where he was.) Of course, I was triumphant. Since the hunt was entitled to rush across a main road, it was impossible to suggest what it could have done to avoid an accident.

To-day, since the judge, Gordon Clark, was very much a country gentleman, albeit with a first-class degree from Oxford, he would not be able to try a case in which his local hunt was a party. Indeed, Cyril Hare, in one of his stories, wrote how a deputy county court judge, who had hunted in his youth, watched a pack of hounds pursuing a fox across country, which was part of the plot of the story. Of course, I had taken the opportunity of telling the Master that I had served in a cavalry regiment, thereby establishing that my heart was in the right place.

Deaf aids were not in those days as they are now. Consequently, deafness was a real problem for many judges. A nice county court judge called Bensley Wells had a small box fitted at the front of his desk; from it there emerged a cord with something at the end, which he fixed in his ear. When evidence in a case was finished and counsel were about to make their closing speeches, he would very ostentatiously lean forward and turn the machine off. Of course, this had the desired effect of making speeches very short. On one occasion he went further. I was acting for the plaintiff and, at the end of the evidence, as my opponent was rising to his feet to make his final speech, while switching off his machine, Bensley said, 'I believe the plaintiff and disbelieve the defendant. There will be judgement for the plaintiff for £400 with costs on scale four,' and was halfway out of the room before my opponent's jaw had finished falling.

An old Chancery judge named Vaisey had a much simpler technique. If he could not hear what counsel were saying, he would make a show of putting in his ear a trouser button attached to a piece of string, thereby giving the impression that he was putting in a hearing aid. This, of course, would result in counsel speaking to him much louder.

In contrast, Roland Oliver had a glass eye. He was a beastly Queen's Bench judge in every respect. A savage sentencer, it was said of him that one could tell whether a plea in mitigation had caused any sympathy in his heart by looking at his glass eye.

He was said to spend his evenings in judges' lodgings playing the violin, while drinking too much whisky. He acquired a reputation for seducing the wives of High Sheriffs. This seemed to me to be wildly improbable, even allowing for the fact that it is difficult to say whether a member of the same sex is attractive to members of the other sex, and he may not have appeared as repulsive to women as he appeared to me to be. But, given the nature and conventions of life in lodgings, it would seem very difficult.

At this time, I suffered very badly from hay fever. I had to inject myself, which I loathed doing, and I could undertake the task only after fortifying myself with a large quantity of whisky. One summer I almost completely lost my voice. I have never won so many cases. At this stage my practice was almost entirely in the county courts, apart for some criminal work. I would arrive at the county court and ask the usher to apologise to the judge for the fact that I had almost lost my voice. Usually, I was acting for an insurance company as a defendant. When the plaintiff had finished giving his evidence, the kindly judge would usually say, 'Mr Ogden, would you mind if I asked a few questions first?' I would croak that I had no objection and he would then proceed to ask the questions which I would have done in cross-examination. Of course, by definition a question asked by a judge is plain, straightforward and readily comprehensible, consequently, if the witness failed to reply appropriately, the judge, as a former barrister, would have his hunter's instincts roused and would be after the witness. When the judge had finished he would say to me, 'I'm sorry, Mr Ogden, I went on longer than I meant to. Are there any questions which you would like to ask?' I would croak out the word 'no' and sit down. The same would happen with any of the other witnesses for the plaintiff. I would then get up and ask the defendant his name and address and ask him to tell the judge what had happened, which, of course, is not the way in which one usually does it. I would ask the witness no further questions unless absolutely necessary and would then sit down. I repeated this process with any other witness. At the end of the evidence, when it was my turn to make the final speech, the judge often said, 'I suppose, Mr Ogden, you would say x y and z?' I would nod vigorously and sit down; my opponent would then make his speech, whereupon the judge would immediately give judgement in my favour. Alternatively, at the end of the evidence, the judge might turn to my opponent and ask him to make the first speech, which was always an indication that he intended to give judgement against him, which he invariably did. I was almost sorry when I recovered my voice.

It must not be thought that all my clients considered my services entirely satisfactory. On one occasion I received a letter from a man complaining about how badly he had been defended. Unfortunately, it was a case in which I had been due to appear but was unable to do so and consequently someone else had done it. It was that person about whom the man was complaining, apparently under the impression that I might have been paid a fee. Of course, that was that.

There was another occasion, on which I appeared for a minor businessman. He struck me as a man who was likely to cause trouble from the moment that I set eyes on him because he came into the room with a shorthand typist, which is the only time I can recollect that ever happened. It was some kind of offence relating to a motor vehicle but not the driving of it; I cannot remember the precise nature of the case. On the day of the hearing an idea occurred to me and I asked my solicitor to telephone and ask for some information. This was duly obtained and we went on to win the case and be awarded costs against the police, which, in those days, was by no means a foregone conclusion. Consequently, it was somewhat to my surprise that a few days later I received what can only be described as a diatribe running to about four typewritten pages in which he complained not only about the fact that I had the idea on the day of the trial, but a general assault upon barristers and the legal profession generally. My recollection is that my reply was along the following line, 'I took your case to a wholly satisfactory conclusion including an award of costs against the prosecution. Since upon one thing I am sure we are agreed, namely, that I will never act for you again, I see little point in answering all your many complaints about me and my profession.' I thought that so short a reply would annoy him immensely, which is what I intended.

Once, a lay client sued me and my solicitor in Guildford County Court. This was very boring because it meant that I had to go down there. I was represented by Raymond Kidwell in chambers. For some reason the case could not come on that day but the judge made some enquiries about it and expressed some views which were rather hostile to the plaintiff, and so after the adjournment he said that he thought that he might discontinue against me. Of course, I told him that was up to him. In any event, his nerve gave and he abandoned the proceedings against both me and my solicitors.

From this time until I took silk in 1968, my practice developed on fairly predictable lines. I started to get High Court work. Initially, this consisted of accident cases, mostly for insurers, which broadened out into policy disputes. As the volume of this increased, I was able to stop going into county courts, doing the small quantity of divorce work, which I undertook with reluctance, and, in my last few years as a junior, all but important criminal cases.

Following Dr Watson's precepts about choosing which of Sherlock Holmes's cases to report, I will recount only a very few cases, on the basis that they may be of interest.

I defended in two murder cases when it was still a capital offence. Fortunately, since I was led in both cases, the main burden did not lie on me, but Joan later told me that they were the only occasions on which she noticed that I was having nightmares. The feeling that if one puts a foot wrong, one's client may be executed, is very nasty. The atmosphere in court reflected all of this; it was very oppressive and everyone was on edge. Fortunately, in neither case was there a conviction for murder. I have completely forgotten about one case but I remember the details of the other quite well. The defendant was a rather attractive young woman who had killed her lover. He had treated her with violence, and I cannot remember whether the defence was self-defence or provocation. Certainly, she did not go to prison. I thought that she was a very nice young woman but, unfortunately for her, she struck me as very vulnerable and likely to be taken advantage of by unsatisfactory men with whom she had fallen in love, and I suspect that through the rest of her life – and she may well still be alive – she probably drifted from one such relationship to another.

A very different case concerned Mr Rosenberg, a Hatton Garden diamond merchant. He made a claim upon his insurers, alleging that he had been robbed of a large quantity of diamonds. His insurers had doubts about whether there had been any robbery at all. I cannot remember, if I ever knew, why they had these doubts, still less whether they were justified in having them. If insurers have such doubts, but have no evidence to substantiate them, they will look at the fine print in the policy in order to attempt to avoid paying out on the claim on some other ground; that is what they did in this case.

I was led by Patrick O'Connor. Mr Justice 'Willie' McNair was the commercial judge – there was only one such in those days – and therefore the case was tried by him. Of course, he was very clever and had vast knowledge of commercial law, but he appeared to live in an unreal world. He could not drive a car, although he was not alone among judges of the time (I have already mentioned Hodgson). He considered that special rules applied in commercial cases and appeared reluctant to believe that cases of fraud occurred, although he must have known of a plethora of them. I forget what our initial defence was but it was a failure, as was our amended defence and our re-amended defence. As the trial progressed, his antipathy to our case increased. One of what were eventually five defences was based on information which insurers had obtained from a New York customs officer, whom they flew to London. Unfortunately, when he realised that he was expected to go into the witness box and give evidence, he slipped out of his hotel and disappeared back to America. Before this happened, we had to apply to McNair for leave to amend to raise this defence, and by this time, Willie was so fed up with us that he refused leave. He agreed to adjourn so that we could appeal his decision, and this we did. This defence was that he had failed to disclose to insurers a fact material to the risks being underwritten by insurers. The fact in question was that his principal buyer had been convicted of attempting to smuggle jewellery into New York and we asserted that Rosenberg had known about this conviction when he applied for the insurance policy.

Willie, who was a good lawyer, should not have refused leave, because Rosenberg was not prejudiced in any way, but Willie's judgement had been affected by his antipathy to our case. Fortunately for us, Lord Justice 'Fred' Sellers, who presided in the Court of Appeal, when allowing the appeal, added that he could not think of a fact more material to disclose. Willie had a very high regard for Fred and when, in some fashion that I cannot recollect, we managed to prove the facts – with the insurers spending money like water – Willie adopted Fred's view and Rosenberg lost.

There was an odd sequel. Rosenberg launched a claim against his insurance brokers, on what grounds I cannot remember and have difficulty in imagining, but I do recollect that I did not think much of his case. Since the same insurers were involved, I again appeared for the defence, but led by another silk because Patrick had been made a judge. The case collapsed when it was discovered that Rosenberg had a suitcase full of tapes which he had failed to disclose in either trial. I think that it was the final straw because it was obvious that his credibility had become non-existent.

It reminds me of a very different case. A client of Beer's had been injured in a road accident. This was not the kind of case which Beer dealt with. Instead of asking me to suggest a silk experienced in this type of case, he instructed a commercial lawyer, Sir John Foster, QC, MP. Liability was admitted and the amount of damages depended upon resolution of a dispute between the doctors instructed by the parties as to the long-term effects of the injuries. John was a brilliant lawyer as well as a good politician who held Ministerial office. However, he was very lazy and seldom read his papers properly before trial, but was brilliant from the second day onwards, having had time to master the case during the first day. He was also very cavalier in his attitude, and a friend told me that, when he was being led by John in the Court of Appeal, at about 11.30 in the morning and without any prior warning to my friend, he suddenly announced that he had to leave in order to go to Paris and that my friend would take over.

Harold thought it proper that he should escort me to the great man's chambers in order to accompany him to court. John and I had walked about two hundred yards towards the Law Courts, when he said to me, 'I will leave the cross-examination of the doctors to you.' Of course, he had not read the papers in a case which doubtless he regarded as trivial and unimportant. Not only was this task the only one of consequence in the case, but cross-examination of expert witnesses requires very careful preparation, especially if the witnesses are distinguished and used to giving evidence – as they were in this instance.

Of course, this outrageous instruction was a fearful blow. I arrived at court infused with rage and prepared to make notes for cross-examination while listening to the evidence of the plaintiff, Niall MacDermot, who was in chambers and at that time a junior, was acting for the defendants. Very sensibly, he spoke to me rather than John, asking whether there was any chance of settling the case. I replied that I thought that it might be possible and we engaged in the usual kind of conversation which goes on in such circumstances, ending with him making an offer. I did not involve John in this because it was plain that he had not read the papers and, even had he done so, I am sure that he had no idea what the appropriate figure ought to be. I went over to where John and Beer were standing and said that Niall had made the offer. 'What do you think about it?' said John. I replied that I was confident that we could push him up further. 'I quite agree,' said John, and Beer murmured assent. I returned to Niall who, after further haggling, made a higher offer. I returned to Foster and Beer and told them. 'What do you think?' said John. 'I think it's a good offer and we certainly ought to accept.' 'I agree,' said John, as of course did Beer and the lay client. I returned to Niall and told him that the offer was accepted and, having told the judge, we all went off, John having earned very much more than I did.

The last case before I took silk which may be of interest to the reader was the 'East Anglian Lime Fraud' in 1964. The first defendant, Griffiths, was an agricultural supplier. He sold lime to the other defendants. At this time there was a Government subsidy to encourage farmers to spread it on their land. The alleged fraud was very simple; Griffiths was said to have invoiced the farmer for much more lime than was delivered and they split the subsidy on the quantity of lime invoiced but not delivered.

The trial took place in Bury St Edmunds, which was and still is a lovely country town. I held a leading brief, Michael Wakeford in chambers being my junior. It was all very jolly. The Angel was the Bar hotel and we started off staying there, but subsequently moved around various pleasant hotels. However, everyone lunched and dined together in the Angel, which had the advantage that one could have the circuit's free sherry at lunch and free wine at dinner. Basically, the case was simple, although the prosecution made it seem otherwise, and it required little effort. It was a fine summer, so that one could sit in the sun in the abbey's gardens after the court rose.

The judge, Richard Elwes, was a very nice man and he had been an averagely competent judge. Unfortunately, he had been ill and asked the Chief Justice if he could try this case so that he would not have to travel from one circuit town to another and would find it less of a strain than trying a succession of cases. This was a grave mistake. Nearly all cases on circuit are short and, usually, simple; I know because I have done it. Long criminal cases have to be tried by a judge sent for the purpose, as was the case with this one. Any civil case of any length was always tried in London or one of the large provincial cities, where several judges were available. Any long criminal case, however simple for defending counsel, is a burden on judge and prosecuting counsel because of the detail involved. The Chief Justice should never have granted his request; it became obvious that he could not cope. The case was prosecuted by Malcolm Morris, QC. Malcolm was an amusing person in the Mess, but very different in court. He was very much an Establishment Man, who was plainly anxious to go on the High Court Bench, which he never did, partly because of this case.

Because of his illness, Richard was very weak and agreed to virtually everything that Malcolm wanted to do, whatever the validity of defence objections. In such circumstances, a sensible prosecutor holds back from doing anything which could possibly be criticised on appeal. Malcolm did not do this, which caused Alun Davies, QC, who appeared for Griffiths, to become very indignant in a way which no one who is not Welsh can emulate. This led to an unfortunate atmosphere. Moreover, Malcolm broke one of the golden rules for prosecutors in long cases: 'Throw away every document and dispense with every witness not essential to your case.' Malcolm went down every conceivable side road, all of which tended to obscure the essential simplicity of the case.

My client was a pleasant and typical Suffolk farmer. His only drawback from my point of view was that his lunch consisted of a mixture of port and brandy drunk from a hip flask. He was very vexed with me when, on the day that he gave evidence, I arranged with a prison officer that he was denied his usual lunch.

The case having maundered on for much longer than it should have done, which was entirely Malcolm's fault, Richard duly summed up and sent out the jury mid-morning. We went to the Angel and had an alcoholic lunch. When we went back to court the jury was still out so we went to the pub next door. This being close to a police station, was not required to keep opening hours provided that the customers were police officers, lawyers and suchlike. The afternoon passed agreeably and we repaired to the Angel for drinks and dinner, and consumed the circuit wine until, at about eleven, we were told that the jury had agreed, Everyone was found guilty and Richard adjourned sentence until the next day.

On the following morning we returned to our places in court, which were rather odd. The dock in the Shire Hall could not accommodate seven defendants and so they sat in a row of seats facing the jury. Those barristers who could fit in sat at the horseshoe table facing the judge, while the remaining four, including a future member of the Court of Appeal, sat in the dock. Griffiths was sent to prison and the rest were fined and we all went home. I had been commuting by car, driving up early on Monday and back on Friday.

Of course, there was an appeal, based on Malcolm's errors and the resultant rulings by Richard. However, it suddenly occurred to me that the indictment was defective. All the defendants had been charged in one count of conspiracy. It seemed to me, rather belatedly, that this was wrong and there were a number of conspiracies between Griffiths and individual farmers. There was a conference of defence counsel, at which I said that I intended to take this point, and it is noteworthy that no one else said that they had intended to do so. We were all permitted to rely on any point raised by another defendant, so my Notice of Appeal was the only one to raise the point.

Gilbert Paull presided in the Court of Appeal. He was very congenial, and had been one of the ablest QCs of his generation, but was not a very good judge. Because, if my point prevailed, it would be unnecessary to consider any other, it was heard first. As soon as I said, 'Our case is that the indictment is bad for duplicity,' all three judges nodded as if they were Pavlov's dogs and I knew that we had won. In the course of my speech, Gilbert said, 'I notice that there were no less than seventeen defence counsel. Why was this point never taken before?' Of course, I was prepared for this question and said, 'It never occurred to me until the trial was over, but if I have to stand in the white sheet of penitence, all I can say in mitigation is that, as I understand it, even now my learned friends for the prosecution do not agree that I am right.' At this, everyone in court, including the judges, burst into laughter except, of course, the miserable-looking Malcolm and his junior.

Gilbert was not to be done out of his fun. 'I am going to ask the same question of every counsel who held a leading brief.' Most were honest and said that the point had not occurred to them until I mentioned it, but two of them could not be said to have been wholly forthcoming. Petre Crowder, QC, was the only Conservative MP that I can remember who served in the Commons for over twenty years but was not knighted. He replied, 'My learned friend Viscount Stormont and I...' and continued to talk for some time without dealing with the question at all and then sat down. The judges looked flabbergasted, but Gilbert obviously thought that it was pointless to pursue it further. Michael Havers, QC, who later became Lord Chancellor, contrived to give the impression that he had thought of the point and was merely biding his time before raising it. This was silly, because, if it had been so, he would have mentioned it at the meeting of defence counsel, would have put it in his Notice of Appeal and would have been the person who would have argued it in the appeal.

After I had finished, Malcolm addressed the court for several days but to no avail, because, once considered, my point was plainly right and the appeals were all allowed.

The whole profession knew about the case because of its length, and because it was, and still is, one of the leading cases in the law of conspiracy. Consequently, whatever chance Malcolm may have had of being appointed a High Court judge disappeared, although I suspect that it was very small anyway. I did not regard him as a very fair prosecutor and he was not a person who should have been made a High Court judge, although he was a nice man. I think that he became a circuit judge, but died of a sudden heart attack shortly after.

I had one ground for complaint. Barristers cannot advertise; publicity is either from newspaper reports or the fact that the names of all counsel are listed in a case reported in the law reports. Although my name duly appeared as one of seventeen defence counsel in *R. v Griffiths*, nowhere in the judgement did Gilbert Paull mention that it was I who had raised the point; as a junior, the publicity would have been valuable, although most people at the Criminal Bar in London knew it, and it rankled for a long time.

Of course, even though it was a Legal Aid case, it was remunerative. Furthermore, during the course of the trial, the ordinary Judge of Assize came round. I did a lot of civil work for East Anglian solicitors, mainly acting for insurers. On three successive days, having arranged with Malcolm that he would call no evidence relevant to my case, I left Michael Wakeford to hold the fort and I did three civil cases in the adjoining court. None of them lasted for more than an hour and a half – a virtual impossibility to-day – and I won all three. Consequently, I earned fees in two courts simultaneously. I should add that, if nothing affecting my client was due to occur, I would often leave Michael in court while I did my paperwork in other cases, being available to rush into court should I be sent for, which did not happen.

In my last few years as a junior, the burden of paperwork was appalling. It consisted of advising and drafting pleadings. So large was the volume that I had three heaps of papers in my room in chambers. One was urgent papers, which I did if not in court when I got into chambers. The second was defences, which were always fairly urgent but, usually, quite simple, so I did these later in the day, when tiring. The third heap was all the rest and was never touched save to move papers to the urgent heap, usually when solicitors asked when they would get them back. At the end of term, I would take them home in the car and spend most of the vacation droning into my tape recorder. In particular, I made sure that I never began the Michaelmas term in October without having done all the papers delivered to me before the end of the legal year in July. I am convinced that helping to unload the car and hearing me droning into the tape recorder during holidays and weekends must have put off any of the children who toyed with the idea of coming to the Bar. This is why so many children of barristers become doctors and so many children of doctors become barristers. They believe that the other job can not possibly be so exhausting.

I was Deputy Recorder at Southend-on-Sea from 1964 to 1971. This was in the days before the Court Act when every borough had its own Recorder, who tried all crimes which were too important for magistrates' courts and not serious enough to be tried by a High Court judge at Assizes. Things were very different from what they now are. When I got off the train, I would be met by the Mayor's car and driven to the court. The Clerk of the Court was either the Town Clerk of the borough or his deputy. At lunch time, I would be driven in the Mayor's car to the restaurant in the airport, which was owned by the borough, and given lunch by whoever was sitting as clerk. At the end of the day, I would be driven to my hotel.

Once, when I was fast asleep, the telephone rang; it was the Chief Constable. He was obviously drunk. 'Come down and have a drink,' he said. 'No,' I said, and attempted to get back to sleep, but I was so angry that I could not do so and would have done much better to have gone downstairs and had a drink with him.

He was a very able Chief Constable but, because of his drink problem, he was foolish enough to put down the cost of his drink to expenses. When this was discovered, he was offered the chance to resign but, very stupidly rejected the offer. As a result he was prosecuted and sentenced to two years' imprisonment; it was very sad.

What made it particularly sad, was that the Deputy Town Clerk told me that had he asked for it he would have been granted a hospitality allowance.

Until 1966 the profession had no central organisation. Each Inn of Court was autonomous. Each called its own members to the Bar and was responsible for disciplining those members. The Bar Council was the trade union and was responsible for the Council of Legal Education, for those who wished to attend it. In 1966 it was decided to set up a central organisation to be called the

Senate of the Inns of Court. Each Inn and the Bar Council nominated members, and I was one of those nominated by the Bar Council. The first meeting was hilarious. In some of the other Inns, but not ours, at Council meetings, or, as some of them called it, Parliament, the Benchers addressed each other as Master. At the first meeting of the Senate, they started to use the same mode of address, but of course that did not apply to me or any other member who was not a Bencher, and after a little while they realised that this was ridiculous and stopped doing it. I did two stints on it and found it to be a very unsatisfactory and unwieldy organisation, which was eventually replaced by the Council of the Inns of Court.

One of the funnier aspects of it related to discipline, for which it was responsible. In the course of setting it up some idiot suggested that disciplinary committees should consist only of Benchers. I pointed out that the two of us who were not Benchers sat as judges, whereas some of the Benchers did not, this put a stop to that rubbish. I was a member of the first disciplinary committee, the chairman of which was a patent lawyer, who, of course, had no experience of criminal cases, which, in effect, this was. The barrister in question was represented by a genial but long-winded QC. It took place on a Saturday and we were not able to retire to consider our verdict until tea-time, at which point we immediately and unanimously decided that the barrister was guilty. I and the next most junior member of the tribunal, the only other member of the tribunal who was not a Bencher, agreed that all that was necessary was a reprimand – the lightest possible sentence. When we mentioned this to the chairman he said, 'But surely we have to listen to what his QC has to say?' 'Certainly not,' I said, 'or we will be here all night. All that you have to do is what we do in a criminal case, and say, "Subject to what you say, we are minded to order that he be reprimanded," and he will then sit down.' Others then agreed with us and, somewhat doubtfully, the chairman did as we suggested and it was all over in two minutes.

7

FAMILY, POLITICS AND OTHER INCIDENTALS

Several things happened in 1960. Edward and Henry had been born and Nanny had been engaged. In many ways, she was an appalling woman and it was certainly a brave moment when, some years later, I gave her notice. However, she looked after the children well and it was not easy to find someone who was prepared to take on three children. The house in Elizabeth Street had only three bedrooms and it was obvious that a move would have to be made. The house in Stanford Road was ideal. It had a basement and three floors above. We were able to provide Joan's mother with a bedroom, bathroom, kitchenette and lavatory in the basement, together with a study for me. A thirty-five-foot room on the ground floor provided a drawing room and dining room, with the kitchen a few feet away. When we moved in, there were three bedrooms on the first floor and a thirty-five-foot nursery on the top floor. It was readily adaptable, so that, later, we converted two rooms on the first floor into one large bedroom and divided the room on the top floor into two and added a bedroom on the same level. As a result each child was able to have its own room. It had a garden at the back, which we had paved, thereby enabling me to park my car there, since it was a corner house. I could drive to the Temple in fifteen minutes in the rush hour.

Also in 1960, I was elected to the Bar Council. This came about in a strange fashion, typical of the way things happened in those days. A Royal Commission led by Mr Justice Streatfeild was set up to report on the circuit system. England and Wales were divided into seven circuits, and judges went round each one three times a year. The South-Eastern Circuit was, and is, the largest. Many years earlier it had been created by the amalgamation of the Norfolk Circuit (East Anglia) and the Home Circuit (counties close to London). Two judges were allocated to it and they started in Norwich, making their way south, sitting in each county town, ending in Lewes. These three peregrinations together occupied the whole year.

The arrival of the judges in each county town was a major event. On the first day there was a church service followed by the opening of the Assize. It was a very impressive event. Because, after the opening ceremony, one judge proceeded to sentence defendants whose solicitors had told the court that they intended to plead guilty, the court was thronged by barristers, solicitors and others concerned in those cases. The judge entered, accompanied by his clerk. Close to his chair were the High Sheriff of the county, who was a local worthy, the Under-Sheriff, who actually did the work, and the Sheriff's Chaplain. There were likely to be others nearby, such as the judge's wife. The Clerk of Assize (a superior kind of court clerk) would then read the Royal Commission. This was a splendid document which gave the Sovereign's authority for the Assize. It was addressed to various people, beginning with 'our trusty and well-beloved cousin', who was, I think, the Lord Chancellor, and a string of other 'cousins' ending with the judges who were going circuit. When his own name was read (there were no female judges) the judge who was sitting in that court raised a black tricorn hat of the kind traditionally worn by highwaymen, briefly put it on top of his full-bottomed wig, bowed to the Clerk of Assize, who bowed to him, and replaced it on the bench and sat down. The document then stated when and where the Assize was to take place.

The Clerk of Assize then said, 'Mr High Sheriff, have you the several writs and precepts?' The Sheriff, who was dressed in a uniform, usually that of his old regiment, if it was the first time that he had to do this, tended to look startled. The Under-Sheriff would bow to the Sheriff and hand him two scrolls. The latter would bow to the judge and hand him the scrolls and he would repeat the process with the Clerk of Assize. The judge would then bow to the Bar, leave court, replace his wig with the ordinary working wig and take off a red, ermine-bordered cape and return to court to start work. All this splendid buffoonery would last about forty-five minutes.

Once, I asked the Clerk of Assize to let me see the precepts.

They were marvellously absurd documents, which looked as if they had been written with a quill pen and were probably the sole occupation of some civil servant shut in a basement. In effect, they ordered the Sheriff to notify people when and where the Assize would take place. The list of people started quite sensibly with magistrates, prison governors and suchlike persons but then drifted into mediaeval fantasy – 'all escheaters and estreaters…' with a threat of 'pain and penalties' which would be visited on him if he failed in this duty. When one became sufficiently senior one was often invited to the Sheriff's lunch and, on one such occasion, I asked one of them if he had done this duty so as to avoid the pain and penalties; he was, as they often were, a wealthy not very bright land owner and was visibly worried to an extent that obliged me to reassure him.

After this diversion to describe a scene which continued until 1972, I return to what happened to me. The South-Eastern Circuit Bar Mess had a membership which consisted of over a quarter of the practising Bar, because everyone who appeared on a circuit had to belong to one and had to charge a 'special' fee in addition to a brief fee if he went on another circuit. Its governing body was the Wine Committee, which had been formed to ensure that there was an adequate supply of wine in the Bar hotel in every circuit town.

At the time of the Streatfeild Commission, the Leader of the Circuit was Tristram de la Poer Beresford, QC, nicknamed 'Chimp', because his face somewhat resembled that animal. He was about five feet tall and habitually wore white spats and a black silk top hat. He was a not very competent silk, who did only personal injury work and was Leader for many years. At the annual Circuit dinner, he made a speech which was barely audible to those seated at a distance. Consequently, it was the practice for his speech to be punctuated by loud demands that he should speak up; it was virtually a ritual. To his credit, this did not appear to trouble him.

Streatfeild wrote to the Circuit Leaders asking for views about improvements to the system and Chimp called an Extraordinary General Meeting of the Circuit. Streatfeild specifically asked that circuits should not reply that there were no changes which should be made. Perhaps predictably, at the urging of the worthy Leader and other old fossils, this was precisely what the Circuit replied as the result of a vote which was unanimous save for one person – me.

I decided to send to Streatfeild my own views and, as a matter of courtesy, sent a copy to the Junior of the Circuit. Following this, the Wine Committee sent a further letter to Streatfeild, without further consultation with members of the Circuit, saying that, while they remained of the same opinion as before, if any changes were to be made, Ogden's ideas seemed sensible. Alas, I cannot remember what I suggested nor what resulted so far as changes due to me, if any, were concerned. However, when the Circuit Junior came to chambers to tell me what had happened, he said that, subject to my acceptance, I had been elected a member of the Wine Committee, which was a self-perpetuating body at that time. Of course, I accepted. They had made the mistake of thinking that, once I was member, I would settle down and cause no further trouble.

When it came to elections to the Bar Council, the South-Eastern asked its members to vote for two candidates, and they were invariably successful. In 1960, Chimp announced that someone's term of office had ended and that a new candidate had to be selected. I said modestly that, if no one else wanted to do it, I was prepared to take it on. This was regarded as a very noble, self-sacrificing offer and so I found myself a member of the Bar Council and continued to be so, off and on, until 1978.

I very soon discovered that I was a born committee man and I found the work extremely interesting. The first thing that happened was that I received a list of committees, excluding the Executive, and was asked which I would like to be on. With growing despair, I looked down the list and saw committees such as Discipline and Consolidated Regulations and began to feel that I had made a dreadful error in getting elected. Then, right at the bottom, I noticed a committee then called Overseas Relations. It occurred to me that, if I joined it, at some time in the future I might be required to relate overseas. It was one of my more sensible decisions and, soon after, I began representing the Bar, at its expense, for over twenty-five years all over the world. The name Union Internationale des Avocats speaks for itself. I noticed that we were represented by Sir Frank Soskice, QC, MP, but that he did not attend meetings; he had a very large practice. At a meeting of the committee, I pointed out that there seemed little point in having a representative who did not turn up to meetings, that he was far too important to care if asked to step down and that I was prepared to take it on and to attend. Of course, this high-minded offer had the obvious result and, in 1962, I found myself at a meeting in Lisbon.

The UIA had been founded shortly after the First World War. Although we were founder members, the American Bar Association, for a reason which I never knew, did not belong, although the New York Bar Association, which had more overseas work than the rest of the American Bar associations put together, did. Doubtless, because my predecessors showed little interest in the organisation, all the proceedings were conducted in French, although English was one of the five official languages. My French was only up to fourth form standards and certainly not good enough to comprehend anything of a complex or technical nature. I decided that it was up to me to remedy this situation, since the Law Society representative, who was a pleasant but ineffectual solicitor, spoke good French and therefore had no incentive to act. Consequently, I simply stood up and spoke in English. This caused total consternation; since it was an official language, they could not refuse to let me do it, also some other representatives who thought that the French had got a stranglehold on the Union rose and congratulated me, saying how glad they were that the English were taking an active part in discussions. What made it more annoying for the French was that I was very much younger than nearly everyone else and it was very galling that this young fellow should have upset the cosy status quo. Once I returned to England, I cemented the position by persuading the Scots to choose someone who would attend, having already persuaded the Law Society representative that he ought to say something occasionally and do so in English.

The UIA Council met each year, and a congress which anyone could attend, took place every other year. The council meetings were more fun than congresses because we numbered only about forty members in all, accompanied by some spouses. We were treated on what could be called a semi-VIP basis and tended to have social events in places in which one would find oneself merely walking through if one was a tourist. For instance, in 1964, before the revolution in Iran which toppled the Shah, I met the Prime Minister, who was later the victim of judicial murder, in his private study, which was small and unpretentious. The Shah allowed the Prime Minister, who was far and away the longest-serving one in the world, to be executed in exactly the same way as Charles I attempted to save his own skin by allowing Strafford to be executed.

Most of the time I was able to talk to other members of the council and their wives in English. Joan was amused by the number of people who told her how good my French was. This was because I would simply embrace them and say, '*Mon cher collègue, comment allez-vous?*' and then stand there and let it all pour over me; of course, such people also remarked on what a good conversationalist I was! I had been on the UIA for about twenty years when, for some reason which I cannot now recollect, the Bar Council asked me to transfer to the Council of the International Bar Association, which was precisely the same as the UIA, except that everyone spoke English all the time.

Eichmann was a war criminal, whom the Israelis kidnapped in South America and brought to Israel, where they tried and executed him. At a meeting of the Union Internationale des Avocats in about 1962, I spoke to the German lawyer who had defended Eichmann. He was very impressed by the mode of trial in Israel which they had retained when we left Israel; in other words, it was English procedure. He remarked very favourably on how marvellous it was to be able to ask his client questions before the court cross-examined him. I thought that it was a remarkable tribute to our English criminal system.

However, I very much fear that the present Lord Chancellor's 'reforms' are likely to result in the total disappearance of independent criminal lawyers in about the next twelve years. Once the Crown Prosecution Service and the Public Defender's Office do all the smaller criminal work, there will be no way in which a lawyer in independent practice can learn the skills which are necessary to conduct criminal cases, and these skills are very different from those required to conduct any other kind of case. I suspect that we will end up with a system in which defendants are both prosecuted and defended by civil servants. This is more or less the American system and is one which I consider to be very unsatisfactory in practice. This is largely because the people who do the work are of low calibre.

It was quite obvious to me when the Crown Prosecution Service was set up that, on the basis of the salaries being offered, no one who was able to get work in private practice would join the CPS. That has happened; as a result the work is done very incompetently, many people are acquitted who should be convicted and many who are convicted have to be acquitted on appeal because of errors made by the CPS. The only advantage of a public defender's office seems to me to be that it will result in a level playing field of ineptitude. Furthermore, further along the line, when it comes to appointing judges to criminal courts, the only people with any experience will be people who were employed by the CPS or the Public Defender's Office, and therefore the quality of the judiciary will also be significantly lowered. This seems to me inevitable and deplorable.

In 1964 I achieved my first success in the field of law reform. In criminal cases the defendant, or his lawyer if he had one, which was by no means the invariable case, was entitled to make the final speech after prosecuting counsel had made his speech. However, this right was lost if the defence called a witness other than a character witness. To add to this illogicality, the Law Officers (Attorney-General and Solicitor-General) always had the right to make the last speech. Since it was generally agreed that the ability to make the last speech was very important, one had to make difficult decisions about whether the value of the evidence which someone could give outweighed the loss of this right. Of course, sometimes one made the wrong decision, and it was particularly horrid if a judge who wanted a jury to convict and thought that he ought to help, said in his summing-up, 'Of course, you might think that the evidence of Mr X might have been very helpful,' thereby implying that he was not called because he was not prepared to support the defendant's version of events.

Plainly, this was unfair. By this time, I was on the Bar Council's Executive Committee, as were the Attorney-General and the Solicitor-General, and one or other and often both of them actually attended every meeting. Without difficulty I persuaded the committee that the law ought to be changed, but it is one thing to get a decision like that made and quite another thing to get it enacted because there is always fierce competition for Parliamentary time. Sproule Bolton, the Deputy Secretary of the Council, helped me very considerably in a number of my various enterprises, of which this was one. We raised the issue with the Criminal Law Revision Committee, which agreed with us and drafted a Bill. The Shadow Solicitor-General was Niall MacDermot, who was a member of chambers, and he readily agreed with us. We were now in a very strong position in that we circularised every MP who had been successful in the ballot to bring forward a Private Member's Bill, saying that the draft Bill would be supported by both Government and Opposition and that, if the MP had not got his own pet Bill to put forward, this one would undoubtedly succeed, giving him kudos in the House of Commons and in his constituency. This duly happened and the Bill went through both Houses of Parliament, meeting no opposition save from Charles Doughty, QC, MP, a backbench Conservative who was so generally regarded as having preceded dinosaurs that his opposition was almost an advantage, and the Criminal Procedure (Right of Reply) Act 1964 was duly passed. My sole regret was that it received the Royal Assent just too late for me to take advantage of it in the East Anglian Lime Fraud.

Like many barristers, I had long been interested in politics. As previously related, I had attended and spoken in debates in the Cambridge Union, partly to hone my powers of advocacy, but also because it attracted leading political figures. I had also been an active member of the University Conservative Association, although none of it to an extent that could interfere with my work. Just before starting my pupillage in 1950, I went and helped John Lowe, who was the Conservative candidate for Gravesend, throughout the three-week campaign. Subsequently, I stood on soap-boxes in the evenings at elections. This was before television and they were regarded as a form of entertainment with a great deal of good-natured banter, although I did feel slightly apprehensive when standing next to a horse-trough filled with water in Cable Street, which was a very rough part of the East End.

Now, I decided that I would stand for Parliament. Without difficulty, I was adopted as Conservative candidate for Walthamstow West. It was usual to fight an election for a hopeless seat and then to attempt to find one which could be won. This seat was an absolutely safe Labour seat. The MP was a run-of-the-mill backbencher. Fortunately, he was a very decent man and there were never any problems between us. The election took place in 1964 and I duly lost, but I received a satisfactory number of votes, by which I mean that the swing to Labour was slightly less than the average for the area, for which, rightly or wrongly, the candidate receives credit. The only unfortunate thing was that the election took place while the Rose Diamond case was taking place. Obviously, my solicitors were not happy about this and I was fortunate to continue to be instructed by them. It also meant that I lost money because during the campaign I had to hand over the refreshers (daily fees) to John Archer, who stood in for me.

Following this I was selected as candidate for Epping. This was a marginal seat and also one of the largest constituencies, having an electorate of over one hundred thousand and it was split up soon afterwards. For me, it was a major problem that it extended from Chingford in the west to Harlow in the east, taking in Waltham Abbey and Epping itself, as well as various small rural communities. Of course, local issues were very different in each part of the constituency. The Labour Government had a tiny majority and it was obvious that there would be another election soon. Therefore, I very frequently found myself having to drive out there in the evenings to attend local committee meetings or other political events like garden parties. It would be idle to suggest that I enjoyed this part of the job. One was regarded as someone who could be patronised by the most stupid men and had to talk to bossy women, of whom there are a great number in Conservative Associations. Joan disliked it far more than I did, partly because she was patronised even more than me. However, she concealed this from me and revealed it only after I decided to abandon politics.

The election was in the spring of 1966. My agent promptly had a nervous breakdown and disappeared. This was a terrible blow, because it is the agent who organises things and knows the technical legal requirements. Fortunately, the extremely nice and competent agent for an adjacent Conservative seat volunteered to act as my agent in addition to looking after his own constituency.

Nevertheless, it made things very difficult. However, it had been obvious to me that the size of the constituency required careful advance planning and I had drawn up a detailed time-table of where I would be throughout the campaign. I would canvass in one area in the morning, another in the afternoon and address a meeting in the evening. Therefore, it was known in advance of the declaration precisely where I would be throughout, say, Day 4, and the officers of the party in the relevant area would make the necessary arrangements; for example, halls were booked for meetings the moment that the declaration was made.

It was very exhilarating but also very tiring. I travelled in an open truck with a microphone, talking whenever it was useful to do so as we sped past posters with my name on them, which appeared to be affixed to every other tree and every other window. On arrival in the area to be canvassed, I would get off the truck and would be joined by the canvassing team. Just as I had helped John Lowe, others came to help me, in particular, Joan, a young man from the Hambro banking family and John Wakeham, who went on to have a most distinguished political career and whom I last saw when I invited him to Grand day in Lincoln's Inn when I was Treasurer in 1998. We were joined by local Conservatives. The team would go ahead knocking on doors and, if someone wanted to talk to me, I would run across and exchange a few words before running to the next person. By running, I mean just that, because with four people going ahead knocking on doors, there was always someone waiting for me. Lunch was provided in someone's house, before we went on to repeat the process throughout the afternoon. In the evening, there was always a meeting. It was utterly exhausting, and in the late afternoon of the last day of the campaign I developed a severe nose bleed, which can only have been due to the stress. Since there was a further swing to the left, we duly lost, but the swing in Epping was less than anywhere else in the area, which was gratifying. I should add that the sitting Labour MP, Stan Newens, was a typically very left-wing man, but we had no personal problems. Some years later, he lost his seat, which was Harlow, a constituency created when boundary revision took place, and he became an MEP (Member of the European Parliament), which I think he still is, ironically representing me! He never achieved office of any kind; what a dismal career for the poor fellow!

I was now poised for selection for a safe seat. I failed to be selected for Hastings in 1968, but had I gone on, I would undoubtedly have been chosen by some selection committee, which would have changed my life completely because I assume that I would have obtained Ministerial office, which would effectively have ended my career at the Bar. However, fortunately, when I got silk a month or so later, it rapidly became obvious that it was no longer possible to have a good practice at the Bar and have a successful career in the House. When I came to the Bar, there were people on both sides of the House who had extremely good practices, e.g. Walter Monckton, John Foster and Maxwell-Fyfe on the Conservative benches and Hartley Shawcross, Frank Soskice and Stafford Cripps on the Labour side. At the end of a day in court, they would simply go down to the House for the evening. But the complexity of cases has altered markedly. A large brief would then be only a few inches thick, whereas now the simplest application results in at least one arch-lever file and my last big case necessitated there being 350 arch-lever files in chambers, while my solicitor in Hong Kong had 2,000. The Lime Fraud in 1966 lasted fifty-one working days and was the longest trial since the Tichborne case in Victorian times; now many cases take much longer.

In politics, reputations are no longer made on the floor of the House because backbenchers get the chance to speak very infrequently. Parliamentary Committees, which were invented not very long ago, are where reputations are now made. Since they sit in the afternoons, practising barristers are seldom able to attend them. David Mellor told me that, after he had been an MP for a few years, he was told by a very senior member of the Conservative Party, 'We have been watching you very closely and you are doing very well, but you must now choose between politics and the Bar.' He promptly gave up the Bar. Certainly, there are now no longer any MPs with good practices at the Bar. It is partly because being an MP is now a full-time job that the calibre of MPs has steadily fallen, with a consequential effect on the calibre of Ministers, most of whom, on both sides, are very mediocre.

I have no doubt that the only solution is to pay MPs very much more; I would double their pay to £100,000 and index-link it. This would stick in the gullet in that most of them are not even worth what they are currently paid. However, it needs about twenty Ministers of ability to run the country properly and one has to attract their successors and then double the number to ensure a similar number on the Opposition benches, perhaps 150 in all. To get them, if they are people of real ability, more has to be offered than less than £50,000 in real terms for life, save for occasions when their party is in office and the Prime Minister wants them as Ministers. Young people of ability who know that they are likely to be earning £100,000 and perhaps much more if things go well, simply cannot afford to do the job at the present rate, particularly, if they are, or hope to be, married and have children. No political leader would dare to advocate such a change; it would have to come from an independent body, probably established to recommend what changes, if any, should be made to their pay, pensions and generally.

Of course, during the 1960s we were troubled by the usual children's ailments, but some merit mention. When we were living in Stanford Road, the children (Celia and Edward) used to be taken to play in gardens in part of the Royal Chelsea Hospital (the home for retired soldiers known as the Chelsea Pensioners). Called Ranelagh Gardens, they were the site of the rather infamous pleasure gardens in former times. They were excellent for children because there was only one gate, where a pensioner was seated, which enabled him to field children trying to escape. (His official duty was to ensure that anyone bringing in a pram had a pram pass, which cost £1, and resulted in the children being under the care of nannies, au pairs or a responsible parent.) They were very well-kept gardens. However, one day, Edward sat down on what proved to be a wasps' nest. The au pair kept a hand over his mouth and the sole result was an incredible number of wasp stings and an understandably fractious child.

When the au pair had a day off, I would often be the person who took the children to these gardens. As a result, I got to know Margaret Thatcher slightly. She was not then an MP but a practising barrister in tax chambers. Had anyone suggested that she would become Prime Minister, I would have been amazed; obviously, I was not very good at identifying future Prime Ministers. Equally, I was amazed at the low calibre of some of the Conservative Ministers or Shadow Ministers whom I met –

Selwyn Lloyd, for example. He had been Foreign Minister at the time of the disastrous Suez affair and had also been Home Secretary. I thought that he was a real lightweight, although he subsequently made a very good Speaker of the House of Commons. I had joined the Coningsby Club, the members of which were aspiring Conservative politicians. I was Treasurer for several years and therefore at dinner, which was in a room in the House of Commons, I was often seated next to the Speaker, who was frequently a Minister. These experiences were the reason for my confidence that, had I pursued a political career, I would have achieved Ministerial office. I should add that being on the Bar Council and also meeting the Conservative law officers or shadow law officers resulted in receiving a certain amount of Government work when the party was in office.

Although I was not present when it happened, the most memorable event concerning Margaret Thatcher at this time was when her twins were expelled from the gardens for several months after they had changed round the small labels which had the names of the plants on them. Many years later, when I sat next to Denis Thatcher after dinner in Lincoln's Inn, I mentioned this episode. He indicated that he remembered it all too well!

An extraordinary event occurred when Celia got appendicitis and had her appendix removed. Initially, she appeared to be recovering normally, but one morning, Joan, who has occasional episodes of second sight, said that we must go and visit Celia at once. When we set eyes on her, it was obvious that something was seriously wrong. The nurse on duty, who hardly inspired confidence when she shook the thermometer before reading it, flatly refused to get a doctor to look at Celia because her surgeon was operating and it was not permissible for another doctor to examine someone else's patient. I went down to the ground floor of this wretched hospital, the Princess Beatrice, and telephoned our GP's surgery. Fortunately, a doctor was in and within a short space of time the surgeon came to look at Celia. It was obvious to me that he was worried. I said that, in my profession, we often thought that a second opinion was helpful and that it really was an occasion when cost was immaterial and I would gladly pay for the best surgeon whose field of expertise it was to be consulted. Soon, another surgeon arrived and the two of them discussed what should be done. They decided, correctly, that Celia was suffering from peritonitis and she was operated on at once. Since peritonitis can cause death very quickly, although it may be different to-day, I am convinced that, if I had not been an assertive and persistent fellow, Celia would have died. This was a major factor in our deciding to abandon the National Health Service and pay the not inconsiderable cost of belonging to a private health scheme. Had I been older, I would have created an immense furore about the incident. I like to think that there are no longer nurses like the one in question.

Henry was a very accident-prone child. In Stanford Road, he managed to bounce down most of the basement steps on his head without coming to any harm. However, he broke his arm when he fell off a climbing frame on to a tricycle below it. A one-in-a-million chance resulted from a half-witted workman knocking out bits of broken glass from a window which fell on to Henry's head as he stood on the pavement outside.

Lucy was a more fortunate child. The only health incident which I can recall was when she developed tonsillitis when we were at Ford Cottage, our holiday home near Bury St Edmunds from 1976. Work called me back to London and I left Joan with Lucy up at Ford, which did not prove much fun for either of them. When we got back to London, the tonsils were removed without difficulty.

Both Joan and I were very fortunate in that we had no incapacitating health problems. I can remember only one occasion when I had to take to my bed with very bad earache, but it happened when I had no court appearances due, which was a rare occurrence. In my forty-seven years of practice, there was not one occasion when illness prevented me from appearing in court.

At some time in the early 1960s, I seriously contemplated leaving the Bar and going into commerce or banking. I cannot now recollect why I did so; I suspect that I may have thought that there was rather a sameness in the nature of the work that I was then doing, i.e. mainly accident cases. Alternatively, I may have thought that I might be able to earn more elsewhere. I rather doubt that it was the latter because I was earning about £10,000 a year, which was quite a reasonable sum in those days. Employment agencies existed but they dealt only with lower paid jobs and there were none of the specialist companies which now publicise highly paid posts. Consequently, I put an advertisement in *The Times*, which said that I was a barrister looking for a job outside the Bar and stating my earnings, so that it could be seen that I was not a failed barrister. The only result of this was a number of begging letters; probably, this was just as well because it is possible that I would not have succeeded outside the Bar.

Fortunately, holidays provided light relief for us all. When the children were young we used to travel on separate aeroplanes. One day when a case was settled unexpectedly we decided to go off on a week's holiday. At such short notice, the only place we could get in was Majorca. Our friends the Blairs had a flat in an apartment block close to our hotel. Every morning we went there and swam in the swimming pool. The Blairs left after a few days, saying that we could continue to use the pool, which we did, getting to know the other flat owners, who were mostly Jewish. Joan went back to England on Good Friday and I went off to the swimming pool, where I was made welcome. I was told that they intended to go to a barbecue that evening and asked whether I would like to join them. In due course we set off in a coach to a farm. When we arrived, we were given lovely pieces of barbecued chicken, after which we went into the farmhouse. There we were given some of the nicest sucking pig that I have ever eaten. Since Jews are not meant to eat pork, I said to my companion that I was quite prepared to eat his share; however, he politely declined. It was a very nice dinner, washed down by large quantities of red wine. Only afterwards did it strike me as very odd that on Good Friday, I, a Catholic, should have found myself eating pork in the company of twelve Jews.

In 1968, we bought a flat in Malta. Before then, apart from taking the children on 'bucket and spade' holidays, our own vacations consisted of loading up the car, crossing the Channel and driving immense distances as far as Italy, Austria and Germany, but mainly in France. We tended to stay nowhere for more than about a night. For lunch, we would buy a roll of bread, ham or suchlike, together with a bottle of wine, and drive up a side-road and into a cornfield, where we would put up our chairs and fold-up picnic table. The harvest would be over so that none of the farmers minded, because, in those days, English tourists behaved themselves and cleared up before they left. Indeed, passing tractor drivers etc. would sound their horns and wave at us and we would raise our glasses in response; of course, there were no drink-drive laws. I suppose it must have rained some days, but not often. In this fashion we would cover great distances, looking at places of interest on the way.

I loathed English 'bucket and spade' holidays. Consequently, we took the children to the French sea-side, where, since my French was not good enough to tell whether or not nearby French people were appalling, we had a jolly time. Three years in succession we rented a house in la Baule, in Brittany. This was a great success. There was an enormous beach with splendid beach clubs into which we would propel the children after breakfast, retrieve them for lunch and do the same thing in the afternoon. In the evening, we would go to one of the many rosette restaurants.

However, in 1968, the country was going through one of the economic crises which were a feature of the fifties and sixties. One of the measures taken was to restrict foreign currency for travel to amounts too small to make a reasonable foreign holiday possible. Malta, for some strange reason, was in the so-called sterling area, and the restrictions did not apply to holidays there. The day after I heard that I had been appointed a silk, I flew there, where Joan was waiting, not having received my telegram giving her the news. As we discovered, this was typical of Malta. We looked at a great many flats and eventually bought the one in which the estate agent lived. It had the enormous advantage that it was furnished and all that had to be done was to buy a few more beds and some linen; apart from that we simply walked in and hung up our hats.

The flat was in St Paul's Bay (which is where the Apostle was wrecked) and was ideal for our purposes. We bought a small boat which was anchored in the bay and the two elder children sailed it around, accompanied by me. As on many islands, you could not sneeze without everyone in Malta knowing about it. On our first visit, I found myself at a drinks party where I was introduced to the Chief Justice. 'I heard you were here,' he said. We rapidly acquired a circle of friends, which made life agreeable. At that time, income tax in Malta was only sixpence in the pound and a great many English people retired there; they were known as the 'sixpenny settlers'. To our amazement, we discovered that, after about our second visit, we knew more Maltese people than they did. Their lives, to the extent they went out at all, were centred on The Club in Valetta, known as God's Waiting Room, for obvious reasons.

Malta was a strange place then; for all I know, it still is. Suddenly, quite mundane things, such as electric fans, would be unavailable; even food such as butter or milk. The one thing which never ran out was the ghastly tomato purée which appeared to be a staple ingredient of the local diet. Cooking was terrible. This was largely due to the fact that it had been a major British base for so long that the Maltese had been indoctrinated by NAAFI food for the troops. It was compounded by what I call the 'Eastern Mediterranean syndrome', whereby most cooked food was neither hot nor cold. The unleavened bread, bought at the local bakery, was extremely good, but was edible only for one meal.

The Maltese were incredibly bureaucratic in an incompetent way. When I realised that I had not received an electricity bill, I wrote asking for one, which they sent and which I paid. However, when Joan next went out there ahead of me, she found that they had disconnected the supply, but not reconnected it. She went to the police station in considerable distress. Although it was after ordinary working hours, the police sergeant ordered the electricity authority to reconnect it at once, which it did. This illustrates another facet of their character; they were incredibly kind, especially when children were concerned. They were very short-tempered but sometimes what one thought to be a violent argument in Maltese turned out to be a discussion between neighbours about, say, electricity charges.

Hygiene was almost non-existent. Sewage ran in the streets. This was largely due to the fact that, in order to avoid the cost of cleaning out the septic tanks, it was a common practice to crack them, thereby enabling the liquid sewage to leak out. The vehicles which removed the sewage were called 'honey waggons'. We invented a game to be played as we drove about whereby, if one saw a priest, nun, etc., one got one point, but the highest number of points, ten, was for a honey waggon. One day, I won because I saw a small boatload of nuns. On arrival, one of the first things one did was to ask which beaches were safe to swim from. Of course, the second was to ask which restaurants sold satisfactory food; it was no more than two or three. The island was so small that one could drive across it within about half an hour or so, even at the speed of about thirty miles per hour, which was all that the roads permitted. This was just as well, in view of the drivers. Coach drivers would sit on only half the seat in order to leave room for the Holy Spirit.

Easter was a good time to visit the barren island, which was largely rock. The place was ablaze with flowers. On Good Friday, one would put on a suit and black tie, which I kept there for the purpose. We visited ten churches on the way to Mdina, the old capital; this was not difficult because there must have been about twenty between St Paul's Bay and Mdina. This secured us a great blessing. Having got to Mdina, we established ourselves in a bar, where, rather inappropriately, I drank brandy, and watched the splendid procession. It began with Adam and Eve and proceeded through history from Noah to the Crucifixion. The various characters were passed down from father to son or mother to daughter. The procession, with every character dressed appropriately, would walk about ten paces and stop. This was necessary because of the large number of heavy floats containing statues, all garlanded with flowers. It was a splendid affair which lasted for several hours. Similar ones took place throughout the island.

The place abounded with nobility; I assume a relic of the Holy Roman Empire. People were referred to in conversation as 'the Most Noble Princess so-and-so'. In the family, conversation was in Italian or English. There was no written language until Mintoff, who was a left-wing Prime Minister, first elected in the seventies, decided that it should be invented. I was very sorry for my middle-aged Maltese friends who were judges; they had to learn it and use it. The same thing happened in Malaysia.

The only problem for us was that, having this flat, we felt obliged to use it rather than go anywhere else. By 1978, ten years after we had bought it, we had no further use for it. Because of the fall in the value of sterling, due to a series of inept Governments, mainly Labour, and the fact that we had bought near the peak of the property boom caused by the sixpenny settlers and people like us, I saw little prospect of selling it satisfactorily. We went there infrequently, twice with my brother, who loved it, but lent it to many friends, who left drink in lieu of rent, which was not very good for us. Out of the blue, I received a very odd letter from a Maltese man, who said that he wanted to buy it. It said that he needed it for his sick wife! It also said that, of course, there was always a risk that it might be expropriated by Government! The truth, as it later emerged, was that he owned a car-hire firm and because the block was built on a steep hill, the necessary support resulted in there being a substantial area outside the garage, on which he wanted to be able to park cars.

There followed a truly hilarious episode. We went to the office of our lawyer, who was a partner of a friend, and the buyer attended with his financial (?) adviser. On being asked whether the sale price was in sterling or the Maltese pound, he immediately said that it was the latter. Since I had the correspondence with me, he had no option but to abandon that contention with alacrity. He then pushed the money, in cash (£7,500 being half the purchase price – at least twice that in value to-day) into the middle of the table. After we had signed the documents, I took the money, whereupon he pushed some banknotes into the middle of the table, saying that they were for his adviser, and invited me to do the same. Of course, I politely rejected this suggestion. After this bizarre episode, we set off to dinner. The money was in Joan's handbag, which she placed between her feet.

This was not the end of the absurdity. The next morning, we went to Barclays Bank International, where I had an account. It refused to take the money. I had never previously come across a bank which refused to take cash. Since we were due to leave Malta the following day, this presented a serious problem, because, of course, to attempt to take it out with us would have contravened Malta's exchange control legislation. Eventually, after a strenuous argument, they graciously agreed to put it into a suspense account, pending authority to release it.

Because of the devaluation of sterling, having sold it for precisely the sum which I had paid for it, I made a profit of about fifty per cent, which was very gratifying.

We enjoyed Malta and the Maltese very much. But I have never been back and have no intention of doing so. It had no satisfactory planning controls and I have been told that it has now been built over to such an extent that it is largely concrete. I would be very disappointed. The same thing happened so far as Penang was concerned. I went there in the early seventies. It was beautiful. There was an unspoilt beach and about one pleasant hotel. When I next went there a few years later, it had been transformed. It was hotel next to bar, next to large block of flats, next to restaurant, next to hotel etc. I never went there again either.

8

SILK AND THE BOARD

1968 was a very important year for me. In February, I received a letter from the Home Secretary, who signed his name 'Jim Callaghan', offering me an appointment as a member of the Criminal Injuries Compensation Board. Repressing the inclination to sign my reply 'Mick Ogden', I accepted.

The Board had been formed only four years earlier. I had been Chairman of a committee of the Society of Conservative Lawyers which had been formed at the request of Edward Heath 'to examine the principles upon which compensation is awarded for personal injuries with a view to making constructive proposals for reform'. It is worth noting that in the Preface, we said, 'Mrs Michael Ogden undertook the very necessary but onerous task of reading our drafts and pointing out passages in which lawyers' jargon or unclear phraseology obscured clarity or caused ambiguity.' I think that this was the first of many such committees that I chaired. Most of our recommendations were subsequently introduced. This did not concern itself with people injured as a result of crimes of violence but, at about the same time, I was Chairman of a Bow Group committee which made suggestions for reform of the criminal justice system, many of which have also been accepted. One of them was that a scheme to compensate victims of crimes of violence should be introduced.

This latter pamphlet gave rise to an interesting experience. On the day of its publication we were staying at the Randolph Hotel in Oxford, in order to go to a play at Stratford-on-Avon.

Chambers sent a message to the hotel, asking me to telephone the BBC, which invited me to be interviewed in 'our Oxford studio'. This turned out to be an unmanned couple of rooms not far from the Randolph, whose concierge held the keys. We duly went and let ourselves into the building and the studio, where I was confronted by a notice which said 'Pull this lever', which I did, whereupon lights came on and machinery started to hum. Another notice on a door said 'Enter'; I did so, and went into a room where there was a microphone on a desk. I sat down and waited, feeling rather silly. Suddenly, I was startled by a voice saying 'Are you there, Mr Ogden?' I was then interviewed in 'our Oxford studio' by a young barrister, Sir Louis Blom-Cooper, QC, as he later became. We then reversed the process and went back to the hotel. It was the weirdest radio interview in which I ever took part, save, perhaps, when Sir Robin Day interviewed me as I sat in a BBC taxi with a large aerial on the roof outside chambers.

The Board consisted of Sir Walker Carter, QC, a judge who tried building cases as an Official Referee, two Scots silks, two English silks and a solicitor. I should have realised that my appointment in place of an English silk who had died meant that I was going to be granted silk in April; being an idiot, I did not. It would have saved me two months of anxiety, since only about one applicant in seven was successful. In 1967, I told Patrick Bennett that I intended to apply the next year and that, therefore, he had a clear run in the current year. He and Oliver Popplewell applied but neither succeeded. In 1968, they applied again, as well as Raymond Kidwell and me. Raymond and I got it and Patrick and Oliver had to wait another year.

Board members were appointed on the advice of the Lord Chancellor or, in the case of Scots members, by the Lord Advocate. Of course, I do not know who put my name forward to the Home Office. Doubtless, as with appointments to silk, various people were consulted. However, it was my belief that it was Gerald Gardiner, the Lord Chancellor, who made the decision in my case, although I like to think that I would have got silk anyway. The reason for my belief is that Gerald, who was a very 'hands on' Chancellor, had been Chairman of a special Bar Council committee which recommended the abolition of 'special' fees. In order to enable one to appear on a circuit other than one's own, one had to be instructed together with a member of that circuit, who received a very small fee, which was almost commensurate with what he did, which was almost nothing. The Bar Council accepted our recommendation and called an

Extraordinary General Meeting of the Bar. I was told that, as the matter primarily affected juniors and not silks, because I was the most junior member I should propose the motion. The meeting was in the Middle Temple Hall and was one of my most frightening experiences. The opposition was led by Elwyn Davies, QC, the Leader of the Oxford Circuit, who was later Lord Chancellor. The hall was so crowded that there were people in the gallery who had to crane round various things in order to see. I made my speech, which was easier because of the loud noises of assent made after my first sentence in which I made the proposal. The perils which had faced me were made very plain when Elwyn's seconder, carried away on a tide of Welsh emotion, declaimed '…and members of the jury', which brought the house down. We won by an overwhelming majority.

Gerald was a very shy commercial silk; if one met him in the street, he would pass by without saying a word unless one spoke first. When he saw the list of applicants for silk, I must have been one of the very few juniors whom he knew on Christian name terms. Moreover, he knew that I was sensible, because we had been in complete agreement on the committee! So far as the Board was concerned, similar considerations must have applied. Compensation was meant to be awarded on the same principles and the same levels as the courts. However, none of the existing Board members were expert in personal injury cases and it was notorious for the meanness of its awards. Doubtless, this was partly due to the Scots members, since damages in Scotland were lower than in England, until the Board's awards had an impact in Scotland, and partly because the youngest member was over twenty years older than me and it is difficult to adjust one's figures in line with inflation. (This problem is now dealt with by the issue of guidelines.) I suspect that someone in the Lord Chancellor's Department, probably Gerald, knew this and knew that I had the relevant expertise.

When at the Bar, Gerald had an enormously large and lucrative practice. This enabled him to do something which I never dared to do. When one went to a consultation with him he did not follow the usual courteous practice of inviting one into his room before the solicitor and lay client, thereby indicating that we had had a brief discussion about the case. We would all go into his room and, as soon as we sat down, he would remove his pipe from his mouth and say, 'In my view, the plaintiff will succeed and damages will be about £X,' or something similar. He would then put his pipe back in his mouth. Needless to say, consultations with him were very short.

Very quickly, I realised that, quite apart from the level of awards, the Board's procedures were seriously defective. Consequently, at the first Board meeting which I attended, I put forward a long memorandum suggesting changes. I prefaced it with a total lie, saying that several Board members had told me that they would be interested in my views. Because they were a decent lot and probably realised that I knew what I was talking about, I got my way without difficulty and without causing animosity. However, I had a difficult time persuading them actually to award proper sums until the following year, when Dennis Barker, QC, who was my age and had similar expertise, was appointed, followed by others.

My first case in silk which was of interest was a few weeks after I was appointed. I defended a soldier in a court-martial in Cyprus. This came about because Philip Otton in chambers had been an officer in a cavalry regiment and a soldier attached to it was charged with murder. On a public holiday, he had been drinking cheap local brandy and, in the course of a brawl, broke a bottle on a table, thereby producing a dagger and, while facing the deceased, had stuck it into his back. Of course, he had not intended to kill, but daggers cause death according to the way in which they are used. The traditional way depicted in paintings is a downwards blow into the chest. Usually, this does not kill because the configuration of the chest wall deflects the knife. However, an upwards strike has the opposite effect. The result of a blow to the back is wholly unpredictable.

The Services always give civilians who are with a Services unit an 'equivalent rank'; this determines whether he dines in the officers' or the sergeants' Mess and other such matters. To my joy, I discovered that the former cavalry captain had the equivalent rank of major-general, while Philip and our solicitor were colonels. As a result, we had VIP treatment at the RAF base; coming and going, immigration and customs were a formality carried out while we were in the VIP lounge. We were last on and first off the plane and on our arrival Philip and I, and possibly the solicitor, travelled in my staff car and, to complete my delight, I had a cavalry captain as my ADC. We stayed in the Headquarters Mess.

The case was as simple as most murders are and we secured a verdict of manslaughter on the ground of provocation and a very satisfactory sentence of three years' imprisonment. However, the circumstances in which the trial took place were appalling. It was in a building in the Sovereign Base Area, an area which the UK had stipulated for when Cyprus became independent, because of its importance as a listening place to spy on Russia during the Cold War. Since it was May, it was very hot and there was no air-conditioning. Later, in the Far East, I had special light-weight clothing consisting of a cotton jacket, which had the sleeves found on a silk's waistcoat and a light-weight silk's gown. Then, I had a heavy silk gown and a coat and waistcoat so heavy that it was rumoured they had been made from a job-lot of material bought from the French after Napoleon's retreat from Russia. Of course, the Army made no concessions to the weather, and the officers who were members of the court-martial board were in heavy Service dress, including Sam Browne belts with swords and decorations.

In those days people were trusted to behave with propriety and at the week-end the Brigadier who was presiding at the court-martial took me for a drive round parts of the island. Of course, we did not discuss the case, but I hate to think of the row which would ensue if that happened to-day.

At about this time, as I have mentioned, I was shortlisted for Hastings, which was a safe Conservative seat. I know that the Chairman wanted me and I suspect that I would have been selected had I agreed to live in or close to the constituency. I said that I would rent a flat there, but what they wanted was a member who, together with his family, would have his principal abode there, and this I was not prepared to do; consequently, they chose the local man. This was quite a common attitude adopted by Conservative selection committees in those days. It was very short-sighted. What is wanted is the candidate who will be able in the House of Commons and likely to become a Minister, not someone who will simply be lobby-fodder and a well-paid welfare worker. The man they chose, whose name I cannot even remember, was doubtless a very good backbench MP and excellent when doing his constituency work, but he never achieved even the most junior Ministerial office and after about twenty-five years retired with a knighthood. I can think of no more terrible way for an intelligent man to spend his life.

My failure to be selected was a blessing in disguise. In the 1950s and 1960s, it was quite common for juniors who had had large practices not to succeed in silk. In this event they were forced to apply for a minor judicial office, usually on the County Court Bench, since, before what I call 'Saint Howe's' 1979 Finance Act, it was impossible to build up an adequate pension fund in private practice. It was also common for new silks to experience a drop in income for a year or so after taking silk. Fortunately, it was almost immediately apparent to me that there would be no drop in income and that I would have a satisfactory silk's practice. Consequently, I told Conservative Central Office to take my name off the candidates' list. Characteristically, I received no letter of thanks for the work that I had done in fighting two General Elections.

On taking silk, one was obliged to continue to act for a year in cases in which one was already engaged and to do so at juniors' fees, although it was common for the brief fees to be slightly larger and to be instructed to lead a very junior junior, who would be paid a small fee at trial. The boring part was having to continue to cope with the deluge of paperwork relating to those cases. Suddenly, in October, the amount dropped away sharply and, of course, in the spring of 1969, I was free of it.

The next few years were spent in establishing a silk's practice, doing a little crime but, mostly, personal injury cases. I can recollect none of interest; it was a question of steady, hard plodding. However, between the summer of 1968 and early 1972, I was given a very interesting and important task by the Bar Council.

In all contested cases, if one party is ordered to pay costs to another party, those costs are determined, in the High Court, by a Taxing Master – in those days, a former solicitor – and in criminal cases by a taxing officer.

Taxing Masters are very conservative and barristers regard them as the lineal descendants of Scrooge. Theoretically, their decisions do not affect us. For example, if a solicitor agrees to pay a brief fee of £1,000, that sum has to be paid even if the Taxing Master decides that the winning party is only entitled to receive £750 from the loser. However, in some types of work there are scales of fees. If the scale fee for settling a draft defence in an accident case is £40, solicitors will not expect a barrister to seek more than that, save in an unusual case. Taxing Masters do not, or did not when I was in practice, increase these fees to take account of inflation.

After the war, there were no scales and Taxing Masters could not be persuaded to increase fees at all. In the early 1960s, I had been a member of a small Bar Council committee which managed to get a scale accepted for personal injuries, but the fees were pretty miserable; it was the same with other types of work. In 1968, when on holiday in Malta, I wrote to Desmond Ackner, QC, who was Chairman of the Bar, suggesting that there should be a serious attempt to get fees increased across the board. To my considerable surprise, he replied, 'I agree; you get on with it.' In retrospect, it was a great compliment to someone who had taken silk only a few months earlier.

It was very interesting. I ran the show by myself without assembling a committee. I would get hold of two barristers who did the type of work in question and we went and negotiated new fees. Of course, I led the team. I started with accident cases, which I negotiated with the Lord Chancellor's Department. I then went on to negotiate fees in areas of work about which I knew nothing at all, such as Admiralty cases (collisions at sea etc.) and Land Registry cases (the Registry paid counsel to advise about ownership of land etc.). All these went well. All the fees negotiated were subject to ratification by the Bar Council, which invariably happened without any questions being asked. It would never happen to-day; there would be a committee with a secretary and a great deal of paperwork.

The most important topic was criminal fees. Until the creation of the Crown Court in 1972, each of the Clerks of Assize on the seven circuits and every Clerk of the Peace of quarter sessions, of which there were a great many, decided the fees for both prosecuting and defence counsel, save in privately funded cases, and there was no appeal from their decisions. I had to negotiate fees for the Crown Courts which replaced those courts, and the fees would apply across the country.

I started my campaign by going alone to see the senior judge at London Quarter Sessions, who became a Senior Circuit Judge when the system changed. I told him that I was authorised to negotiate new fees on behalf of the Bar Council and continued, 'Of course, quarter sessions across the country look to London Sessions to give the lead.' One could see him visibly swelling with self-satisfaction and, of course, I had him and ended up with very satisfactory fees. I then went to see the Clerk of the Peace (if that was his title) at the Central Criminal Court, which was the Assize Court for the whole of London and also the Court of Quarter Sessions for the City of London. Known then and now as the Old Bailey, it was the most prestigious criminal court in the country. Of course, I started by showing him the fees agreed for London Sessions and saying that if that inferior court was paying those fees, the fees at the Old Bailey ought to be much higher. In the course of the discussion, I mentioned what barristers were paid for doing Order 14 summonses. Since these applied only in civil cases, I am sure that he had little or no idea what they were. Instead of saying so, he let me go on. Naturally, thereafter I mentioned them quite a lot, but by then it was too late to admit his ignorance. Again, I came away with a very satisfactory new scale and, very importantly, the scales of fees for both these courts included brief fees in all run-of-the-mill cases.

It was now time to negotiate the fees which were to apply when the Crown Courts took over on 1 January 1972. What happened was incredible.

I took two of the leading silks at the Criminal Bar with me; this, as will be seen, was probably an error. The Government fielded a team of six. At the end of the table was a deputy secretary in the Lord Chancellor's Department (the number two position). On his right sat someone from the Treasury, the Home Office, the Chief Taxing Master and, at the bottom of the table, two taxing officers from the Old Bailey. The Chief Taxing Master's job did not involve dealing with fees in criminal cases. Consequently, within a couple of minutes the entire dialogue was between us three and the two taxing officers at the end of the table. This should have been predictable to Government; how were any of them, save the taxing officers, able to express any views about, say, what fee should be paid for a plea of guilty in a burglary case compared to a contested shoplifting case?

When the second meeting took place the Government team was reduced to the Chief Taxing Master and the two taxing officers. However, I had lost the two QCs, who were each engaged in long cases. It had seemed to me that it was best not to replace them, since their successors might well have vanished by the third meeting, which would have made us look a bit silly. Also, since, once I took silk, I had begun doing far more criminal cases than I had done in my last few years as a junior, I was confident that I could manage on my own. Nevertheless, what I was engaged in were negotiations which, subject to the Bar Council's approval, would determine the incomes of nearly all the Criminal Bar for years to come. Had they known it, I suspect that they might not have slept easily in their beds. It was also extraordinary that the Government were content for the negotiations to be conducted by two junior civil servants. In view of the sums of money involved, it was, to my mind, extraordinary that it all came down to what the three of us agreed, since, as I have said, the Chief Taxing Master, who had the unusual name Graham Graham-Green, while being a very nice, sensible man, knew nothing of criminal cases.

I spent a great deal of my time negotiating compromises in personal injuries cases, and during my years on the Bar Council I had had many dealings with the LCD. As a result, I was well able to cope. On occasions like that, a good reputation is very helpful. I had had dealings with one of the taxing officers when he had had another job in the LCD. We had got on well and he knew that I was sensible and reliable. They produced a draft scale, which, as a result of what I had said at the first meeting, contained considerably better fees than those which I had negotiated at the Old Bailey; it was now my task to improve still further the ones which really mattered. I started by saying that I thought that one of the proposed fees was too high. There was a stunned silence. 'Too high!' 'Yes, it really does not merit so much.' It was at once obvious to them that they were dealing with a thoroughly trustworthy person, who was to be relied upon when we moved from this very unimportant fee to those which really mattered to the Bar! My intention from the outset, as I had

Training for the Army championship in Austria, 1947, which the 16/5 Lancers won

Wedding, December 1951

Photograph for election leaflet, 1966

Day sworn in as Q.C. (wife, daughter Celia, son Edward) April 1968

At home before attending Grand Day in Lincoln's Inn 1998. Left to right: Count de Borchgrave d'Altena (Celia's husband), Joan, the author, Edward, behind Professor Hamish Miles (Edward's father-in-law)

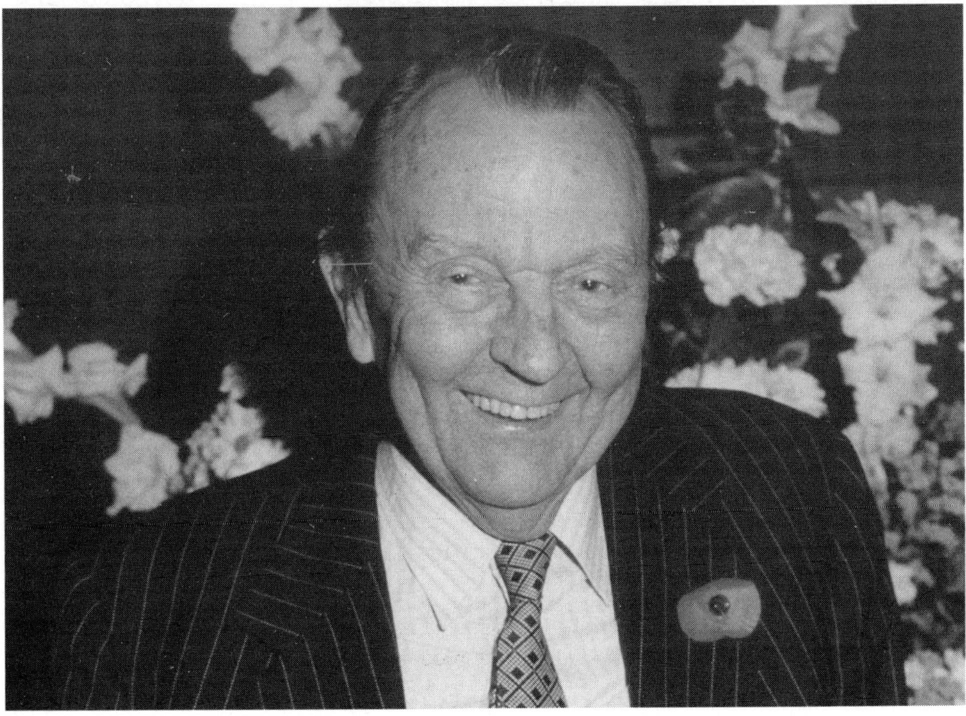

At a function in Lincoln's Inn when treasurer 1998

made plain, was to raise criminal fees to the same level as those paid in personal injuries cases. It seemed to me that a simple personal injuries case was on a par with a simple criminal case and that the same applied to larger, more complex cases, although the scales did not concern themselves with the biggest criminal cases, such as complex frauds. This I achieved. Unfortunately, in later years, this did not continue so far as criminal cases were concerned because the Treasury increasingly exercised control in all areas of Government expenditure, which, in my view, has had an unfortunate effect on many aspects of Government; quite simply, the Treasury does not seem to care whether work is done well or badly as long as it is done as cheaply as possible. They could exercise their influence on criminal cases, because both sides were usually funded by Government. But in personal injuries cases, the 'going rate', which is what Taxing Masters have to base their decisions upon, is set by trade unions on one side and insurers on the other.

The whole of this exercise was very interesting and the results extremely satisfactory. Of course, I was thanked by the Bar Council but I am certain that the Criminal Bar as a whole, and probably most of those who benefited from other negotiations, were wholly unaware how much their increased incomes were due to my efforts.*

At about this time, I was instructed in the Third London Airport Inquiry. Heathrow and Gatwick existed; Luton, which has in practice become the third London airport together with Stansted, was then of no consequence, and for some reason was not at that time considered for that position. Three inland sites and the Maplin Sands, off Southend, were selected for consideration by a Royal Commission, presided over by Eustace Roskill, who was a clever commercial judge. Predictably, people who lived near the inland sites strongly objected to a large airport being constructed nearby. For reasons which I never asked about, Southend Corporation were very anxious to have it on the Maplin Sands; certainly, it

* Since writing these memoirs, I was told that it took the Lord Chancellor's department 10 years to recover from my fee negotiations. Flattering but, if true, since all the fees were fair, I can only assume that the people with whom I negotiated were thought by their superiors to have been insufficiently Scrooge-like!

would have resulted in the creation of a very large number of jobs. I had been Deputy Recorder of Southend for about seven years and had got to know the Town Clerk and his deputy very well. I was instructed to appear for Southend but on the basis that, unlike those appearing for opponents of the inland sites, I would not get the extensive expert back-up which they did. In effect, I and my junior, Michael Wright, were told to do whatever we thought best.

The inquiry took place in the large decaying ballroom of what was then called the Piccadilly Hotel, about two hundred yards from Piccadilly Circus. An agreeable perk was that I was able to lunch every day in the hotel's quite good restaurant at the expense of the corporation.

Counsel for the tribunal was Arthur Bagnall, QC. This is an odd task in that in one sense counsel for the inquiry is independent but is working for and at the behest of the tribunal. Arthur was a very able Chancery practitioner, who became a judge shortly afterwards. I knew him well because we lunched on the same table in the Inn. He was very amusing and had a quick wit. His personal life was unusual, to put it mildly. It was said that he had only to enter any London nightclub and all the girls would greet him by his Christian name. Since he had a very large practice, it was extraordinary that he had the time and energy to do it. He died young and, not surprisingly, in spite of having been a high earner at the Bar, left an estate which, was virtually bankrupt. His conduct at the inquiry was astonishing. He cross-examined the experts who gave evidence on behalf of opponents of the inland sites as if they were on trial for fraud at the Old Bailey. This resulted in one of the most embarrassing incidents of my professional life. The three QCs representing the opponents of the inland sites came to me and said that because I was calling no expert witnesses, I was plainly impartial in the matter and would I speak to Arthur and ask him to behave himself. Of course, I had to agree. I told Arthur of their complaint and said that I had to agree that they were right. He was absolutely devastated, as was to be expected. Thereafter, his behaviour altered, but it was a very unpleasant experience.

The tribunal made a complete mess. There was only one planning expert among them. There was one economist, and all the others seemed to rather fancy themselves as such. At that time 'cost-benefit analysis' was a very fashionable planning concept. It consisted of drawing up a balance sheet which included putting a value on everything. For example, what was the value to the nation of the Brent geese which abounded near Southend, and of a Norman church which would be affected. The most important and, as it turned out, the decisive factor was 'passenger-user costs'. It would take about twenty minutes longer to get by the proposed high-speed rail-link to Southend than to any of the inland sites. A value was put on twenty minutes of a businessman's time. This seemed to me to be a very dubious approach. I doubt whether many businessmen do an extra twenty minutes' work if they have a shorter journey to the airport, but one could not argue about some value being put on this consideration. However, they then went on to value the time of a holiday-maker. The final absurdity, which really should have caused them to stop and reconsider, was when the calculation took account of a baby's time! Calculating passenger-user costs for twenty or so years produced so large a figure that it heavily outweighed any and everything else. On this half-witted basis, they came down in favour of one of the inland sites, the planner on the tribunal dissenting.

Eustace was a very arrogant man and thought that they had done a splendid job. At the dinner attended by all members of the tribunal and all counsel involved, he suggested that judicial inquiries were plainly the right solution to all major planning applications. When I did not express fervent agreement, he was quite vexed, saying, 'Well, Michael, you were only a fringe-man in the inquiry,' a comment which I heard with equanimity. The Government duly rejected the Commission's conclusion and nothing was done thereafter, resulting in Luton and Stansted becoming the de facto solution. Thereafter, I teased Eustace once or twice by saying that I had won on appeal. The Department's Permanent Under-Secretary (the senior civil servant) subsequently told me that they had been so appalled by the report that they had determined never to have a judge-led inquiry again, and they have not done so.

Lawyers are very good at deciding what went wrong about something, e.g. what caused a plane or train crash, but we are not trained to evaluate future events. However, recently I have rather changed my mind and think that it might be a very good idea if one or two important planning inquiries were to be conducted by judges. At present, they are conducted by senior planning silks. Like nearly all large planning cases, they take much longer than they should. Although Roskill got the wrong answer (it should have been Maplin) he got through it in two or three months. As I write, a planning silk is taking what is expected to be about a year writing a report on an application to build a fifth terminal at Heathrow, the hearing having taken several years. It is ridiculous. Recently at a dinner in Brasenose, I said that the whole thing would have taken less than a year if I had been the inspector, whereupon my host, a professor of law who is a member of the Ogden Working Party (a treat yet to be endured by any reader who perseveres that far) said, 'Having seen the way that you chair meetings, I have no doubt about that.' There is little discipline exercised in planning inquiries in that people are allowed to ramble on endlessly and repetitively, and planning silks pick up these bad habits. What I would like to see is a major inquiry being undertaken by a tough, robust, sensible, no-nonsense Queen's Bench judge, of whom there are a great many.

In spite of all that I have recounted, I enjoyed that inquiry, to which I was able to walk most days because of a run of good weather, going through Kensington Gardens, Hyde Park and Green Park, arriving in Piccadilly only a few hundred yards from the hotel. It also resulted in a gratifyingly large cheque, which was very welcome to a young QC with a wife and four schoolchildren to support. (For some years all four of them were at boarding school or university – thank heavens that by then I had a decent practice.)

In 1971, I was appointed Recorder of Hastings. It really rather served the burghers of Hastings right that, having failed to select me as Conservative candidate, they were now lumbered with me as Recorder. Richard Wells had been at Downside with me. He was far too kind and gentle to make a satisfactory barrister and he joined the Lord Chancellor's Office. In the 1960s, I had been on a Bar Council committee which had complained that there were far too few county court judges, as a result of which wholly inadequate people were being asked to sit as deputies far too often. For once the Bar had responded to an appeal for comments and we were able to annex a formidable number of letters to our report; of course, names were left out. I remember that one such letter began: 'This case was tried by an elderly, deaf, stupid deputy at hearings spread over a period of eleven months.' Our report had the gratifying effect of the immediate appointment of four judges and more later. Shortly afterwards, Richard came into my room in chambers, saying that he 'happened' to be passing by, and asked me for the names of those whom I regarded as unfit to sit. There flashed across my mind a picture of all those decrepit people, and I replied that none of them, save one whom they would not appoint because of his heart condition, was any good; that was our point, I said.

It was Richard who telephoned me to ask if I would be prepared to accept this appointment; of course, it was not his decision. It did not last very long. The Crown Court came into existence the following year, so I was the last Recorder of Hastings, which made me feel like a dinosaur. However, it was quite fun. I was responsible for judging all cases in Hastings and St Leonards too important for magistrates but not important enough for a High Court judge at Assizes. Michael Wright, later a High Court judge, agreed to be my deputy and, between us, we got through the list at a proper rate, wasting no time. On my first visit, I sent for the senior police officer in Hastings and asked what his principal problems were. 'Like all seaside towns, it's drugs' – as far back as 1971! Fortunately, one of the first cases was a young man who had been charged with possession of a small quantity of cannabis. Quite wrongly, one of the police officers' statements said that, while he was questioning the defendant, another youth had said, 'Glad you've got him; he's a pusher.' This gave me my chance. The defendant was about to emigrate and I gave him a conditional discharge. However, when sentencing him I said that, of course, I ignored this remark, but I added, 'Had I thought you were a pusher, I'd have given you seven years.' On the front page of the local paper appeared the headline 'Seven years for drug pushers says Recorder'. Next time I was in Hastings I asked the same police officer how things were going. 'Your remarks about drug pushers had a marvellous effect; they've all gone to Brighton.' I doubt whether the Recorder of Brighton thanked me.

For about the only time, Joan accompanied me to court to watch me be inducted – wearing a brown dress, as she reminded me when I told her that I was about to write about Hastings. What a memory! My recollection of her being there is what happened at the buffet lunch which was given to celebrate the event – with the Mayor, etc. A barrister cheerfully told me that he intended to appeal a sentence of imprisonment which I had passed on his client. 'Oh yes,' said Joan, 'it really was too long.' 'Good luck,' I said to the barrister; but there was no appeal.

In marked contrast, it was reported to me that a police officer said, 'That's more like it!' following my sentencing in the first case which I tried. (My predecessor had been a kindly fellow who tended to put everyone on probation.) I do not believe that I was a harsh sentencer, since in the whole of my time as a part-time criminal judge, I was successfully appealed only once – an appeal against sentence – and I was arrogant enough to think that the Appeal Court was wrong. Sentencing, like assessing damages in a personal injuries case, is not an exact science and all that one can hope to do is to make a decision which is within acceptable limits.

The most memorable thing about Hastings, which could probably be said about most such courts, was how efficient the set-up was. The Clerk of the Peace was an elderly local solicitor, who did the job part-time with the assistance of his secretary. A few days before the court sat, he would send all the papers up to me with a suggested list for the first day of those cases in which he expected a plea of guilty. I do not think that I ever disagreed with his assessment. On the first day, I would expect to deal with no less than fourteen pleas of guilty. Of course, to-day there are fewer pleas of guilty but each of them seems to take much longer than they did then. Needless to say, the court staff is very much larger. In short, it is now far more expensive and less efficient.

The Clerk of the Peace seemed to know most members of the jury and after they had been sworn in, would say, 'Mr So-and-So, would you act as foreman, please.' Since the standard textbook contained no prohibition against this being done, I kept quiet on the basis that it could hardly be said to constitute a valid ground for appeal, even if the Appeal Court said that it was wrong.

I was rather sorry when the job disappeared and I was simply a Recorder of the Crown Court, with no responsibility or interest in the court in which I was sitting. Fortunately, a few years later I was asked to sit at the Old Bailey, which was more interesting.

9

TWO HIGH-PROFILE MEN

I may have given the reader the impression that I sauntered effortlessly from one triumph to another. Of course, this was far from being the position. Like everyone else, I made mistakes and lost cases which I should have won. However, one tries to suppress such memories and, since I am not in the confessional, I see no reason why I should mention them. The two cases which I am about to relate cannot be said to have been won in the ordinary sense, but one, although lost, was successful and the other, although never tried, was certainly not lost.

Robert Maxwell

It was in 1971 that I suddenly found myself propelled into *In Re Pergamon*, as it had started life, but was now *Maxwell v Department of Trade and Industry*. It is unnecessary to go into details of the very complex issues; it is sufficient to say that the general allegation was that Maxwell had distorted and concealed matters in his business transactions and the Department had appointed company inspectors to investigate and report on the complaints.

When I said that I was propelled into the case, it was no exaggeration. The case was already being heard by a judge named Wien. Initially, it had been conducted by Sam Silkin, QC, who was later Attorney-General. For some reason unknown to me – and one does not enquire into such matters – he withdrew from the case, and for some days Maxwell conducted it on his own. He discovered, as others have done, that conducting cases in court is more difficult than might appear to an observer, and I was asked if I would take over. The task which faced me was formidable. As Lord Denning said when the case reached the Court of Appeal, the inspectors' report covered 209 pages of close type and the transcripts of evidence were even longer. They covered 366 pages of close type and the hearing had lasted 12 days. I took the judge through 30 criticisms made of Maxwell and went through them in detail.

When I arrived in court, Maxwell was asking a witness a whole lot of irrelevant questions and Wien looked at me curiously as I went and sat next to Maxwell. When he had finished, he said that I would be taking over, and I rose and asked for a four-day adjournment. 'How can you possibly hope to master this case in four days?' said Wien. I replied, 'I would probably not be much better off if I had a month.' Of course, he had to grant the adjournment, which he might not have done if I had asked for a month.

The Department took the case extremely seriously; not only did they instruct Godfrey le Quesne, QC, but Gordon Slynn, later a Law Lord, and Peter Gibson, later a Court of Appeal judge, being then Common Law and Chancery Treasury counsel respectively, i.e. permanently retained to work on behalf of the Crown, together with another junior. Doubtless it has happened, but I cannot recall another case in which both Treasury counsel were instructed. As if this was not enough, Raymond Kidwell, QC, was instructed to lead the same three juniors on behalf of the inspectors, although their interests were identical with those of the Department. The reason for all of this was not just the point of principle involved but the fact that Maxwell was an extremely high-profile and controversial businessman who had been a Labour Member of Parliament.

I had two things going for me. First, I was leading Tony Grabiner, who is now a Life Peer and has one of the best practices at the Bar. The other was that Sam Silkin had very kindly given me his very detailed notes, without which my position would have been absolutely appalling as opposed to being merely appalling.

Wien, before whom I never appeared on any other occasion, had the reputation of being a very unpleasant judge. However, he was so grateful for the fact that I had taken over from Maxwell that he treated me with the highest consideration. I staggered through the case in what I flatter myself was a creditable fashion and in due course Wien, predictably, ruled against us.

This was far from being the end of the story. The application had taken place while the inspectors were still conducting their inspection and, as soon as we had finished before Wien, I had to appear before them. There are always two inspectors, a barrister and an accountant. The latter was a former president of the Institute of Accountants and the senior partner in a large City firm which provided the back-up team. Since I cannot recollect him ever saying anything, I was unable to form any view about him. Owen Stable, QC, was in a set of chambers above us and I knew him quite well. He had an eccentric appearance in that he wore the striped trousers and black coat which was virtually our uniform in those days, but the coat was made in the form of a hacking jacket and he wore a wing collar. His father had been a High Court judge who, because of the type of spectacles which he wore, was known as 'Owlie'. Owen wore similar spectacles and this, coupled with his jacket, caused the sharp-tongued judge Melford Stevenson to call him 'the racing correspondent of the *Church Times*', which delighted the profession. During the hearings, he would leave for lunch wearing a boater. He was somewhat out of his depth and made the fatal error of pursuing every possible allegation, no matter how trivial, although they had quite enough serious and substantial allegations to consider. Thus, a man had asked Maxwell if he would buy his factory and Maxwell did so on behalf of one of his family companies. The man had not asked whether Pergamon would buy the factory but, inexplicably, the inspectors devoted a chapter of their report to decide that he should have bought it for Pergamon. Not surprisingly, the Department found the report deeply embarrassing.

Of course, I had to work very hard. After each day we would have a long meeting during which I was taught about the matters to be considered the next day, and this would be continued before we went off to the inspectors. Every lunchtime, we would get into Maxwell's Rolls and go to the Savoy, where we continued to discuss the case unless, as often happened, Maxwell discussed business with someone else. This probably went on for only a few weeks but it felt like a lifetime. Then for some reason which I cannot remember, Maxwell instructed me to tell the inspectors that he did not propose to attend to answer any further questions.

He was not entitled to do this and could have been imprisoned for contempt had he refused to comply with a demand by the inspectors that he should change his mind. However, they decided to do nothing about it.

It was following the publication of the report that we found ourselves in the Court of Appeal, which I had to fit in during the Summerland Fire Inquiry in the Isle of Man. Our point was simple. Since the inspectors' proceedings are held in private, a person who might be criticised in the report does not know what other witnesses have said, still less, what the inspectors are minded to decide. We said that the inspectors should have given Maxwell the opportunity of commenting on what other witnesses had said. Since the inspectors failed to do this, we said, they were in breach of the rules of natural justice and we asked the court for a declaration to that effect.

Tom Denning was extremely hostile to Maxwell, who was just the kind of man Tom detested. The case lasted for five days, following which I returned to the Isle of Man. A week later judgement was given against us. Of course, Maxwell decided to take the case to the House of Lords. It was necessary to seek leave from the Lords and I duly found myself before a committee of three, headed by Lord Dilhorne. To-day it would be unthinkable that he should have sat, since, as Reginald Manningham-Buller (known to the Bar as 'Bullying-Manner') he had been Conservative Attorney-General when Maxwell was an MP. We were given short shrift and leave was refused.

Sometimes people say to me, 'You lost that case, didn't you?' I reply, 'It depends what you mean by lose.' It is true that we lost before the Trial Judge, the Court of Appeal and the House of Lords. However, by then the events in question had happened many years before. There was now a Labour Government and Sam Silkin was Attorney-General. What made it wholly impossible to take steps barring Maxwell from holding office as a director and, still more, to contemplate prosecuting him, was the incredible fact that Harold Wilson had asked him to take over two ailing companies, which entailed him becoming chairman or managing director of them. So, Maxwell was able to continue to run large companies and to perpetrate the thefts which led to his death.

An interesting footnote to the affair was that although the

courts had decided that the inspectors had behaved fairly and had not breached the rules of natural justice, the Department evidently thought otherwise, because, in all subsequent cases, inspectors did precisely what we said ought to have been done.

It was an extremely high-profile case and was very advantageous to a fairly new silk in that my name became known to a great many people who might have heard little or nothing of me and who now knew that I was capable of conducting such a large, complex case.

Over the years, I conducted other cases for Maxwell, as did a great many other QCs; he was constantly engaged in litigation, often using a writ to scare someone into shutting up. On one occasion, having bought a business, he went to visit it, saw two people he disliked and dismissed them on sight. They sued, and he tried to justify his conduct. I told him that he was bound to lose. 'No, Michael, you'll tear them apart in cross-examination.' 'You can't make bricks without straw, you need to give me some straw.' Although he had about ten City accountants working until midnight at vast expense, he never did so, and we lost. At least he had the grace to say that I had warned him. Had he sent all his work to me, it would have been almost a full-time occupation.

He was an extremely difficult man to work for and would constantly ask me to do things which I refused to do. There were occasions when, after I had rejected a series of suggestions, he would make one which all my instincts told me was a bad idea, but, because I could not put my finger on why it was not a sensible thing to do and could not see that it would do any harm, I agreed to do it; invariably, I regretted it. However much he would argue, he never pushed it to a breach. On one occasion, he said, 'Michael, if you won't do it, I'll just have to go round the Temple and find someone who will.' 'Well, Bob, that's what you'll have to do.' He did not.

He had scant regard for professional niceties. One evening, as I was about to let myself into the house, the telephone started ringing. 'Michael,' he said, 'the *Sun* is threatening to sue me if I publish a story tomorrow.' I told him that, for once, since Joan was away, I would go the *Mirror* building if he sent a car for me. 'Splendid, come and eat some caviar with me while we wait for a time-lock to let us get a tape out of a safe.' A Rolls appeared and I went to his office, where I found the largest pot of caviar that I have ever seen and a bottle of vodka. Also present were a solicitor dragged up from Tonbridge, the editor of the paper in question and a couple of people who said nothing and I never understood why they were there. After consuming a great deal of caviar and enough vodka to be close to impairing my judgement, we listened to a taped conversation with a tennis player who should never have talked to one of Maxwell's people because she had a contract with the *Sun*, after which I said it was all right to publish and I was driven home. Of course, I charged a higher than normal fee for working out of hours.

There was a similar occasion when he dragged me out of the house in the evening and we were driven down to the duty judge's house near Hampton Court, where I got an injunction preventing the *Sun* from publishing a story as the clock struck midnight.

He was a terrible bully and once caused a female solicitor to burst into tears in my room with one unkind remark. When he tried, he could be charming. If he came to my house, which he did several times at weekends, he would always ask Joan about the children, whose names he would remember.

I had not seen him for some time before his death. He had got into appalling financial difficulties and resorted to stealing funds in one of his companies. He often sailed close to the wind but I had never thought that he would resort to out-and-out theft. He disappeared off his yacht in the Mediterranean in the middle of the night. There were suggestions that he had been pushed but I never believed that. He was a brave man, who had won the Military Cross. I believe, as does Tony Grabiner, that he realised that there was no escape and preferred to commit suicide rather than face the ignominy of appearing in the dock at the Old Bailey and being sentenced to a substantial period of imprisonment. He was an interesting and very able man but a thorough rogue.

Bernard Cornfeld

Bernie, an American, was an amusing character. He was very small and wore a yachting cap at all times, even during consultations. He ran a savings company called Investors Overseas Ltd

(IOS). It was aimed at American Servicemen in Europe, of whom there were a great many in the seventies. The sales technique demonstrated in the textbooks provided for the salesmen were fairly nauseating, although probably no worse than many others. The manuals showed cartoons in which the potential buyer was called 'Mr Prospect'; the product was described, as was every question or objection which might be raised by Mr Prospect, followed, of course, by the retort which dealt with the problem. I had the impression that the wretched salesmen were expected to learn it all by heart.

Bernie was the last person who should ever have been in charge of a mutual fund because he was a gambler, and the present regulatory controls did not then exist. In the United States, banks still failed and here one large insurance company did so.

IOS had three flat years to start with but this period was followed by about ten years of great success before, again, there was a problem. Public interest was much increased by Bernie's spectacular personal life, and the press featured photographs of large numbers of attractive ladies and stories of dubious conduct.

Consequently, when IOS got into trouble, the Press became hugely excited in it. Three journalists wrote a book entitled *Do You Sincerely Want to be Rich?*, which had been one of Bernie's slogans. Needless to say, it was a thoroughly bad book, which I was obliged to read from end to end when on holiday in Malta. From Bernie's viewpoint, what mattered most was an allegation that he had circulated a false prospectus. The allegation was that in a graph showing IOS's success, the first three flat years had been omitted. In fact, the management of the company had changed hands at the end of those years, which doubtless accounted for their omission. More to the point was the fact that no one who saw the chart as it should have been would have been affected in the slightest degree by the fact that the first three years had been flat, since the following ten, which had been spectacularly satisfactory, would have been what mattered to the prospective investor. Furthermore, as Bernie plaintively said, 'Why am I receiving all the blame? I did not prepare the prospectus; it was done by a leading London firm of solicitors and a leading merchant bank. Why am I receiving so much blame for not noticing this small, immaterial error contained in a very long document?' It seemed to me to be a valid point. As Managing

Director he was responsible, but it was a trivial error not caused by him.

However, the three reporters were employed by a Sunday paper with a large circulation, which serialised extracts from the book. This achieved widespread publicity, not only here but abroad. Bernie consulted Hans Beer, who came to me. Hans's idea was that we should launch libel proceedings against the paper as a measure of Bernie's resolution to clear his name. This had the merit of stopping all further public discussion of the case in this country, because it was *sub judice*. Philip Otton was my junior. Hans Beer telephoned him on a Sunday and asked him to speak to Bernie, who was in America, who insisted that he also spoke to his mother (!) and he was asked to draft a writ for service the next day, which he duly did.

Of course, since many of the American Servicemen were serving in other parts of Europe, complaints were made in those countries, and these included a criminal complaint in Switzerland. Bernie's mother lived there and he was unwise enough to pay her a visit. He was promptly arrested and thrown into St Antoine, the prison in Geneva. I was acting for Bernie in another, smaller, case which was coming up to trial, while Hans was looking after a number of his affairs. Consequently, we flew to Geneva to see him. As a matter of courtesy, Bernie's Swiss lawyer took us to make a call on the *juge d'instruction* who was in charge of Bernie's case. He was a young man in his thirties. To my amazement, in a very prominent position on his desk, was a much-thumbed copy of *Do You Sincerely Want to be Rich?* It was plain that the judge relied on this piece of journalistic rubbish very heavily. From then on I have had a low opinion of Swiss justice, which has been confirmed whenever I have had anything to do with it.

When we went to see Bernie, we found him quite cheerful. He had remembered his Jewish roots and was therefore able to send out for excellent kosher food. I noticed with interest what I subsequently noticed in a prison in Beijing: that, as in England, there was a pervasive smell of cabbage over-cooking. Fortunately for him, Bernie's expensive kosher food must have smelt and tasted much better.

When it came to bail, the Swiss had a curious habit which was consistent with their nature. In fraud cases concerning foreigners they tended to grant bail, which was set at a very large sum and had to be deposited in cash, whereupon the defendant was expelled from the country and told to come back on the date fixed for trial. Of course, the expectation was that he would never be seen again and the Swiss would pocket the bail money without having incurred the cost of his keep pending trial and, if convicted and sentenced to prison, his further cost of keep.

Bernie, having been released on bail, had come to stay in London where he had a large house near Hyde Park Corner. Unfortunately, another incident occurred which necessitated my services. Bernie was charged with attempted rape. A young, naked girl rushed out of his house in the middle of the night crying rape. Bernie had arranged for a young girl to be sent from America to London en route to Switzerland, where she was to look after his horses. It was she who had rushed out of the house and was the cause of Beer and Ogden having to act for Bernie again. As will be remembered from my account of Bernard Gabriel Grealy, who had been falsely accused of blackmail, Beer was a solicitor who was not only very clever but was prepared to use unconventional means. On this occasion, he contrived to discover who the girl's American attorney was and began a correspondence with him, asking how much money his client would accept for agreeing not to come to London to give evidence. When he received a letter saying that the woman would stay away if she was paid the very large sum of money stipulated in the letter, he ended the correspondence.

In due course, we found ourselves at Bow Street Magistrates' Court, where Bernie was due to be committed for trial to the Old Bailey. The young woman was present and I looked at her with interest. She was Puerto Rican and had the misfortune to have a complexion which was the colour of the kind of mud found in harbours. Equally, it has to be said that the sight of Bernie, who besides being very small, had a small beard and was doubtless wearing his yachting cap, would have been terrifying.

The representative of the Director of Public Prosecutions obtained authority to accept a plea of indecent assault, to which Bernie duly pleaded guilty. The case was heard by the Chief Metropolitan Magistrate, Evelyn Russell, whom I knew well to be a sensible, level-headed man, which was an important factor in advising Bernie to plead guilty to indecent assault. I told Evelyn that my instructions were that the woman had been procured to come to London for the specific purpose of having sexual relations with Bernie, but had doubtless lost her nerve when the small bearded gnome in the yachting cap had come into her room, and she had bolted out of the house into the road, where she had to cry rape to account for her behaviour. I showed him the correspondence. Of course, it was decisive. While he had no idea where the truth lay, any more than I do, the correspondence removed from his mind any idea which might have been present as to a custodial sentence. He imposed a modest fine and Bernie, Hans, my junior and I repaired to a very good restaurant, where we had an excellent and very alcoholic lunch. It is always a relief when a case like that goes right, because it is a great responsibility to advise someone to plead guilty if it is possible that it might result in a prison sentence.

Bernie is generally remembered as a crook. He was not. He never stole a penny from IOS. When his case came on for trial in Switzerland, the little man elected to turn up and was duly acquitted. I was told that the judge who tried the case was so angry that it had been brought that he ordered the complainants to pay Bernie's costs. Furthermore, one of the speculative deals which Bernie engaged in, which was of a kind wholly unsuitable to a mutual, was the purchase of Alaskan oil rights, which eventually proved very remunerative.

Once the Swiss litigation was finished, we dropped the libel action. Bernie was not the kind of person who would have appealed to a jury and he did not need the money. However, before this happened, my second junior, Nicholas Strauss, had to appear before a Master in relation to a summons that the paper should provide more detailed particulars of its defence. 'Ah,' said the Master, having read the documents drafted by Philip, 'words by Otton, music by Strauss.'

I did not meet Bernie again. He returned to Los Angeles, where he continued to be photographed with large numbers of young women and continued to give rise to stories about his sexual activities. He died at a fairly young age, doubtless due to a mixture of sex and drink in immoderate quantities.

10

THE SUMMERLAND FIRE INQUIRY

In November 1973, I was instructed in the Isle of Man fire disaster. A leisure centre in Douglas, called Summerland, was consumed by fire, with considerable loss of life. As an independent state, which happens to have the same monarch and various agreements with the UK about matters such as defence and foreign affairs, the Isle of Man has its own lawyers but, being basically a tax haven, they were not skilled advocates. Consequently, all interested parties were represented by English silks and juniors, together with a local lawyer, who was seldom present but useful for administrative purposes. It was a Royal Commission, presided over by an English judge, Joe Cantley. My junior was Graeme Hamilton from chambers.

I was acting for the Commercial Union, who insured Trust House Forte, the owners of Summerland. Other parties consisted of a team representing relatives of the deceased and people injured, insurers of an architect, sub-contractors, the local authority and the like. It has been my experience that major disasters are often caused or contributed to by several acts of negligence, and this case was no exception. My clients had been guilty of a number of negligent acts, including locked safety doors and suchlike. It was obvious to me that there was no hope of avoiding severe criticism on a number of grounds, and I told insurers that our best course would be for me to make a statement at the outset of the inquiry admitting responsibility for a number of shortcomings, as a result of which other parties would concentrate their fire on each other rather than us. Insurers agreed and I did so, with the anticipated result. Much of the inquiry was taken up with consideration of whether there had been breaches of the fire regulations in the design and construction of the building.

I formed a very unfavourable view of the island. The inquiry lasted from November to February and, throughout, the weather was very depressing. I had not known that it was possible to have deep fog and torrential rain at the same time, often accompanied by strong winds, which caused tons of pebbles to be blown on to the esplanade. In the summer, it was a low-grade tourist resort much patronised by people living in Liverpool and thereabouts, and must have been appalling at that time, but for different reasons. When we were there most of the hotels etc. were closed, adding to the dismal atmosphere. Most of us, including other members of chambers, stayed at the hotel, which had a casino. Doubtless because of this, the bar was open long after usual closing hours, thereby attracting all the local drinkers and making the bar so intolerably full that, often, I retired to the casino, not to gamble but because it was quieter. A number of the locals took pity on us, doubtless partly because we were new faces, and invited us to dinner, but, as is the case with the Channel Islands, many of the people living there were tax exiles and such people are often neither interesting nor good company. With the exception of noble people who live in such places when they are old, in order to protect their estates for their children, it seems to me bizarre that people who are so wealthy that tax ought not to matter much, should go and live somewhere where they would otherwise not wish to live, in order to avoid tax. Of course, because it was a high-profile case, numerous journalists and other media people were there and they were much more interesting.

So far as I was concerned, the inquiry went well and the result was as good as could be expected. Afterwards, Joe Cantley paid me the compliment of telling me that I was the only counsel who never asked an unnecessary question, although that was probably rather overdoing it and was more a reflection of the fact that he did not get on at all well with some other silks.

It is an indication of how hectic life was that I had to leave the inquiry for a few days in order to conduct the Maxwell appeal in the Court of Appeal and, as soon as it ended, had to prepare for the Stevenage Development Inquiry, which, in turn, I had to leave because it overran, so that my junior had to make the closing speech.

The Isle of Man case was an interesting experience, as well as being remunerative, but not particularly pleasant, although the fact that Graeme was my junior made it more agreeable. One curious aspect was that we all commuted between the island and London at week-ends. The inquiry sat earlier on Fridays and finished in time for us to catch the plane for London, and we all flew back on Sunday evening. Manx kippers are very good and I had a standing commission to buy them for us and some of our neighbours. On one occasion I remember reflecting that, when I was called to the Bar, it would never have occurred to me to find myself in a queue at a florist's shop at an airport in the Isle of Man in order to buy kippers.

In 1973 I had a weird case in the House of Lords. A man driving his wife's car was involved in an accident when he was on his way to a nightclub. The issue was whether at the time of the accident he was acting as 'servant or agent' of his wife. Tom Denning, who was extremely good in persuading fellow members of the Court of Appeal to adopt ridiculous decisions of his, persuaded them that the man was indeed acting as servant or agent of his wife. This was an utterly preposterous decision and I was brought in after the Court of Appeal hearing in order to conduct the case in the Lords. Reggie Manningham-Buller, the former Lord Chancellor, was a member of the court. In the course of argument I said to them, 'If anyone would like to see my old AA road guide, it's quite obvious that he was travelling in the opposite direction to home from his place of work.' Of course, the rules against introduction of new evidence in the House of Lords are very strict; however, Reggie had not the slightest hesitation in saying that he would like to see the *AA Gazetteer*, and so I handed my dog-eared copy over to him. He took one look at it and said, 'Oh yes, I see,' and as far as he was concerned that was the end of the case. Of course, I won it without difficulty.

I was Chairman of the Bar Council's International Relations Committee at a time (1974–5) when it was very popular for American lawyers to come over to Europe pretending that they were increasing their knowledge of foreign law, which enabled them to put the whole trip down to expenses which were not taxable; a loophole which, thank heavens, was subsequently closed.

It became quite obvious to us that in effect, we were being bribed by a few glasses of whisky with whatever State Bar was doing this trip and, of course, we resented this. I let it be known that we would not co-operate in any of these affairs unless I was satisfied that it was genuine. Consequently, when the litigation section of the American Bar Association wanted to come to London, they asked for my agreement to join in, and I was subsequently told by the chairman that I had given him a terrible time cross-examining him about precisely what it was that they intended to do.

However, once I was satisfied that it was genuine, I put on a special show for them. I took the main hall in the Law Courts on a Saturday morning and we proceeded to have a mock trial. It was a rape case and the rather attractive victim was a member of the Bar. It was very interesting. The English lawyers (barristers taken from my chambers) proceeded to examine and cross-examine the complainant in the morning and also made a final speech. In the afternoon the Americans (lawyers from the litigation section) did the same. Of course, the American team was not present in the morning so that they would have no unfair advantage in the afternoon. I acted as judge. It was a very instructive affair because it was quite obvious that our people were infinitely better than theirs. They perceived it, and spent the rest of the little trip explaining that this was just rather unusual and generally they were much better than the two Americans who had taken part in the mock trial. As a result of this affair I was made an Honorary Member of the litigation section.

How I came to be instructed in the Stevenage Development Inquiry I do not know, since I did not do planning work. The Government had made a policy decision to double the size of all the New Towns near London and I suspect that it was an Attorney-General's nomination, which came to me because I was known to him as a result of being on the Bar Council. Stevenage had the merit of being only an hour's drive, whereas ghastly Harlow was well over an hour. I doubt whether Stevenage was less ghastly than Harlow, but, except for looking at the proposed development site, I saw nothing much of it save the road to where the inquiry was held and from there to the Development Corporation's offices, where we had lunch. It confirmed me in my view that planning work is very boring. Inspectors, who are civil servants, do not have the authority or inclination that judges have to attempt to ensure that cases proceed at a reasonable pace. People were able to ramble on at will, which lay people usually did, and there was endless repetition and duplication. All the inspectors duly approved the Government's proposals with very minor changes.

However, before the decisions could be implemented, there was a change of Government, and one of the few sensible things that Tony Benn, who was the new Labour Minister, ever did was to refuse to implement any of the plans. Ironically, the present Labour Government has suggested doing virtually what the Conservative Government had proposed in the inquiry, in which I acted for it.

The reason why I had to leave the Stevenage Inquiry before its end was because I had accepted my first brief in Hong Kong. It was a case of 'throw your bread on the waters and it will come back sandwiches'. When I was a junior, a pupil would pay his pupil-master a pupillage fee of one hundred guineas. That practice ceased many years ago, as did the practice of solicitors paying a fee for their indentures, which amounted to the same thing. Now, the wheel has turned full cycle and, while all pupils must be paid a minimum sum, £7,500 in 1999 I think, good sets of chambers will pay about £17,500 in order to attract people of high quality. However, since the universities are currently pouring out far more law graduates than are needed, partly because law is a cheap subject to teach, since it requires only a few lecturers and a room for them to lecture in, about 350 people apply for the three places on offer. Since they can apply to only about twelve sets, many fail to get in anywhere. Hardly a sensible arrangement, since they have acquired large debts getting that far (£17,500 is not unusual).

In the early 1960s, Lincoln's Inn had asked me to take on a Hong Kong pupil for nothing, which I did. Ronald Arculli was partly Chinese and partly Pakistani. In 1974, he asked me to go out and lead him. Shortly afterwards he transferred to being a solicitor in one of the best Chinese firms in Hong Kong and sent me more work. He prospered enormously; he was asked to be member of the Legislative Council, and was appointed an MBE for his services. All four of my pupils have done well but he has been the most successful.

I had never been to the Far East, where I was destined to appear in many subsequent cases. It was utterly fascinating. In those days, there were no non-stop flights. The plane would put down once in Europe, usually Rome or Frankfurt, once in the Near or Middle East and once in the Indian subcontinent. A first-class seat was always part of the deal, and then it truly was first-class, with excellent food and a sitting room on the upper deck of the 747s, when they came into service, where there were comfortable armchairs and a bar. Of course, there was jet-lag and in those days I refused to do any work until one clear day had elapsed after my arrival.

On this occasion I appeared for Gordon Wu, who was a very able architect. Hong Kong island is simply a large steep mountain sticking out of the sea with large blocks of flats built all the way up to the Peak. There had been a torrential rainstorm which had caused landslides, resulting in a number of flats being washed away, causing considerable loss of life. A Chinese friend had been buried up to his neck in mud for several hours, while his wife lay dead in bed beside him. As a result of this calamity architects who had designed the buildings were prosecuted. We had no defence but the prosecution agreed to accept a plea of guilty on the basis that Gordon, who was the Authorised Architect, had not personally been responsible, the error having been that of subordinates. I suspect that the member of the Legal Department who prosecuted was happy to do this because he did not understand what had been wrong. This became plain when the magistrate asked how great was the error. The man prosecuting was grateful when I said that I would explain it to the magistrate. This I did, but not quite in the same terms as I would have used had I been prosecuting! In these circumstances, there was no question of Gordon being sent to prison and he was fined a fairly small sum. Afterwards, he said to me, 'I will never be an Authorised Architect again!' Subsequently, although he constructed many large buildings, both in Hong Kong and in China, I believe that he adhered to this resolve. He and Ronnie must have been happy, as will be seen.

Throughout my career, chance has played a large part. The Inn might well have asked someone else to take on Ronnie. If so, I might never have got to the Far East because the nature of my practice and the chambers that I was in would have tilted the odds against it happening. In that event, I would have missed a part of my career which I found particularly interesting as well as highly remunerative.

1975 was an important year for me. James Miskin, who had been Leader of the South-Eastern Circuit, was appointed Recorder of London, i.e. senior judge at the Old Bailey. I was elected to succeed him. I have always regarded this as a great honour, since it was not a matter of appointment but election by my peers. As I have mentioned before, the governing body of the circuit was the Wine Committee, so-called because its original function was to ensure that there was an adequate supply of wine owned by the circuit available in the Bar hotel in all assize towns, which was available free to members when on circuit. Unfortunately, for some mealy-mouthed feeling of political correctness, it is now called the Executive Committee. Having been elected to it in 1960, I had remained on it and had been the first person to hold the newly-created post of Recorder of the Circuit, which existed in order to take some of the administrative burden from the Leader. Election of Leader was by the Wine Committee and was for five years.

The circuit mirrored the circuit of the Judges of Assize. The South-Eastern was the largest of the circuits, stretching from the Wash to the South Coast and from the East Coast to the Hampshire border, and over a quarter of the members of the Bar belonged to it. Although I had the assistance of the Treasurer, Recorder and Junior of the Circuit, it was quite a demanding job. There were six sessions messes, e.g. Sussex and East Anglia. For each sessions mess there was a joint committee consisting of its chairman, a representative of the Crown Courts and the local Law Society, which discussed problems. Although I did not attend all their meetings, I felt obliged to do so from time to time, which entailed the disagreeable necessity of going to, say, Chelmsford on a Friday evening in order to attend the meeting and the dinner which followed it, getting back home at a very late hour.

I had to deal with complaints by judges about misconduct by barristers which did not merit formal disciplinary proceedings by the Bar Council, and I would have to reprimand the barrister. There were also complaints by sessions messes about circuit judges. These I dealt with by getting one of the judge's friends to speak to him, mentioning that the ultimate sanction following complaints by the local Bar and Law Society was removal to a different court some distance away, which would involve the judge in long journeys to work or having to move house, which happened on one occasion.

The Lord Chancellor's Department sent numerous communications which entailed action by me. One disagreeable task was when they wrote saying that it had been reported to them that some Assistant Recorder was not up to the job. Had I replied that I agreed, the person would probably never have been given either a part- or full-time appointment in the future. Happily, in each case some wretched court clerk or suchlike person who had made the complaint had got it wrong. On one occasion, it gave me great pleasure to report that the man in question made no secret of the fact that he knew nothing about crime, which was hardly surprising since he was a commercial silk, but that he was learning fast and would obviously make a competent judge. I added that, if he made a mistake, it was preferable that he should do so when trying a simple case of burglary than when he was a High Court judge trying a murder. I was very pleased when, some years later, he was made a High Court judge, but I was charitable enough not to write to the Department about it.

Because I had been on the Executive Committee of the Bar Council for most of the time since 1962 and, in particular, Treasurer in 1972 to 1974, I had had many dealings with the Lord Chancellor's Office. I regarded it as unreliable and untrustworthy. In those days, nearly all those in it had arrived there only because they had failed at the Bar. I believe that this caused many of them to have a chip on the shoulder, which caused them to resent those who had been successful. As a result, they endeavoured to indicate that they were very important and powerful. All of this made it very difficult to deal with them and was in marked contrast to civil servants in the Home Office, which was the department with which I had most dealings. Fortunately, because they were mostly inept, it tended to produce a more level playing field, but it was very tiresome. Of course, it did not apply to all of them and things are much better today, partly, I suspect, because many of them are not lawyers.

The most amusing meeting which I had with them was one in which I was merely an observer. In about 1976, David Napley was President of the Law Society. He was a very able but not very likeable man. In the course of conversation, he said to me in rather belligerent tones, 'The Bar Council never supports the Law Society when it tries to get solicitors' fees increased' – he knew that I had negotiated fees for the Bar, which had been satisfactory. 'You've never asked me,' I replied. A few weeks later, he telephoned and asked me to go with a Law Society delegation to talk to the Lord Chancellor about fees. I walked to his office and got into his large, black hearse-like Rolls, which I thought rather inappropriate for people with a begging bowl, and went to the House of Lords. The Lord Chancellor, Elwyn Jones, sat at the end of a long table, with his civil servants on his left. The Law Society team sat on his right, with me at the end of it, showing silent, moral support. David fancied himself as an advocate and he deployed the very strong Law Society case with skill. Unfortunately, I cannot remember what it was, but he said something which caused all the civil servants to sit up with raised hackles, and all was lost. It was a remarkable demonstration of the advantages of a divided profession, with barristers as advocates being chosen by solicitors.

My other abiding recollection of David was equally humorous. It was at the American Bar Association meeting in Atlanta, which was preceded by a church service. The Law society had resolved that its President should have a ceremonial robe. David's predecessor decided that the robe should be of two colours divided vertically. Since he was Welsh, the robe was in the Welsh or Cardiff rugby football colours, which were red and mauve. Since David was small and had an olive complexion, the poor fellow looked unbelievably comic.

By 1975, I had been a member of the Criminal Injuries Compensation Board for seven years. None of the other members were unpleasant, which was just as well since three of us would spend a week at a time together, usually including four nights in a provincial hotel. The country's economic affairs were increasingly unsatisfactory and the Government announced that there would be a wage freeze, which did little good. Board members' fees had not been increased since its inception in 1964. Unsurprisingly, members felt that they ought to be increased before the wage freeze took effect, particularly since there was rampant inflation.

Like a number of wealthy men, Walker Carter had little interest in money. Moreover, he was doing the job of chairman on an unpaid basis, since he was a judge. He was extremely reluctant to do anything and I said that, since I had experience of fee negotiations with Government, would he care to leave it to me, and he readily agreed. We had a very strong case and I was able to negotiate new fees with the Home Office quickly and satisfactorily. They were index-linked, thereby avoiding future similar problems.

Unfortunately, that was not the end of the matter. The practice was for a Board member to be paid a fee when he dealt with a case, but if he made an interim award, no further payment was made until a final award was made; obviously, this represented a compromise between only one fee being paid no matter how many times interim awards were made, and an award being made each time. Walker interpreted the letter from the Home Office which set out the new fees as meaning that only one award was to be made. This caused a terrible row, which Walker could easily have averted by asking the Home Office. However, he was a very stubborn man and the row intensified, culminating in Sir Ronald Morrison, QC, who was the Deputy Chairman, demanding to see the correspondence with the Home Office. This caused Walker to resign in a huff, saying that, obviously, he had lost the confidence of Board members. He had being doing this unpaid job for eleven years and I suspect that he was glad to have found a reason to stop.

This had come to a head in August, while I was on holiday in Malta. At that time telephone contact from Malta was almost impossible and, seven years after applying for a telephone, we were still without one. When we got back to England, I telephoned Walker and attempted to get him to change his mind but, not to my surprise, he stubbornly refused to do so, adding that I and two others were the only Board members that he was prepared to speak to again. Plainly, that was the end of it. 'If you won't change your mind, do one last thing for us,' I said. 'Get a decent chap to take over.' 'The Home Office wanted you,' he said, 'but I told them that you were much too busy.' I was so amazed that I was not even angry that he had not asked me first. Suffice it to say that he agreed to speak to the Home Office again and I duly got the job, but paid, of course.

Obviously, the Department's dealings with me about fees played a part in its decision, in that I was someone with whom they had spoken, and they must have decided, after consulting the Lord Chancellor's Department, that I was someone who would be satisfactory. Sometimes, thereafter, I wondered whether they repented of their choice. Of course, the first thing that I did, even before I was appointed, was to ask whether they had intended to alter the pay arrangements about interim awards; unsurprisingly, they replied that they had not.

The fees that I negotiated proved very satisfactory. When the Board was founded, the daily fees for sitting to hear appeals were those for Assistant Recorders, which was rather insulting considering that we were all senior silks or senior solicitors. However, fees paid to members who made the initial decision were so much per file. Doubtless, this was based upon an estimate of how long it would take for a civil servant to deal with it. QCs work much faster than civil servants. Most of the cases were simple and we were able to deal with the thirty cases a week sent to us without it interfering with our practices. I asked each Board member to sit on appeals for forty-three days a year, it being easy to do at least twenty of them during vacations. As a result, anyone doing this part-time job was able to earn the equivalent of a circuit judge's salary. Of course, in addition to these fees, I was paid for being chairman. Since it was assumed, correctly, that I had a large say in who was appointed, I was never so popular.

In the ordinary way, barristers do not run anything. If one is Head of Chambers, one is in one sense in charge of chambers, but one has very limited authority; anything of any importance is a matter for all members of chambers and is decided at a chambers meeting. Consequently, to find myself in charge of a Government department, albeit a very small one, was very exhilarating. I think that, when I left the job, there were about three hundred Civil Servants and about thirty Board members. All the

Board members were either silks or former Presidents of the Law Society. The reason why the solicitor members were former Presidents was because, in those days, the job carried an automatic knighthood. It was very important to keep down the percentage of appeals and it seemed to me, I think correctly, that a decision by 'Sir X' or 'Mr Y, QC' was more likely to be accepted by an unrepresented claimant than one by 'Mr Z', who might be thought to be a civil servant.

Theoretically, if I wanted another Board member, I would ask the Home Office, which would consult the Lord Chancellor's Department, which would produce a name, and the Home Office would ask me whether that person was acceptable to me. This seemed to me to be highly unsatisfactory in that, competence apart, I might not consider the person to be someone with whom I would like to spend a week away from home. I agreed with the relevant person in the LCD, who was a very nice, able person, a list of names from which he would pick one when consulted by the Home Office, which then asked me if I was happy to have appointed someone, whose name I had already agreed with the LCD. This worked very satisfactorily and resulted in a 'happy ship', which was sometimes far from being the case with judges on circuit.

Scotland was different. Appointments were by the Lord Advocate, with whom I had to negotiate each time, having consulted the Scots members. Usually, the person whom I suggested was acceptable. However, if there was a change of Government, the equivalent of Treasury Counsel were all replaced by the new Government (incredible!) but the senior one, the Home Depute, would be appointed to the Board. On one occasion, the existing Scots members were aghast, telling me that he was virtually a Marxist. When I went into the room to meet him, all I could see was a pair of legs, the face being concealed by the *Financial Times*, above which could be seen a pall of cigar smoke. Immediately, I concluded that what I had been told was almost certainly wrong. This view proved to be correct. He was a very pleasant, competent man with no hint of being an extreme leftist. Later, he was made a Labour peer but, unhappily, died shortly after.

I got the impression that Walker Carter had let the civil servants run the Board, simply deciding things when asked to do so. I was very much a 'hands-on' chairman. As was the case when asked to negotiate the Bar's fees with Government, having been put in charge of the Board, I proceeded to run it. The way in which civil servants work could not be more different from the way in which barristers work. We are used to making instant decisions when standing on our feet in court, knowing very well that asking the wrong question, or the right question in the wrong way, can have dire effects and may even lose the case. Civil servants tend to write long memoranda and, if the point is of consequence, will tend to get approval from as many others as possible, so that no blame can be attached if things go wrong. The way in which I functioned was very different. On a fine day, it was a pleasant half-hour's walk to the Board's offices in Russell Square. I would look in about once a week and ask the Board's secretary what was happening. He would tell me the nature of a problem and, usually, I would say, 'How about doing X?' 'No, because of such and such.' 'Well, how about X+Y?' 'Yes, but…' 'Well, what about X+Y+Z?' And thus we reached a decision.

Of course, some decisions require much more thought, but, in my experience, they are very much in the minority, and even in such cases one's instant reaction usually proves to be the right answer. This was very much so in my practice. A mechanic who listens to a car engine which is misbehaving may say, 'I think it's the something-or-other.' If cross-examined he might well not be able to produce a satisfactory explanation, but he is usually right. Sometimes, I would get a feeling that a case which looked sound was not. I never disregarded such feelings. Once, Hans Beer said to me in his heavy, guttural, Viennese accent, 'Michael, do you tell me that as a matter of law, or because you feel it in your bones?' 'Hans, I feel it in my bones.' 'Ach so; I trust your bones.'

Once the civil servants realised that they were protected if I made a decision, that I could not be promoted and few decisions were such as could lead to my dismissal, even if wrong, they were very happy with this strange way of running things. On my part, I seldom wrote communications for circulation within the Board, save for memoranda to the Board members. Again, so far as they were concerned, I simply made decisions and seldom asked them first. Board meetings were invariably over before lunch.

One of my principal difficulties was that I could never argue my case for further resources directly with the Treasury, but had to do it through the Home Office, which had many other competing interests. This was particularly important because our workload was constantly increasing, and with an inadequate number of staff our backlog mounted.

The Board was not fettered by any procedural rules and I could experiment. It functioned as civil courts then did. There was an opening speech by the applicant's advocate, if he had one, followed by the applicant giving evidence about what he said had happened. This seemed to me to be a waste of time and I stopped it. Instead, the advocate would be asked whether there was any thing of importance not contained in the applicant's statement in his application, or any error; if not, cross-examination by the Board's advocate took place. This saved a great deal of time and is now the practice in the Commercial Court.

However, another experiment was a disaster. In those days, people paralysed from the waist down had a short life expectancy. Consequently, an award was likely to be too high or too low. I decided that, in one case, I would make an award each year until he died. Each year the case came back to me and I made an award. But he lived for years and the administrative costs were out of all proportion. I did not do it again.

About this time, I prosecuted in a murder at Maidstone. The defendant had strangled his lover and pleaded guilty to manslaughter on the basis that he had acted only after provocation in a moment of fury. The prosecution's pathologist said that the woman had been throttled for three minutes; the defendant's said one minute. When I cross-examined I said to the defendant, 'When a pathologist speaks of a minute he is not using that word loosely; he means sixty seconds; let's see how long that is.' I asked the judge to order that no one in court should move or anyone be allowed in while we did the experiment. He agreed and I took out my pocket watch, which, in those days, we all wore at the end of a watch-chain across our waistcoats. I said 'Now!' and watched my watch until I said 'Now!' at the end of a minute. It was a very large court and the burden of silence was immense. 'It's a very long time, isn't it?' I said to the defendant; 'Yes,' he replied in a depressed voice. I am confident that this made certain the Guilty verdict, which was swiftly returned. The circumstances of the offence were such that I doubt whether he served more than about ten years.

As Chairman of the CICB I was interviewed a great deal by the media. I had certain rules; for example, I refused to be interviewed on any radio or TV station which was not a national one because I would have spent my entire time doing so. As it was, I was interviewed far more than I would have wished, particularly at the time of the annual report. However, on other occasions, if something of an interesting nature from a media point of view blew up, I could expect the hyenas to pounce upon me. Happily, I very soon learnt how to deal with them. It was necessary to be utterly firm at the outset about the content of the interview, and I always made it plain that I would refuse to answer any question which went outside that ambit and terminate the interview immediately.

There was one splendid occasion when the BBC did something dreadful, the nature of which I cannot now recollect, which caused me to write a letter to the Director General. I said that in view of its latest act of misbehaviour, I would refuse to be interviewed by the BBC unless it was live or, if recorded, on terms that either the whole of the interview was to be broadcast or none of it, or any cuts to be made were agreed with me. I received a letter from the Director General saying that he could not agree to that. I then wrote a further letter saying that I feared that he had not understood correctly what I had said in my first letter. 'What,' I said, 'I tried to say was that I would not give an interview unless those terms were accepted and if those terms were not accepted there would be no interview.'

Obviously, this was not something to which the BBC was accustomed. All Members of Parliament are prepared to be interviewed at any time, and any member of the public who is caught up in some event doubtless feels flattered to be asked to be interviewed. Of course, that was not my position. They did not appear to appreciate that there were some people who did not care tuppence whether they appeared on television or the radio or not.

In any event, my second letter resulted in the most gratifying climbdown by the Director General in which he said that he perfectly understood what I had said and was very sorry for any misunderstanding, and furthermore he hoped that the incident would not impair the excellent relations which we had enjoyed over the years. Of course, the last observation was a joke so far as I was concerned but I let the matter rest.

Thereafter, of course, I adhered to what I had said in my first letter and the BBC, and indeed ITV, had to accept my terms or no interview took place. Invariably, my terms were accepted.

The job brought one jolly perk. The Board belonged to the International Crime Victims Compensation Boards. This resulted in an annual trip to a meeting in the USA or Canada, which was not very useful but I regarded it as my holiday, so far as the Board was concerned.

11

HONG KONG

In 1976 I did my first big case in Hong Kong. It should never have happened. Paul Lee was the Managing Director of a company, of which Gordon Wu and his partner Henry Lee were non-executive directors. I appeared for Henry Lee. Paul Lee was dishonest. Either the accounts or a prospectus was dishonest. All the non-executive directors were prosecuted on the ground that they must have realised that the document was dishonest. It was ridiculous. The inspector in charge of the case had recommended that only Paul Lee should be prosecuted. However, the case was sent to a lawyer in the Government Legal Department, who took the contrary view. One of the other defendants was Donald Cheung, a solicitor, who became a friend and was responsible for me being instructed in the largest and most remunerative case in my career.

Two other London QCs were instructed. This being so, the prosecuting lawyer, an Australian, was asked if he would like to be led by a London silk but he declined, saying that he would 'see off those Pommy bastards'; a comment which reached our ears. It was his second mistake.

Judges in Hong Kong were mostly of fairly low calibre. However, fortunately, our judge was a man of considerable ability. The case was a very high-profile one and was usually on the front page of all the Hong Kong papers. The principal witness was Paul Lee, who had already pleaded guilty. Of course, his cross-examination lasted for a very long time. Clearly, he was lying and the longer he was cross-examined by us all, the more obvious this became. Our only problem was one of the co-defending counsel. Theoretically, he was being led by an English silk who lived and practised company law in Hong Kong, but the cross-examination was left to his excitable Chinese junior. The three English silks had the embarrassing task of telling the leader that his junior was doing more harm than good and should be told to sit down and shut up; which he did. Fortunately, the harm which he did was of scant importance but one did not know what might have happened.

Eventually, we reached the happy situation that every submission made by us on a point of law was accepted and every submission by the prosecution was rejected. By the end of the prosecution's case, Paul Lee's credibility had been utterly destroyed and the prosecution's morale had been shattered. A London QC arrived just before the end of the prosecution's evidence, appearing on behalf of a banker in order to make a submission that there was no case to answer. John Willmers was a very competent QC but extremely good at putting people's backs up. He walked straight into court from his aeroplane and did just that within minutes of his arrival. It was ridiculous because he had no idea what had been going on during the weeks before his arrival. Fortunately, he arrived too late to do any harm.

After submissions of no case to answer had been going on for only a few days, devoted at that point mainly to assertions that the indictment was defective in various ways, the prosecution threw in the towel against all the non-executive defendants, the banker and even an in-house accountant against whom I thought they had a strong case. This left one junior employee of the company, who was convicted. Kemy Bokhary, now a judge in Hong Kong's Final Court of Appeal, had been a pupil of Ronnie Arculli, who had been responsible for my being instructed in the case. He is now a judge in the Final Court of Appeal, but at that time was a junior appearing with one of the London silks. A few weeks ago, he told me that I was responsible for the final straw which broke the prosecution. I had forgotten, but he said that I had demanded that the prosecution should list every piece of evidence which they alleged corroborated Paul Lee's evidence, since it was evidence of an alleged accomplice. The prosecution's note-keeping had been so bad – it was before the days of satisfactory transcripts – they found that they were wholly unable to do it.

The inspector in the Independent Commission Against Corruption who had advised that the non-executive directors should not be prosecuted was worried about the effect that the case might have on his career. How it came about that the prosecution had been forced to give us copies of his report I cannot remember. Plainly, it would have been unfair if any blame attached to the inspector. The two other English silks (I did not bother Willmers) agreed that, as the senior silk, I should write on behalf of the three of us to the Commissioner of Police saying that he was in no way at fault, that what had happened would not have happened if his advice had not been disregarded and that he had done a very good job. Shortly thereafter, he wrote to me saying that he had been promoted, which he attributed to my letter, and for some years he sent me Christmas cards.

Henry Lee invited me to lunch with his family in the Jockey Club. He was late and I was sitting with his wife and elder daughter. His wife spoke no English but said something to her daughter, who said to me that they wanted to thank me for saving Henry from prison. I nearly burst into tears.

One of the pleasures of long cases in the Far East was that part of the deal was that Joan could come with me, both of us travelling first-class. Since the children were still at home and some at school, on this occasion she was able to join me for only a limited time. We had a nice flat with an amah, called Ah Won, who, flatteringly, asked if she could come back to England with us! It is the most work-hard, play-hard place I have ever visited. There was a dinner or a party every evening and we very quickly acquired a large number of friends, many of them Chinese. I found them easy to work with and far from inscrutable.

I am not a gambler, but I always enjoyed being invited to races there. I was the guest of a steward, and went to his box, which contained two large round tables seating about fifteen people, and had a splendid lunch. At about the end of lunch, racing would start. If one had not finished, there was closed-circuit television in the box. Otherwise, one walked outside on the balcony to watch. The tote had a window immediately outside the box, where I watched with interest as little old ladies put hundreds of pounds on each race. I put on ten dollars each way (the rate was ten to the pound). This was the minimum stake. If I had put on a hundred pounds, I am sure that people would have said, 'Michael cannot be a very successful silk, if he can only afford a hundred pounds.' As it was, I think that they said, 'Michael is very strange, he does not gamble, he only puts on ten dollars each way to give himself an interest in the race.' The Chinese are addicted to gambling; like the Maltese, many of them tend not to insure their possessions.

That same year, we bought our cottage in Suffolk, which served us well as a second home for twenty-six years. It shows how times have changed that when I telephoned the solicitors to ask if the purchase was completed, they were amazed that I should be doing so from Hong Kong. It is a very nice, thatched, listed building, which consists of three cottages thrown into one. The first was built in the sixteenth century and the other two in the seventeenth. A previous owner had put in good central heating and double glazing. It has four bedrooms, sleeping seven people comfortably, and two bathrooms.

The small village, Dalham, is very pretty and most of the houses in the centre are also listed. There is a small stream through the middle of the village, which is usually dry, but is very necessary after heavy rain. It had been deepened after a very bad flood but, on a later occasion, it again overflowed and water came into the sitting room, but, fortunately, not enough of it to cause serious harm; after that I had a soakaway constructed. After we had bought it, we spent Christmas there, having to eat off some kind of trestle table, because our dining table had not arrived.

It is noteworthy that I had no difficulty running the CICB while being in Hong Kong; the single member cases were sent out in the diplomatic bag, as also happened when on holiday in Malta.

However, a splendid attack upon me was made in the London *Evening News* in a leading article. A police officer had been injured by the IRA bomb explosion outside the Old Bailey. I had nothing to do with his compensation claim made to the Board. Quite correctly, because the scheme obliged us to do it, the Board member deducted from thc award the £2,750 which the officer had received as sickness benefit, and it was this that attracted the splenetic fury of the newspaper. The article contained the following marvellous piece of purple prose:

> The only sanity in doubt is that of the handful of men who decide these sums of compensation – the Criminal Injuries Compensation Board under Sir [premature by thirteen years!] Michael Ogden, a 50-year-old Q.C. In the public eye to-day he stands accused of meanness pushed to the limit of incredulity.

Of course, I complained and an apology was duly published among a page of car adverts in the most inconspicuous position possible.

In 1977, I was made a Bencher of Lincoln's Inn, i.e. a member of its governing body. It is a wonderful kind of club. Apart from being a cheap place to have a good, quick, working lunch, there are a large number of dinners. There is one after the monthly council meeting and others for special events. For as long as I can remember, the other Inns have conceded that our food is the best and our wine infinitely so.

Obviously, I was also very busy at this time conducting cases in England but none that I can remember which were of particular interest. However, when I was in Hong Kong in 1978, having finished my case, I made a courtesy call on the Attorney-General before I left. In the course of conversation, he told me that he did not know how he was going to cope with a forthcoming long prosecution, saying that he could hardly ask a London silk to come out for such a long time, at which I said, 'I will, if you like,' which, I assume, is what he hoped for. Thus, I embarked upon what was known as the 'Mongkok Conspiracy'. It was a prosecution of thirty-five police officers for corruption.

Mongkok is on the Chinese mainland beyond Kowloon, and the corruption seemed to involve many at the police station of the rank of sergeant and above. They accepted bribes from anyone who could be persuaded to offer them, particularly in the red light area. At one establishment there was found a meticulous record of all bribes paid. It looked as if a bribe was paid to any officer who asked for one, including, to my amazement, mounted police.

I was instructed by the Independent Commission Against

Corruption. My junior was a not very good Australian lawyer from the Legal Department, but, fortunately, the ICAC officer in charge, who had been an inspector in Essex, was very good and, after a few days, I made it plain to him that he and I would have to run the case without relying on my junior for much. I was put up in a large Government flat on the Peak, this being the best place to live before air-conditioning. When I arrived in May the Peak was enshrouded in cloud and remained so for several weeks. It was like being in a plane.

Every day, two cars would arrive for me. I travelled in one and the other carried my large metal trunk, which contained all my papers, none of which we could leave in the court building for fear that the police would rifle through them. My car was on the ICAC radio link, which was useful. Joan was able to come out for a few weeks and I could pick up the microphone and say 'Tango Three for Island Control, over.' 'Island Control to Tango Three, over.' 'Tango Three, please telephone my wife and say that we need three bottles of whisky to-night.' 'Island Control, wilco, out.'

The trial had to be in a court large enough for all the defendants, and the one chosen was even further into the New Territories, which meant a three-quarters of an hour journey from the Peak, under the tunnel and out through Kowloon. Since most of the defendants had Cantonese as their first language and three had Shanghaiese, there had to be simultaneous translations at all times into two languages. This was done, without headsets, simply by two interpreters shouting loudly. The noise was frightful. Of course, there were no good restaurants in the area, but they found a nice little duck restaurant opposite the San Miguel brewery. The walls were entirely covered with white lavatory-type tiles, so the noise was indescribable, but the food was very good and they kept a table each day for our team, which usually numbered about five. What Bill Silke, who tried the case, did for lunch I do not know.

I had not been asked to advise on the prospects of success. Unfortunately, all our principal witnesses were corrupt policemen who had been granted immunity on agreeing to give evidence for the prosecution. All of them went back on their evidence, which was no great surprise to me, and it was almost by chance that I secured two convictions. I persuaded the Governor that they should attempt to prosecute one of them on the basis that he had committed perjury either when he signed his sworn statement or when he gave evidence. They secured a conviction which was upheld in the Court of Appeal, but it was overturned by some idiots in the Privy Council who decided that the precise occasion had to be specified – half-witted!

Subsequently, when I was sitting as a judge at the Old Bailey, there was a good example of the injustice caused by this foolish decision. The defendant was accused of attempting to obtain money by deception. He had claimed a reward from a bank for notifying the police of an impending bank robbery; the prosecution asserted that it was a fraudulent claim. The defence was that it was a genuine claim and that the defendant was one of the conspirators but that the raid had been called off after he had contacted the police. The jury acquitted. Prosecuting counsel then told me, correctly, that the defendant could not be prosecuted for conspiracy because the prosecution did not believe that this is what had happened and there was no evidence to support it, other than what the defendant had said during the trial. Not surprisingly, the jurors looked stunned. Of course, because of the Privy Council decision, had he been prosecuted for conspiracy and given evidence contrary to that given in the trial before me, he could not have been prosecuted for perjury.

However, before the Mongkok trial, I was instructed to support convictions against another five police officers, including an English superintendent, on other corruption charges. The ICAC officers had misbehaved by showing witness photographs of the defendants before they went to identity parades. I persuaded the Court of Appeal that in four cases it did not matter because the witnesses already knew the officers, and I suggested that they should allow the appeal in one case, a Chinese sergeant, which they did. The ICAC was very pleased about this result.

During the course of the Mongkok trial, the Legal Department sent me some papers so that I could advise on a proposed prosecution. I was able to work on them during a typhoon. Since I was staying at the top of the Peak; our building took the full brunt of the storm, causing me to work in the passage with all the doors closed in order to avoid the risk of broken glass. The proposed defendant had moved money from country A to B to C to D and back to A all on the same day, for no apparent reason.

Plainly, no one does that for an honest reason and, when looking at some of the other circumstances, it was clearly fraudulent. The Legal Department was troubled because they could not point to a motive but I advised them to proceed on the basis that one would appear in due course, as it did.

I was told that the man was in Malaysia but likely to leave it in the near future, and therefore to draft an indictment ignoring the relevant extradition treaty. He duly vanished and I thought no more of the matter.

Some time later, while eating breakfast in Glasgow, where I was sitting on the Criminal Injuries Board, I read in the paper that the man was being questioned by police in California. I wrote a short letter to Hong Kong, saying that it ought to be possible to extradite him from there. Some considerable time later I was told that he had been brought back to Hong Kong, where he produced an out-of-date passport to the immigration officer, who promptly said that he must go back to America! The police protested in vain and the senior immigration officer confirmed the decision, which was only overruled by the chief immigration officer, who had to be dragged out of a dinner party.

I was unable to do the case as I was committed to something else, which was just as well because it turned out to be a horror, involving assertions by the defendant that it was a conspiracy by a foreign bank; he was convicted.

About two years later, when I was in Hong Kong, the Attorney-General came to see me in my hotel, looking very worried. It had been discovered that one of the two counts in the indictment was not covered by the extradition treaty with America. 'If you look at my instructions, you will see that I was specifically instructed to pay no regard to any questions of extradition,' I said. 'They have been lost,' he replied. Fortunately, the sentences on the two counts were concurrent so that the Attorney-General was able to admit that he was wrongly convicted on that count, but that he still had to serve the full sentence.

The case was conducted by two very senior London criminal silks, but neither they, nor the lawyers who conducted the extradition proceedings in America had noticed that one of the offences was not extraditable!

* * *

I especially remember two lawyers from my Hong Kong days. Charles Ching was a splendid chap who ended up as a judge in the Final Court of Appeal. My abiding recollection of him is when we were drinking Beaujolais in his room in his Hong Kong chambers, doubtless after we had just finished a case, and there was wine dribbling down from the corner of his mouth because he was quaffing it in large quantities. I knew him from about 1974 onwards and met him on very many occasions.

The incident which sticks in my mind particularly was when he was Chairman of the Bar. At that time the Hong Kong Bar was dissatisfied with the large number of London QCs who were being allowed into Hong Kong to conduct cases. I got the impression that this is because we charged lesser fees than they did. In any event, when Charles Ching, who was then one of the leading QCs in Hong Kong, was Chairman of the Bar, he was, of course, responsible for advocating this policy. However, when I was out there doing a case, I met him on some social occasion and he said to me, 'Michael, this case you're on will finish this week, won't it?' 'Yes.' 'Well, do you think you might stay on and lead me in the case which I am doing next week?' Of course, this was very comic coming from the mouth of the person who was meant to be at the forefront of the fight to limit the number of London QCs coming to Hong Kong.

The next day his solicitors telephoned me and asked how much I would want to be paid for leading Charles. I said, 'I don't mind what you pay me, I really don't mind at all as long as you pay me more than Mr Ching, I will be happy.' I am glad to say that my confidence was not misplaced and I received a more than adequate fee for leading him.

The other lawyer is Kemy Bokhary. He is my grand-pupil, being a pupil of Ronnie Arculli's. On one occasion I was leading him in a case which involved development of a site; the nature of the litigation I cannot recollect, but it necessitated us going to the site in question and looking at it. It was on an incline, and as I was walking down the path in the centre of it, followed by Kemy, I suddenly noticed a flicker of movement behind me on my left side. I did not pay much attention to this until Kemy shouted, 'Michael, run! There's a cobra behind you.' Of course, I did. Fortunately, the cobra was as worried about me as I was worried about it and made off at an angle, and that was the end of the incident.

However, for some reason the case reached the Privy Council and Kemy has reminded me that when I was addressing the court and we were looking at the plan of the site, I mentioned in a conversational way, 'Oh yes, that is the point at which I was chased by a cobra.' I thought nothing of it and went on but Kemy told me that the members of the Privy Council were transfixed by this piece of information and obviously would have loved to have heard more about it. However, I had not noticed their interest and merely went on to deal with what I was meant to be doing, leaving them, I fear, somewhat unsatisfied.

By 1979, I had given up all criminal work except for the occasional murder. Michael Havers was Attorney-General. He told me that he was not satisfied that all Treasury Counsel were doing complex fraud cases competently, and asked me to go down to the Old Bailey and lead them in one or two cases, so that they would learn how to do them. This was a great compliment.

He was quite right: in the first of these cases, I deleted more than half of the indictment on the basis that if one could not get a conviction on one of four or five counts, it was unlikely that one would get one if one had twelve, and to have so many counts might well confuse the jury and result in an acquittal.

The next thing that I did was to summon Treasury Counsel and the representative of the Director to a conference. I said, 'Let us first consider the position D5 and D6, the wives of D3 and D4. Does anyone think that, if convicted, the judge will do any more then wag his finger and tell them not to do it again?' No one spoke. 'I assume then that we will discontinue against them and suggest that they give evidence for the prosecution.' No one spoke. 'Let us now consider their husbands. They are fringe men; tell them that I expect them to plead guilty but would they like to give evidence for the prosecution.'

Of course, all four leapt at the chance; it would make all the difference between going to prison or not because they were able to say that they were repentant and were helping the prosecution. This caused the principal baddie, a solicitor, to plead guilty. This left one defendant, an estate agent – this was one of the earliest mortgage frauds – who was found guilty after a trial lasting a few days. Had I not done what I did, the case might well have lasted several months with seven teams of lawyers, all of which would have cost a great deal of money.

I did about three such cases. However, after the last, I wrote to the Deputy Director of Public Prosecutions thanking him for his letter telling me that I would have my daily fees increased to the largest ever paid to prosecuting counsel at the Old Bailey, but adding that, unfortunately, they were smaller than my clerk would ever agree to in a privately paid case, and I did no more of them. Nor did most people who had a reasonable civil practice.

One fine summer's day at the week-end we all went out to Kensington Gardens. The au pair foolishly left the window open in her bedroom, which was on the first floor. As a result, a thief climbed up a drainpipe, got in and stole Joan's best jewellery. In itself this caused no problems, save that Joan would have wished to have had what was taken rather than what was bought in its place.

Some time later, when we were having work done to the house, we went out to some formal occasion and when we came back it was necessary to put away the jewellery. My study where the safe was kept was full of furniture, which meant it was almost impossible to reach the safe. I had gone to bed first and therefore Joan decided to put the jewellery in a 'safe place'. Unfortunately, in the morning she could not remember which was the safe place. The house was searched from top to bottom but the jewellery was not discovered. Of course, I had to report the incident to my insurance brokers, while telling them that I was utterly confident that it had not been stolen and would turn up in due course. After a while, I was told by the brokers that the insurers could not let the matter drag on and they wanted a formal claim made. Consequently, I did this. We were duly paid out and more jewellery was bought. Some months later, when the contents of the display cabinet were being cleaned, a clinking noise was heard in one of the silver jugs which was in the cabinet. Of course, this was the safe place. In one sense, this was very fortunate for Joan because I had not got the heart to say that one lot should be sold, and therefore she doubled the amount of her best jewellery. Had I been a mean-minded soul, I might have thought that she had done it on purpose! Anyway, it could be regarded as proper compensation for the heroic achievements in bringing up the children with little help from me. If not working abroad, I usually came home and collapsed in a chair in a comatose condition until revived by whisky. Of course, I had to repay the insurers what they had paid me.

Apart from incidents like this, the reader will have noticed that I have not said much about my family life. However, I feel there is one thing I should mention. Celia was coming up to her 'O' levels. I discovered that the good nuns at Woldingham had allowed her to abandon most subjects of any value, so I did what I regard as one of my finest feats of advocacy. I said to her, 'Ask any of your friends who have elder brothers or sisters. They will confirm that if you can get into Oxbridge, it is three years of parties. Of course, you have to do a certain amount of work, but nothing very strenuous.' Obviously, she made enquiries which confirmed what I had said, because she set to in order to acquire the five 'O' levels necessary for matriculation. An elderly lady was dragged out of retirement in order to teach her Latin. Because she had been taught French rather badly, she decided to take up Italian. She duly passed.

When she went up for her interviews at Oxford, she first went to the college of her first choice, which was Lady Margaret Hall. There she had what she subsequently described as three Celia Ogden Fan Club interviews. She then went on to Somerville, which was the college of her second choice. It had been a long hot summer's day. Having been kept waiting for a very long time, as she described it, she went in and saw a large woman dressed in tweeds, who was seated behind a large desk. 'Hear you're a mediaeval historian,' said the large lady. 'Jolly hockey sticks, bully for you,' said my dear daughter. The rest of the interview went along similar lines. Needless to say, she was not accepted by Lady Margaret Hall but was accepted by Somerville. I suspect that the battleaxe at Somerville had also had a long hard day and was fed up with good little, young girls who made remarks such as 'I am very interested in mediaeval monasticism, miss', and that it was a great relief to have someone with a bit of red blood coursing through their veins.

Subsequently, Celia rather thought that she might have regretted it. She came down after three years and said, 'Daddy, I got a solid third, but I never missed a party.' When it came to Lucy going up to Oxford, Celia suggested that they might remember her too well at Somerville and so she went to Balliol.

Another family reminiscence: Joan and I had a most interesting trip to Persia, before the revolution, when (as mentioned earlier) the Council of the UIA met in Tehran. There were probably no more than twenty of us, and we were received by the Prime Minister in his own room. I thought it a poor omen for the future that immediately outside the French windows, there was stationed a soldier in full battle kit including a sub machine-gun.

On our first night, we stayed in a hotel in the centre of the city. On turning on the wash-basin tap, our suitcase in the opposite corner quietly filled up with water. Thereafter, we stayed in a good hotel on the very outskirts of the city. By this I mean it was literally at the edge of the desert; the grass of the hotel garden stopped abruptly at the point which the fully extended garden hose could reach.

We were taken to see the jewels which represented the backing for the currency, including the Peacock Throne, which they had looted from India. However, when we arrived we had to go away again because our hosts had through incompetence failed to realise that it was not due to open for an hour. Consequently, they took us to a club, which was far more English than any club in England. In particular I noticed that all walls appeared to be painted in brown Windsor soup. Most of the group dutifully went upstairs to a room opened for them but a German, a Yugoslav and I noticed a bar and promptly went into it. Chairs lined the wall, occupied by disconsolate-looking British males. We went up to the bar and the German said to the Yugoslav, 'Well, you bloody partisan, what are you going to have to drink?' Needless to say, the looks on the faces of the people in the chairs were interesting.

Unfortunately, Joan was attacked by mosquitoes when we were eating blinis; at that time, she did not know that she was susceptible to them. Consequently, she had to stay in the hotel while I went down to Isfahan to see the marvellous temples and on further south to see Persepolis, which, in my view, is one of the finest of ancient sites, matched only by Palmeira.

The governor of the province gave a reception for us, at the end of which he told us that he had arranged for us to go to a nightclub. Of course, we had high expectations; the reality was very odd. In a garden, there were several tables covered with damask table cloths and bottles of whisky, brandy, wine and other beverages. A band was playing 1920s dance band music. When I was introduced to the governor at his reception, he said, 'I have two daughters at Roedean.' It was interesting that, although the Persians, being Muslims, were teetotal, they poured out enormous glasses of alcohol because they had no idea of the proportions necessary for, say, whisky and water. It was a fascinating trip.

Every year we invited representatives of foreign legal professions to the opening of the Legal Year. As a member of the Overseas Relations Committee I was expected to ask some to dinner, which was usually pleasant, although tiring. The following evening there would be a dinner in one of the Inns or the Law Society. In those days, the Law Society dinners were not very good and the aged waitresses were worse. On one occasion, one of them was serving mashed potato. Two guests had their heads close together and, in order to serve between them, she lightly tapped one on his bald head with the spoon which she was using to serve the mashed potato. He reacted with stoical calm but I have no doubt that he recounted what he probably thought was typical British behaviour to his colleagues in his own country.

I was continuing to go to Hong Kong quite frequently. A year might go by and I would not go at all but the following year I might go five times. Two occasions stick out in my mind. Once I was on holiday in Madeira when I was urgently summoned and had to fly back to London immediately, then on to Hong Kong the following day. On another occasion we were on holiday in Malta and I had to fly to Rome and then on to Hong Kong, arriving with little more than my holiday clothes, and I had to borrow someone else's wig, gown and court coat.

However, there was one even worse occasion. Again, we were on holiday in Malta and intended to travel from there to Vienna for an IBA conference, go to Budapest on an IBA trip and on to the Court of Appeal in Hong Kong. Since the Austrians always insist on a white tie ball in addition to black tie affairs, I was travelling with all of this kit, clothes for court as well as holiday stuff. All went well until we reached Budapest. It was before the fall of communism and, while there had been no signs of it during our pleasant stay, there was a major problem when we came to leave. We had all arrived in Budapest on coaches but I intended to fly from Budapest to Hong Kong. As we were packing, the telephone rang and a voice said, 'It has been decided at the highest level that everyone who came on the coach must go back to Vienna on a coach.' Had I agreed to this, I would have lost a day and arrived a day late in Hong Kong. I went down to the hall, stood several yards from the duty manager and shouted loudly at him. This I continued to do for some time. Had I not have been with an International legal association, I would probably have been arrested. As it was, it was the concierge, interestingly enough, who picked up the telephone and spoke, and then told me that I could go to the airport. Obviously, he was the senior secret service man in the hotel. When I got to the airport there were no problems and I arrived in Hong Kong via Frankfurt on time. It was an interesting experience.

I think that it was on this occasion that a very nice judge, called Pickering, said, when granting my application for admission to the Bar to do the case in question. 'It only remains to wish Mr Ogden, one of the most faithful members of the Far Eastern Circuit, a happy visit.'

Unlike Pickering, the Right Honourable Sir Dingle Foot, QC, MP, a member of the distinguished Foot family, was a rather unpleasant man – possibly because he always gave the appearance of suffering from a hangover, which was probably true. How he came to be appointed Solicitor-General I do not know; certainly, he was no good in the job. Since I was on the Bar Council, I came across him from time to time, but never with much pleasure. It appeared to me that, after he ceased to hold that appointment, his practice seemed to consist largely of cases in black Africa, the West Indies and on behalf of their inhabitants in this country. I prosecuted him in a murder in the Court of Appeal in which he attempted to run the defence of duress, at a time when it was uncertain whether such a defence was available in murder. When I received his list of cases which he intended to put before the court, I noticed that he had omitted the only one which might possibly give him any assistance. I drew his attention to the case but he did not mention it to the court and immediately he had finished, Geoffrey Lane, the Chief Justice, gestured to the other two judges to join him. This was a clear indication that he intended to suggest that the appeal be dismissed at once without the need for retiring to consider it or to call on me to reply. I stood up at once and said that I should draw the case to their attention, which I then did. When I had finished, Geoffrey thanked me for having done so, saying that I was quite right to have done it, but nevertheless went on to dismiss the appeal. Dingle's conduct in failing to draw the court's attention to the case was quite extraordinary.

Even more extraordinary were the circumstances of my involvement in his death. I was working in Hong Kong when Dingle arrived in order to conduct an appeal in the case, which had suddenly come to life after many years. Had it been otherwise, I doubt whether he would have been instructed. He was very drunk when he arrived off the plane, and went to the Mandarin Hotel, where he ordered a sandwich and promptly choked to death on it. A memorial service took place in the Methodist chapel, Methodism being the nearest to his religious faith. At the front on one side of the aisle were the members of the Court of Appeal before whom he was due to appear, consisting of a Catholic, a High Church Anglican and an agnostic. On the other side of the aisle were me, Peter Rawlinson, who was also a Catholic, and someone whose faith was wholly uncertain. Because the widow was not present, the entire event was televised, so that one had to keep a suitably reverential face throughout, which is not an easy thing to do during a long service.

The first thing that happened when I got back to London was that I received a set of papers asking me to advise his life insurers whether they could repudiate liability under the policy because of misdisclosure of his drinking habits. I had before me his family doctor's notes, from which it was quite obvious that they could. The estate was virtually insolvent. The insurers were decent people and offered to pay a small sum which made it just solvent. I sent for my opponent and showed him the doctor's notes; without any hesitation, he accepted the offer. I assume that the unfortunate widow had to exist on an MP's widow's pension, which cannot have been very much. Doubtless, Dingle had drunk what money there was. It was a very sad tale.

Still on the subject of overseas visits, on two occasions, I had to represent the bar at the Rentrée, the opening of the French Legal Year. The ceremony itself was extremely boring. It consisted of sitting in a large hall while the two top students read out their papers. Once, a member of the Paris Bar said to me, 'Could you understand a single word that the second student said?' Since I knew very little French, I was able to say with truth that I had not. 'No,' she said, 'he comes from Provence.'

We had to be dressed in our full court kit and, of course, with our full-bottomed wigs, knee breeches, jabot and buckled shoes, we acted everyone else off the stage. On one occasion, when I came down in the hotel lift, the doors opened and I was revealed to a group of Americans. It was the only time in my life when the phrase 'he fell back in amazement' came true. I must have appeared to them as a ghost of a member of the *ancien régime* on his way to the tumbril. The corridor which led to the hall was lined by the Republican Guard. As I approached, the commander of the guard called them to attention and saluted, which he had not done for any of the people in front of me. I said to the member of the Law Society who was with me, 'Is there anyone of importance behind me?' 'No, it's for you.' So I passed along, graciously indicating my acknowledgement by giving a small wave with my gloves.

However, in the evening, there was a splendid party in the crypt under the palace, the place where Marie Antoinette had been imprisoned before execution. It was very comic but enjoyable; a combination of an enormous drinks party with a buffet.

At about this time, as I have said, I stopped doing ordinary criminal cases and only did an occasional fraud case. Partly, this was because crime did not pay nearly as well as civil but also because ordinary crime is rather boring. As the Count said in *Fledermaus*, 'Seen one, seen them all.' There are a very limited number of ways in which one can murder someone.

The last of these cases which I agreed to do was a murder

which I found rather interesting. The unfortunate murdered man was paralysed from the neck down. He wanted to commit suicide but, because of his condition, was unable to do so. His parents eventually agreed to do it for him by putting a polythene bag over his head. They pleaded Not Guilty of murder, but Guilty of manslaughter by reason of diminished responsibility. When I read the medical reports provided by the defendants' doctor, they were total rubbish. The instructions from the Director of Public Prosecutions said that I could accept any plea that I considered proper. This was an obvious invitation to accept the manslaughter plea. I did not feel able to do so. I spoke to the Deputy Director and said that on the basis of the available evidence, it was plainly a case of murder; if the jury wanted to bring in a merciful verdict, they were entitled to do so but it was not for the prosecution to do so. I added that I had no doubt that the jury would do so, but this was an immaterial consideration. He was reluctant to agree, so I said that I was very happy to go with him to meet the Attorney-General and if the latter agreed with him, I would readily change my mind. A little later, he phoned back and agreed to what I said.

When the trial took place, it was not very difficult to discredit the defendants' doctor. In spite of the fact that this was a heart-breaking case, the jury was out for seven hours before returning a manslaughter verdict, which I considered vindicated my view. Although I considered that the verdict was a just and proper decision, a better doctor engaged by the defence would doubtless have written reports which would have enabled me to accept the plea of manslaughter in the first place. It was further vindicated when the defendants gave a television interview on the steps of the law court saying that there was nothing wrong with them mentally at all. Had I accepted the pleas tendered, there would have been a real risk of severe criticism in the media.

A major obstacle in many cases is the mandatory life sentence required in the case of someone convicted of murder. As in all other cases, the trial judge should be able to determine the sentence.

One of the most interesting cases with which I had to deal with in my capacity as the Assessor of Compensation in miscarriage of justice cases was the well-known Confait case in 1981. In my assessment I said, 'It is an appalling and extraordinary story', and so it was. The three claimants had been prosecuted for murdering Confait and of arson of his flat. Three of them were convicted of murder and two of them of arson. There was an unsuccessful appeal but about three years later the convictions were quashed. The Home Secretary agreed that the claimants should be paid compensation. However, before this was done, a retired High Court judge was appointed to conduct an inquiry. He concluded that one of the claimants who had been found guilty of murder was in fact guilty of murder, as was the one who had not, and that all three were guilty of arson. Of course, this was a highly embarrassing result. Nevertheless, Sir Walker Carter proceeded to make assessments, doubtless with the consent of the Home Secretary. In each case he awarded £1,000, stating that he did so disregarding the inquiry findings.

About five years later, rumours from prisons reached the Home Office, as a result of which the case was reopened. The result made the case even more embarrassing. The Home Office pathologist who had conducted the post mortem had wrongly identified the murder weapon. Confait had been strangled but the ligature found round the neck had been changed, doubtless because the original could have been connected with the murderer. Worse, the pathologist had got the wrong date of death. Of course, this meant that, because all three claimants had valid alibis for the correct date, the signed confessions made by all three claimants were of no value. Consequently, the Home Office accepted that none of the claimants was guilty of any offence and the case was remitted to me for reassessment

My difficulty was writing an assessment in terms which were not denigratory of what had gone on in the past; it was not easy. How the retired High Court judge reached the conclusions which he did, I do not know. In addition, Walker Carter's assessments were ludicrously low, given the fact that he was ignoring the decision of the retired High Court judge. The pathologist came out of it badly as, of course, did the police, since they had obtained signatures to false confessions. I awarded each claimant £15,000, together with other sums for loss of earnings and other claims. The present value of those awards would be very much greater.

By the time that I made my award, the identity of both of the men present, one of whom must have been the true murderer, was known, but there was insufficient evidence for a prosecution, since each blamed the other.

Of course, I had by now quite a large number of Chinese friends. However, if ever I was arrogant enough to think that I was beginning to understand the Chinese, something happened to show me that I had not begun to do more than scratch at the outside of the egg. For example, I learnt that they had the curious tradition of visiting the family grave on a particular date each year. Everyone sat round or on the grave and had a picnic and the ancestors were told what had been happening to the family during the past year. Another interesting custom was how to behave when invited to a banquet. My recollection is that it is after the first course that the guests raise their glasses and toast the host. It is very impolite to eat much rice, which arrives towards the end of the meal, because this might indicate that one had not been given enough to eat. At the end of the meal, no one thanks the host but simply gets up and leaves.

Throughout the world there are similar customs which are a trap for the unwary foreigner. For example, it is considered rude in Germany or Austria to cut a potato with a knife. For this reason, potatoes are usually served in small cubes, which have been fried. In Arab countries, one can get into terrible trouble if one uses the wrong hand to eat, and in the Far East generally, it is essential to remember to take off one's shoes before going into a temple and one must remember never to sit with one's feet pointing towards the Buddha. However, it appears to be perfectly acceptable to play football inside a temple courtyard or to urinate. In Austria and Germany, if one is offered more food or drink and wants to receive it, it is very important to remember to say 'please' rather than 'thank you'. In the United States, one should never ask for whisky if one wants Scotch because it will invariably result in one been given rye or bourbon, both of which I consider disgusting.

I had an insight into Japanese customs when the Bar Council asked me to receive a delegation of Japanese employed by a Government organisation who were interested in something or other, the nature of which I cannot now recollect. They duly came to chambers and we had a conversation, during which they presented me with an embroidered fan and that, I thought, was that. However, a year or two later I found myself in Tokyo en route between Hong Kong and San Francisco. I was there for only twenty-four hours and knew only one person in Tokyo, who kindly gave me lunch. I remembered this organisation and asked if I could call upon them, which I did. It was an interesting experience.

I was led into a room and given a cup of tea and various people came and bowed at me and then went out. I was then taken into a second room, where I was given another cup of tea. As on the first occasion, I took only one sip, and a smaller number of people were brought in and bowed at me. I then went into the main office which was about a hundred yards long and fifty yards wide being on the open plan basis with no partitions, and in one corner on a small dais was the Managing Director's desk. We went in there and I sat down at his desk, where of course I was given another cup of tea and two more people were brought in to bow at me. I assume that I had gradually been introduced from people of lower rank to people of higher rank. After I had discussed with them whatever the topic was which had brought them to London in the first place, I was asked if I would like to go out to dinner with them. It was then 5 p.m., which is a rather strange hour for me to have dinner. Nevertheless, I agreed unhesitatingly and we went off to a little restaurant close to their office, where of course I had to sit virtually on the floor at one of those little tables which are about four inches off the floor. In retrospect I wonder how anybody who suffers from an infirmity manages to do this and, if not, what provisions are made for them. In any event, there were five Japanese and they produced a very good dinner except that I am not very partial to the Japanese delicacy of raw fish. In the course of the evening I was told the nearest they could get to the name Ogden in Japanese was Inner Temple. I thought this was rather funny but refrained from reporting this back to the Treasurer of the Inner Temple on my return to England. On hearing that I was Inner Temple, the waitress who was serving us – literally scurrying around on her knees – was even more deferential than before.

After dinner we went out and the two senior Japanese said that they had to go off home but the three others would take me to a bar, which they did. While having a drink there, the senior of them said to me, 'Is there anything else that you would like to do? Absolutely anything?' Of course, I knew what he meant and he knew that I understood what he meant. I have no doubt that if I had accepted it would have been their duty to accompany me. However, I said that I was feeling rather tired and had to fly to America the following day and therefore excused myself and went off to bed. In retrospect, I rather wish I had accepted the invitation, even though stopping short of what it was all about. I think that the young Japanese were probably very disappointed because, as I understand it, part of their system is that they enjoy perks, and going with me would have been a duty and also a perk.

I should repeat that I have never felt easy with the Japanese because of the way in which they behaved during the last war and I was very glad that I never had to do any work with them. I simply do not believe that people change in one or two generations.

Celia was married in 1981. Before the wedding, since I had a long case in Hong Kong, she and her brother Henry came out to stay with us in the large flat with which we had been provided. This enabled her to get a great many clothes made at prices which, in those days, were very much cheaper than they were here. Joan instructed me to buy a pearl necklace for her, which, again, was much cheaper than would have been the case here, particularly since all the negotiating was done for me by a lady who lived in Hong Kong. It was always my policy when buying something which was in the least bit expensive to get a local person to accompany me because it made all the difference in the world.

I remember on one occasion when I had been so busy that I was unable to buy Joan the birthday present I had intended until the day of my departure. I got Ronnie Arculli to come with me and what ensued was a typical example of what I have in mind. In Hong Kong people very often speak in Cantonese and English at the same time, in the sense that they may be speaking Cantonese but you will suddenly hear a word or a phrase in English thrown in. Thus, having decided what earrings I wanted to buy, the price tag on them became wholly immaterial and Ronnie negotiated the deal for me. He was doing this in Cantonese but suddenly I heard him say, 'What, only fifty per cent off, you can do better than that!' I have no doubt that if I had been doing the negotiating myself and had, with great difficulty, negotiated a reduction of twenty-five per cent, I would have gone back to London boasting about it.

When it came to the wedding, things became a little complex. Celia's husband is a Belgian diplomat who is a Count of the Holy Roman Empire, that title still being recognised in Belgium. They decided that it would be best if the civil wedding took place in Brussels and the religious ceremony in London.

It so happened that on a trip from Hong Kong, when I changed my route back, I had gone into a local travel agent and bought tickets for Joan and me. The travel agent pointed out that at the end I would find a ticket from London to Amsterdam. She explained this by saying that owing to the mad IATA rules, it was actually cheaper to give me a set of tickets ending with a flight from London to Amsterdam than to give me a set of tickets on which the flight ended in London. Of course, at the time I merely put these tickets into my desk and thought no more of them. However, now that we had to go to Brussels we used these tickets to go to Amsterdam and have a very pleasant weekend there before travelling by train to Brussels, or, to be more precise, Waterloo.

The wedding ceremony took place in a small civic building with the Mayor sitting with a cummerbund of variegated colours round his stomach. Albert and Celia were seated in front of him and the rest of us behind. Everything had to be notarised by his secretary. Consequently, both Albert and Celia had to produce various documents such as certificate of birth, in Celia's case accompanied by a translation into French. In Albert's case the situation was worse in that he had to produce amongst other things, his certificate of completion of national service. I can only assume that had he not been able to do so, he would not have been able to be married. After that, he had to produce some sort of certificate of his patent of nobility and also a letter of consent from the King. After this bizarre ceremony, we went off to the usual reception.

So far as the religious ceremony in England was concerned, we faced the problem that one cannot be married in public twice to the same person unless, of course, after a divorce. Consequently, the service took place in the private chapel of the Jesuits in Farm Street. Of course, this is a small chapel and only members of the immediate family were able to attend. The chapel was full, since a great many of Albert's relations came over from Belgium. As the wedding reception was in the evening, obviously I had to provide them with lunch. Therefore, we set up a number of tables in the drawing room as well as the dining room, and hired a cook to serve lunch. Of course, the problem of placement had to be faced, as Belgians expect to be seated in appropriate order of precedence at any function of importance. However, knowing nothing of Belgian orders and the precedence of one rank over another, this would have been a hopeless task. Luckily, I managed matters to everyone's satisfaction, as one of them said to me, 'I congratulate you on your placement because you have so arranged the seating that it is quite obvious that there is no placement and therefore no one can be offended.' I should add that all of this took place on a day between two of the coldest nights of the century, and when we went off to the wedding I actually had to carry Celia from the house to the car so that she would not get her clothes dirtied by contact with the snow.

In the evening we arranged a reception in the Great Hall in Lincoln's Inn. Of course, some of Celia's friends would not have known what Albert looked like, and therefore we decided that Celia should wear her wedding dress to the reception and Albert the morning clothes in which he had been married that morning. This curious arrangement worked well and it turned out to be an extremely satisfactory affair. Fortunately, no such problems arose in the case of the weddings of our other children.

12

1982

Except for the year when I was Treasurer of the Inn, this was the only year for which I kept a diary. For some extraordinary reason, Edward gave me a large diary for Christmas and so I felt obliged to use it. Looking at it, my overriding thought is how on earth I managed to do so much.

First of all, I had a large arbitration, which was the only occasion in the UK when I led two silks and a junior. One of the silks was because there was a point of European law of which I knew nothing. The case was very interesting. In effect, the oil company for which I was acting was engaged in sanctions-busting. This came to light and caused the deal with the other oil company to fall through. Since the price of oil had moved dramatically, it was a question of which company would have to bear the loss. The main reason why we lost the case was that the principal of my oil company did very badly in the witness box under cross-examination. Nevertheless, we ought to have won the case because I had no doubt that the other oil company knew perfectly well what the position was, but the arbitrator decided otherwise. Nevertheless, it was very interesting and remunerative. I understand that the successful company never succeeded in getting its money.

One night after that, I had just got into bed and was about to turn off the light when the telephone rang. It was someone who had been a pupil in chambers. 'Where are you?' I said. 'In Fiji.' I knew that he was employed by the Government of Fiji. 'We are in a terrible mess.' 'How can I help?' 'It's a criminal case which has gone terribly wrong but the trouble is there are a great many papers.' 'Well, it so happens that the case which I was due to do next week has settled, would it be a help if I came out?' 'Would you really?'

Of course, thirty-six hours later I was on an aeroplane. These days this might seem less extraordinary than it then was but in those days few barristers did cases abroad at all and to go somewhere which is literally almost halfway round the world was very unusual.

In appearance, Fiji was much like other islands in the Pacific but what made it different was the large Indian population which we had transported in the nineteenth century for some purpose. The Indians were very hard-working but the native Fijians were quite the reverse. Furthermore, most of them appeared to be mildly intoxicated throughout the day. I was in the capital, Suva, staying in a hotel immediately opposite the Government building where I worked. As I went to work in the morning, I would notice a group of Fijians, doubtless Government servants, who had a pestle and mortar and were busy pounding pieces of coconut which were in a muslin bag lying in water. After a time, this would produce a drink which was very mildly intoxicating but if consumed throughout the day would have the obvious effect and, of course, meant that the following morning they were only topping up with alcohol. Inevitably, the Indians acquired all business and commercial work, which vexed the Fijians, while the Indians were also vexed because they could not own land. Some time after my visit the Indians were unwise enough to cause the election of a Government in which Indians were the majority. This caused a rebellion and many of the Indians were forced out of Fiji.

The case had indeed been a disaster. The most senior civil servant in Fiji had been charged with conspiracy with a company which had a monopoly in flour. He had been convicted but the conviction had been set aside by the Court of Appeal, which consisted of Australian judges lent by the Australian Government. We appealed this decision to the Privy Council, where I duly, and quite rightly, lost. During the hearing, I was, I thought rather unfairly, asked whether I summed up the law in the same way as the judge had done when I was sitting as a Recorder! The truly honest answer would have been no, but, of course, I prevaricated and replied that I was a belt and braces man.

For some reason, this case resulted in another one entitled *Attorney-General of Fiji v Director of Public Prosecutions of Fiji*. It was in fact just what the title of the action said that it was. A law had been enacted placing the DPP under the control of the

Attorney-General. The DPP, for whom I acted, asserted that this was constitutionally unlawful. It was an extremely comic situation. We lost; again, quite rightly.

I did two other arbitrations that year; one of them was rather strange. I was acting for Arab princes. They had invested in a consortium which was going to build a leisure complex near the Pyramids in Egypt. The Egyptian Government was a member of the consortium, its contribution being the grant of the land by presidential decree. The work began but the President's political opponents, looking for opportunity to attack him, claimed that the land was of archaeological value. Ancient remains were suddenly found on the site, probably put there in order to support the allegation. The President felt in a weak position and revoked the grant by another presidential decree. By this time, a great deal of money had been spent and a claim was made upon Lloyd's underwriters under a confiscation, expropriation policy. Lloyd's repudiated the claim on the ground of failure to disclose material facts when proposing for the policy.

It was one of those cases which looked all right when one started but the more it went on the less satisfactory it looked. I received a report from an expert witness and, having read it, asked my solicitors why, since the expert said something on page x, did he say what he did on page y? The expert wrote back saying, 'What would Mr Ogden like me to say?' Needless to say, this did not improve his standing in my eyes. As things went on, skeletons started trying to edge their way out of cupboards and I was rapidly losing confidence. I was also told that there might be problems about calling the princes. On the other hand, remarks were being made to Lloyd's that it did not look as if Lloyd's really wanted work from Arab countries. I took the papers with me to the cottage, where I was telephoned by my solicitor three days before the arbitration was due to begin to tell me that underwriters had increased their offer from $US 0.5 million to $US 11 million. Immediately, I said, 'Take it with both hands and run.' 'Thank God!' he said. I was very glad not to have had to fight the case.

I went to Hong Kong three times that year. One of the cases was somewhat unusual. I was acting for the Royal Hong Kong Jockey

Club, which had suspended a rider for not trying hard enough in a race. His lawyers had managed to persuade a High Court judge that this decision was wrong and I was brought out to do the appeal, which I had little difficulty in winning.

Rather splendidly, I was put up in a little flat at the very top of the Jockey Club next to the racecourse and was able to eat in their excellent restaurant downstairs. I was also able to go up to the stipendiaries' little perch on the very top of the racecourse in order to watch a couple of races being run. In addition, I was taken to watch a disciplinary hearing immediately after a race before the stipendiaries. It was nearest to a drumhead court martial than anything that I have ever seen before or since.

I did two very important cases in England in 1982. One of them, *McLoughlin v O'Brien*, was on what is called nervous shock. This is lawyer's jargon for post-traumatic stress disorder occasioned by being involved in or seeing some horrible sight. In this instance, it was because of an accident on a road in which a man and his four children had all been seriously injured; one actually died. The hospital had been stupid enough to allow the widow to see them all while they were still in the accident unit with blood and mud all over them. Not unnaturally, it had an appalling effect upon her. The point at issue was whether one could obtain damages in such cases if one had not actually seen the accident, which was what my opponent contested and what many people thought that the law was.

Anyway, I went to the House of Lords and we succeeded, and that is still a leading case on nervous shock today.

The other case also arose out of a road accident. A man had been killed and his widow sued for damages. I was for the defendant insurers. In this case the issue was how much of the man's earnings could the widow claim as being her dependency. This point had never been decided properly before and when we conducted the case I was aware of the fact. I told my insurers that if we were to succeed, in view of the identity of the trial judge, who was over-sympathetic to plaintiffs, it would be essential to take the case to the Court of Appeal, which we duly did, and got a result which was very satisfactory for them. This has remained the leading case in the field to this day.

* * *

Although I had started sitting as a Deputy High Court judge in the Queen's Bench Division in 1977, at this time I was continuing to sit as a Recorder at the Old Bailey. This was quite pleasant, not only because the cases were more interesting than those which Recorders at other courts dealt with, but also because the Sheriffs of the City gave one a free lunch every day, to which they invited guests, and one could meet some quite interesting people there.

It is said that a well-known actor was once foreman of a jury at the Old Bailey in a case in which the judge was Edward Clarke. Edward was very nice chap socially but appallingly pro-prosecution on the Bench and behaved very badly. Reportedly, when the jury in question retired to consider its verdict, the actor said to the other jurors, 'I want you to answer three questions. First do we all agree that the defendant is guilty?' 'Yes.' 'Second, do we all agree that the judge is a shit?' 'Yes.' 'Third, do we all agree to acquit the defendant?' 'Yes.' This illustrates very well the great danger that any judge runs if the jury gets the slightest impression that he is not being impartial and is favouring the prosecution.

Of course, throughout this time the Criminal Injuries Compensation Board continued to occupy much of my time, although it did not interfere with my practice in any way. In particular, when we published our annual report there would always be a flurry of interest on the part of the media, and I see that this year I gave four radio interviews on one day and another one on another. There were also problems dealing with the Home Office.

When I received a letter saying that 'Ministers have decided that...' going on to mention a number of things which I did not want at all, I decided that I would go and see the Home Secretary, Willie Whitelaw, who was a very nice man. I thought something strange was going on when on the way to his room his private secretary said to me, 'On this occasion the Home Secretary will see you without any other Civil Servants being present save for myself.' This was a very unusual situation in that one usually sat facing the home team of Civil Servants with the Home Secretary at the end of the table. Instead, he was simply standing in the middle of the room and as I came in he gestured me to a chair.

He then said, 'Mr Ogden, you are owed an apology; no Minister knew of the existence of that letter.' On hearing this, of course, I started to make deprecatory gestures with my hands but he raised his right hand. He was a large man and he had a very large hand and it looked very awe-inspiring. 'No, Mr Ogden,' he said, 'you are owed an apology,' which he proceeded to give in very stately terms. More to the point, from my point of view, he told me that I could forget that the letter had ever been written. As a result, I went away very happy and the civil servants at the Home Office left me alone for quite a time. Usually, I dealt with the Minister of State. David Mellor was by far the best, being both very competent and helpful. Most of them were mediocre, like MPs generally, and are of even lower calibre now. As I have said before, this situation can only be improved, and then, only over a period of time, if all of them are paid about twice as much as they are now. Mr Blair's reliance on people created peers and 'advisers', together with his disregard of Parliament, which verges on contempt, hardly constitutes 'parliamentary government' and is probably modelled on the American presidential system. It is rather sad.

Looking back on it it is very remarkable that I managed to run the Board even when I was in Hong Kong. I would simply telephone once a week and ask what problems there were and, if there were any, I dealt with them over the telephone. I had one rather unfortunate experience. One of the members of the Board, a QC, simply did not do the papers that were sent to him so that they accumulated until they reached a maximum, at which point the Board staff no longer sent him any until he sent some back. Unfortunately, he continued not to do them. For some reason, I was not told about this for some time, and when I was told, of course I spoke to him and he promised to deal with it right away. This he did not do, so I had the very disagreeable task of writing to him demanding that he resign from the Board, which he did. It was not a pleasant experience.

In that year, a friend of mine sitting as a Recorder had to deal with a very unusual case. The defendant was accused of a sexual offence which could only be committed if one was a man. The defendant asserted that 'it' was a female. Consequently that was the point which the jury had to decide. The jury found the defendant guilty, thereby indicating that it was satisfied that the defendant was a man. My friend duly sentenced him to a term of imprisonment, whereupon the Prison Service immediately sent him off to a women's prison!

Lincoln's Inn gave a dinner in 1982 for the Queen Mother, who told me that she would like to visit Hong Kong. The next day I asked her Comptroller whether she meant it. He said the Queen would 'not allow it'. I had had no idea that the Queen exercised such a degree of control over other members of the Royal Family.

I was told that Lord Hailsham, when Lord Chancellor, wrote a letter to the Top Salaries Review Body saying that he was very disturbed that he had heard that some barristers were earning about £20,000 more than High Court judges. Someone must have spoken to him, because he wrote a second letter saying that he had made a mistake and that some barristers earned about £100,000 more than judges. Since some barristers earned about £250,000 (and much more now), he would have been nearer the mark if he had said that his first figure had had a nought left off it! It only goes to show how easy it is for a Lord Chancellor to become wholly out of touch.

I was also told the following story about the fraudster Horatio Bottomley. He was sitting in prison sewing mailbags when a judge, who was visiting the prison, caught his eye. 'Sewing, I see,' said the judge. 'No, my Lord,' said Bottomley, 'reaping.'

Each year in the Board's annual report, I liked to give the media a ready-made story which I hoped that they would print and not look around for something to attack us about. This year we said that some courts were far too lenient towards violent criminals. This had a spectacular effect; far more than I had anticipated. It was interesting that all the comment was favourable and, of course, it was particularly gratifying that the Prime Minister said in the House of Commons that she agreed. The only person who was unhappy was the Lord Chief Justice, who was very vexed with me and told me that that kind of thing was none of my business, which was probably true. However, I remained unrepentant and I like to think my remarks had some effect.

In November I was asked if I would be chairman of a working party consisting of representatives of all the legal and actuarial professions in the United Kingdom. It arose because the actuaries had been complaining that judges were not awarding sufficiently high damages in fatal accident and personal injuries cases in so far as things like loss of earnings and costs of care were concerned. I agreed to be chairman of this working party and noted in my diary, 'Sounds very tedious.' This proved to be wholly inaccurate. It is, I think, the thing for which I am now best known throughout the Bar.

It was very hard work because actuaries are very clever but also very precise people. At the end of our deliberations, when we had decided what we were going to do, I said to them, 'The tables themselves are easy and will be prepared by the Government actuary [who was a member of the working party] but when it comes to the explanatory notes we must make sure that they are readily comprehensible. We must assume the most stupid circuit judge in the country and before him are the two most stupid advocates in the country. All three of them must be able to understand what we are saying.' Consequently, what I had to embark upon – because, of course, being chairman I had to write the explanatory notes – was to translate what could be called actuary language into plain English. This was very difficult indeed.

At last, we finished our work, which was published in 1984. It had some impact on the judiciary but not as much as I would have wished. I told the actuaries that unless and until they did further work to provide for contingencies other than mortality, e.g. the fact that the man might have lost his job or been killed in another accident or suffered long-term illness or something of that nature, the courts would not give full effect to our tables. Finally, they did it and we produced another edition of the tables.

Eventually, the Law Commission, one of whose members was on the working party, published a report supporting us. Armed with this I was able to persuade the Government to bring in legislation and in 1995 there duly appeared a Civil Evidence Act, which, to my joy, said in a marginal note: 'Admissibility and proof of the Ogden Tables'. I said to the lady who had the conduct of the legislation, 'Of course, it is very gratifying to find oneself immortalised in a statute, but why?' She said, 'Well, if you remember, your pamphlet was entitled *Actuarial Tables with Explanatory Notes for use in Personal Injury and Fatal Accident Cases*. We couldn't waste all that space, and because everyone was calling them "the Ogden Tables" we thought that we would do so too.'

However, even this did not persuade the judiciary to accept the Tables until a case was taken up to the House of Lords in 1998, and the Judicial Committee ordered all courts to adopt the Tables. Since these affect all the most seriously injured accident victims and widows of accident victims, the impact was considerable and all awards of damages in the biggest cases went up very significantly. As a result, my children tell me that people often say to them, 'Is your father the author of the Ogden Tables?' And when I went to a political dinner a few months ago someone said to me, 'Are you Ogden of the Ogden Tables?' 'Yes,' I said. 'Ah,' said someone else, 'I've read them.' 'Oh,' said the Shadow Minister who was present, 'What are they? Explain.' All very gratifying to an already inflated ego!

At the end of the diary I wrote some comments in December 1992 explaining some of the entries which otherwise would have meant nothing to the reader and also tying up loose ends. I ended by saying, being now aged sixty-six, I would no longer be capable of undertaking the volume of work, the long hours and the stress described in this diary. I said, how I managed I didn't know, but it had been an interesting read. It has been an even more interesting read in the year 2001 as I sit here dictating this.

I should perhaps add that it was not all work and no play. We went up to the cottage in Dalham frequently at weekends and during the longer holidays and enjoyed it very much. We also went on very enjoyable holidays in France during which we drove phenomenal distances – once, right down to the South of France and up as far as the Pyrenees and back. It is really quite extraordinary looking back at it, how I had the energy to do that kind of thing.

We also visited Albert and Celia when he was ambassador in Baghdad. It was a strange place. Saddam Hussein was in power but at that time was not so frightful as he now is. The whole of Baghdad was littered with enormous great posters showing him in various guises, e.g. soldier, devout man, etc. There were separate queues outside shops, one for men and one for women, and it was to be expected that if one saw a man walking along leading a donkey or a camel that his wife would be following behind carrying anything that needed to be carried.

We had to get permission to go and see Babylon, which was a great disappointment because there was virtually nothing to see, and I gather it is now worse since the wretched man has reconstructed it with his effigy all over it. However, when we went down to the river Euphrates, just where the Hanging Gardens would have been, we did have an enormous feeling of great antiquity. On our way out we came across a group of schoolgirls wearing immaculate white little uniforms, and obviously they wanted to practise their English once they learned our nationality. Each would say, 'How do you do?' and one was expected to reply appropriately. Obviously, I got it wrong on one occasion because the little girl said, 'No, you are meant to say so and so,' which I understood to mean that that is the way in which they had learnt it by rote in their school.

Albert presumed that the residence was bugged, which he enjoyed because he was able to say what he liked about the regime in the drawing room, knowing that the person listening to the tape would hear it. If he wanted to have a truly private conversation he would go out into the garden. Apparently, one day the wife of an ambassador was telephoning a friend in her home country, Pakistan, I think, when suddenly a little voice said, 'Speak in English. I cannot understand what you are saying.'

Obviously, it was not a pleasant posting for them. It was made more onerous for Albert because, since the United States had broken off diplomatic relations, he had to take under his wing the United States Embassy, which therefore flew the Belgian flag although there were two American diplomats left behind who actually did the work. Nevertheless, it was an additional burden upon Albert.

On our way back we were on a really frightful plane. It was dirty and a no-smoking sign actually became detached from the ceiling and started waving about. The whole flight was very unsatisfactory and I wrote a very stiff letter of complaint to the Managing Director of British Airways. Shortly afterwards, I received a letter from someone writing on his behalf in which the writer said that the Managing Director was deeply distressed to hear about my experiences and nothing like that would ever happen again, etc. Of course, this was the usual bugs letter, i.e. a standard form letter. Unfortunately for the writer, the letter said that the Managing Director was troubled about my experiences on my flight from Bangkok. By now I had recovered my temper; I wrote a further letter to the lady, saying that she had misunderstood what I was complaining about; that it was last year that a plane from Bangkok had broken down in Delhi and I had had to be put up overnight, but that I do not believe that I ever bothered to complain about that. I, I said, was complaining about a flight from Baghdad. Of course, this put a terrible penance upon her because she could not just push a button to produce another bugs letter and therefore had to write one specially, which I thought served them all right.

(The origin of the phrase 'the usual bugs letter' is not widely known. Before the 1939 war a passenger in a train sleeper wrote complaining of bugs in his bed. He received a reply expressing deep regret and saying that it had never happened before and would not do so again. Unfortunately, it still had a note attached to it saying 'Send usual bugs letter'.)

13

MISCELLANEOUS EVENTS HERE AND ABROAD

One of the great advantages of working in the Far East was that I was able to buy round-the-world tickets. If one goes to, say, Hong Kong and back, that is the equivalent of two-thirds of the way round the world. But if one goes all the way round, the cost of the round-the-world ticket is not significantly more. Of course, since I only went to these places because I was doing work there, I also had the advantage of first-class tickets. The round-the-world ticket enabled one to go anywhere covered by the airlines provided that one kept going in the same direction. One therefore had to work out one's route very carefully to ensure that at no stage did one plan going even minutely in the wrong direction. It did enable me to visit places and people whom otherwise I would never have seen. For example, I got to know very well a woman who was on the Alaska Compensation Board for Victims of Crime and on one occasion when going to work in Hong Kong, I was able to travel by way of Juno, Alaska, and call on her, something which in the ordinary way I would never have attempted to do.

Another such occasion was when the Council of the International Bar Association was invited to go to Beijing after it had held its meeting in Japan. Beijing was itself the usual dusty dirty place that one expects to find in the Far East, although rather more so than many, save Indian, cities, but travelling there on a semi-VIP basis was extremely interesting. Of course, like any tourist, I visited the Forbidden City and other such sights, but what was particularly interesting was being able to sit in the Great Hall of the People in order to hear the speech of welcome. We also were able to sit in those splendid armchairs with antimacassars which one often sees on television.

I always got the impression that the Chinese officials attempted to guess what questions they were going to be asked, and had learned a schooled response which was the same whoever one asked. The art was to try to find something which they had not considered. I fixed upon the question of independent lawyers. These firms of lawyers were ostensibly independent but in fact employed by the Ministry of Justice. On every occasion I would ask: 'If the Minister of Justice sent for the independent lawyer and said – "Bring me the file which contains all the papers in the case in which you are acting for a foreign company against the Chinese Government" – would the independent lawyer be obliged to comply?' The answers were splendidly different. They varied from 'Of course' down to 'Well, he would not be blamed if he did so'. From these answers it can be gauged how truly independent those firms were, although I believe the situation may be better to-day.

My old friend and fellow Bencher, George Carman, QC, has recently died. He was a fascinating character, in that he was extremely good with juries. Justifiably, this resulted in him earning a great deal of money and because his forte was libel he gained a great deal of publicity. It was a very different story if he appeared before a judge without a jury.

I was against him on two occasions. The first was in Chester, where I appeared for two businessmen who alleged conspiracy against the Chief Constable of Lancashire on account of the actions of the Regional Crime Squad and a local businessman. George and Ben Hytner, QC, acted respectively for the two defendants. They were in the same chambers but did not get on well, which was greatly to my advantage. The case was tried by Bill Mars-Jones, who was a very pro-establishment judge and should have been George's natural ally. However, they got across each other in a spectacular way, very much to my advantage.

Every day I would make an application to Bill saying, 'As a result of the discovery of documents which you ordered yesterday I have a further application for discovery of other documents.' George would then get up and seek to argue that I should not get that order. In the course of this he would always say, 'As your Lordship knows, I am acting on behalf of the Chief Constable.'

At this, one could see clouds of steam erupting from Bill's head, together with a small balloon which read, 'After four or five days I might be expected to know for whom you are acting.' In any event, Bill would always make the order. George would then say that as it was a matter of great importance, he would like a few minutes' adjournment to consider his position, i.e. was he going to consider going down to the Court of Appeal in order to get the order upset, as one could in those days, but after a few minutes would return saying that in the circumstances he had decided to proceed. This went on for several days.

After this hilarious case had gone on for several weeks I was made an offer by the businessman, which I accepted, and we all went home to London.

The other case in which we were against each other was in Manchester. The question was: 'Did my machine burn down George's factory?' My expert was the Professor Emeritus of Electrical Engineering in Newcastle upon Tyne University, which takes a special pride in the standing of this faculty. George had as his expert a lecturer from the same faculty. Of course, this was quite fun for a start. However, late in the day, George's solicitors got hold of the man who had designed the machine and, to add to the gaiety of nations, he had been a pupil of both the other two and had been offered but rejected a place in the faculty. His evidence would have been that both the other two had misread the electrical drawings! At this, I said to George, 'This is an impossible situation, let us split the case down the middle.' George readily agreed and we decided that we would telephone our respective claims managers at the next adjournment.

Meanwhile, the trial judge thought that he might helpful by saying, 'I don't see why I shouldn't believe the driver of the machine.' This was not something which he should have said since it was in the middle of the plaintiff's evidence and he had heard none of my evidence at all. Fortunately, George, as an honourable man, did not go back on our agreement and at the adjournment we went and telephoned. I said to my claims manager, 'Forget what I said in the consultation last week, the position is now as follows.' He gave a sigh and said, 'Michael, I suppose what you're telling me is that, yet again, the expert has let us down.' 'Yes,' I said. 'Well, you'd better go ahead and do it.' George and I duly announced the settlement of the case and went back to London; the judge, probably but wrongly, thought that it was his remark which had brought about a resolution.

I participated in a very odd arbitration all about asphalt; I cannot now recollect the details. It took place in the ballroom of the National Liberal Club, which was a remarkably decayed, cavernous room in which the members of the arbitration huddled in the middle. It lasted a reasonably short length of time, which was just as well, because Ronald Arculli telephoned and asked me to go and act on behalf of one of his partners, who faced an allegation of insider dealing. In Hong Kong insider dealing was not a criminal offence but if found guilty of it one lost a great deal of 'face'.

I said that, because I had done so much work for the firm, I would do the case for nothing but merely on the basis of having my expenses paid. As a result Joan and I went out to Hong Kong and were put up in the usual suite and had a very jolly time. Happily, we succeeded. Of course, the partner could not lose face by not providing a gift in place of fees. Consequently, on the last day that we were there, a messenger came round with two little Chinese purses, always in red if they were a gift, inside which were two watches. Mine was the poor man's gift consisting of a Chopard gold pocket watch and chain which I subsequently discovered to be worth something over £1,000, while Joan was presented with a Rolex Oyster with little diamond and ruby chips on the face, which was worth something over £3,500; the present-day values would of course be very much greater.

On our way back from Hong Kong we stopped in Bangkok for a couple of days. When we went to leave, we discovered that our Singapore Airlines flight which should have taken us to Singapore in order to board another plane for London, had been delayed and we would miss our connection. I could not afford to spend another day in Bangkok and it was arranged that we should travel by Air France. This meant that we landed in Paris and had to transfer to a little plane which went from Paris to London – very different in terms of comfort from the aeroplane which had made the longer flight. It also meant that we were decanted at Terminal 2 rather than Terminal 3.

I went to Customs and declared the two watches, saying I had no idea what they were worth. In Terminal 3, which at that time, dealt with international flights, I am sure that this would have caused no difficulties but in Terminal 2 this obviously caused the Customs officer a great deal of trouble. He looked at Joan's watch and got out his Rolex brochure and said, 'Is it genuine?' 'I suppose so.' 'Might your friend have given you a valuable present?' 'Yes.' At this he looked very troubled and turned the brochure round so that I could see, and pointed out that it was the most expensive Rolex in the catalogue and there would be a figure of several hundred pounds by way of duty, but he would go and talk to his superior. He went off and then came back and with a very apologetic look said he was awfully sorry but that's what he had charge us. Of course, on these occasions, when it comes to it the cheque which one has to sign is not very large and I did so without any feeling of discomfiture. But this was quite plainly something that upset the Customs man. Looking sideways, he noticed my watch and said, 'Well, let's say seven pounds for that!'

During all these years when I was travelling to and fro between London and the Far East, Joan had the Herculean task of contriving to look after the home and the children and, when they were old enough to be left or when all of them were at school, coming out to be with me. Of course, the number of times that she could do this increased greatly, culminating in the period of my last big case before I retired.

At about this time, I had to go to the House of Lords in a case in which my opponent was seeking leave to appeal. It was a reinsurance case, the answer to the problem being, in my view, fairly straightforward, but it involved a great deal of detail. The Committee consisted of three, namely Lords Bridge and Brandon, together with retired Lord Chancellor Elwyn-Jones. They were late asking us to come in and I said to my people, 'I suppose that, as usual, they are deciding the case before it begins and I can assure you that if Bridge and Brandon agree, that will be the end of it.'

Within thirty seconds it was apparent that Bridge and Brandon did not agree; the former being for me and latter against. The person who had to decide whether leave should be granted was

Elwyn-Jones, who was, so to speak, only there for the beer. His worried little Welsh face looked anxious throughout the hearing and, very sensibly, he decided that since he plainly didn't understand the case at all, it was best to agree with the person who said that leave should be granted. As a result I got a brief on the appeal which I should never have got, because it was quite obvious that the appellant was wrong.

The Bradford Football Club fire was a rather unusual disaster. One of the stands at the ground had a typical slatted floor so that rubbish could and did fall between the slats and accumulate below. During a match someone must have dropped a lighted match or cigarette end or something of that kind which fell through the slats on to the rubbish below and set it on fire. The fire spread rapidly and engulfed the entire stand. A match was being played at the time and so the terraces were full. Initially, no one paid much attention to this little fire underneath the stand and it was only when it took hold that people standing above it realised the danger that they were in. Consequently they began moving in different directions to try to escape it but, of course, if they went sideways they were moving towards people who did not realise why they were being pushed along and naturally were somewhat resistant. Equally there were difficulties in getting out on to the football pitch from the stand because it meant getting over the barriers which had been erected to prevent precisely that happening during or after the course of a match.

As a result of all of this, a number of people were killed and many more were injured, including police officers who had run across the pitch in order to try to help people to get over the barrier. The game in question was being televised and therefore, for once, there was film of the disaster taking place. It was somewhat horrific, and I was obliged to watch it on a number of occasions. One of the incidents which stuck in my mind was when a man walking away from the fire suddenly had his hair ignited by the heat of the fire, which was in fact some thirty feet from him. He was walking along the terrace and appeared to be wholly unaware of the fact that his hair was on fire. I have no doubt that he was one of those who died.

I was instructed to appear on behalf of the Police Federation and another set of lawyers appeared on behalf of the relatives of those killed and others who had been injured. However, the arrangement between the solicitors was that I should lead the two teams.

There was no doubt about the liability of the football club but considerable doubt as to the extent of its insurance cover, and the insurers were not prepared to reveal this to us. This was why we sued the local authority so that we could get our sticky little hands into a bottomless pocket. In order to win against the local authority we had to establish that the Fire Brigade had failed in its duty to inspect premises of this nature properly, if at all.

On the day that I was due to cross-examine the Chief Fire Officer the new Beaujolais arrived. I discovered this when I went down to the little bistro where I and my team usually had lunch. The team was about six to eight people and so, with confidence, I ordered a bottle. However, for good reasons, none of my team turned up. Since I have always been allergic to leaving undrunk wine which I have paid for, while I did not consume the whole bottle, I certainly consumed quite a lot of it. This had no adverse affect upon my performance; indeed, subsequently I was congratulated upon a very positive, forceful and incisive cross-examination. Whether or not this flattery was justified I do not know; however, it was certainly a cross-examination which completely destroyed the Chief Fire Officer's evidence and meant that we were bound to win against the local authority, which we duly did.

One aspect of the case which was quite amusing was the fact that it was tried by the same person who had tried the Summerland Fire Inquiry. This was Joe Cantley, who had been a judge when he tried the Summerland case but had retired and was now sitting as a Deputy High Court judge. By chance, I happened to have retained the report which he made after the Summerland case and at the beginning of my opening speech I read to him a couple of paragraphs from the beginning of it. This pleased the old boy very considerably and for the rest of the case we got on very well, just as we had at Summerland. Equally, just as at Summerland there was someone he did not get on well with, so too, the counsel for the local authority managed to get across him, which also was to my advantage.

* * *

At about this time I was instructed on behalf of a trade union called SOGAT (Society of Graphic and Allied Trades), which was in dispute with another union with which it had amalgamated. In effect, they wanted me to act for them to obtain a divorce from this other union. This was a case quite unlike any which I had ever conducted before; indeed, so far as I know no such case had ever been tried before. My clients consisted of those at the bottom end of the employment ladder, such as those who tied bundles of newspapers together, drove the vans and suchlike. The executive committee would come and have a consultation with me every month or so and these very large men, and one rather attractive woman who later became a life peer, would sit in my room and ask me exactly the same questions that they had asked during the previous consultation.

In due course the case came to trial, but just before it started, we were able to come to an agreement as to the nature and terms for the divorce, subject to the approval of the executive committee. Consequently, we asked the judge to defer coming into court and I was taken to the basement ballroom of a hotel in Southampton Row, where all the executive committee were seated behind little school desks while I, my junior, instructing solicitor and the leader of the trade union in question sat at a little top table. The trade union leader, who was a very sensible man named Bill Keys, got up and said, 'Brothers, Brother Michael here thinks he's got a good deal for us and so I'll ask him to tell you about it.' This I duly did and they agreed with what I had suggested. It is, I think, the only occasion upon which I have ever been referred to as 'Brother Michael'.

After postings in Brussels and Baghdad my daughter Celia and her husband Albert had two foreign postings, Santiago in Chile and Lima in Peru. Two more different places it would be difficult to imagine. One has to remember that in South America, like other places which are forested, such as Borneo, there were simply settlements at various points and there was very little communication between them by land and any communication that there was would be by sea. Consequently, they all grew up quite differently and just as Lima is very different from Santiago so Rio de Janeiro is very different from Buenos Aires.

Chile was a nice place with beautiful food and good wine, and it had largely settled down following the appalling conduct of Allende and the arrival of Pinochet, who though widely reviled in left-wing circles in Europe, was highly admired by anyone who was not a revolutionary in Chile for saving them from a Marxist Cuban-style Government. The Chileans were very fond of the British, although I doubt whether they still are following our treatment of General Pinochet. This was because Admiral Cochrane had come round the Cape and up to Santiago at the time when it was occupied by the Spanish. Upon the arrival of this British warship the town rose up, the Spaniards fled and they gained their independence, for which they have always thanked us. So much so that at one party a woman said to me apropos of the Falklands War, 'Whenever we heard that you had had a victory we opened a bottle.'

Admiral Cochrane, or Captain Cochrane as he then was, had done exactly the same thing for the Peruvians but I think that they have wholly forgotten the fact. Of course, Peru is a very interesting place; on an earlier occasion I had been to the ancient city of Machu Pichu deep in the jungle where the ruins were only discovered about forty or fifty years ago. The only difficulty about visiting it was that it occupied about three days because one had to fly from Lima, which is at sea level, up to a very high altitude. One had to rest at Cuzco, the provincial, theft-ridden capital, in order to get over altitude sickness, which is rather like jet-lag, before proceeding on one's way. It is one of those places where you spend a lot of time and effort getting there, and having stood looking with admiration at the ruins for about forty-five minutes or one hour, one says to oneself, 'Seen that, done that,' and goes away.

One of the more amusing incidents about this journey was on our way down from Machu Pichu to the train in a coach. It was a very winding road and when we came towards the first bend there was a little boy at the side of the road who cried out 'shoe-shine shoe-shine'. We looked at him with some surprise, but when we came round the bend there was the little boy again: 'shoe-shine shoe-shine', and when we went round the next bend there he was again, and so on all the way down the mountain. What he had done was to come down a track of stones which had been laid by his ancestors at the time when Machu Pichu was inhabited and, being small, young and athletic, he was able to come straight down this track at a much greater speed than our coach was able to negotiate the bends. Of course, at the bottom he was rewarded with large sums of money by all the passengers.

I had been on this trip long before Celia and Albert were posted to Peru but I visited them there on a couple of occasions. On one, we went to the top of the Andes to a place called the Colca Canyon, which is twice as deep as the Grand Canyon in America. It is a most extraordinary place; it really is the rooftop of the world so far as South America is concerned. One could see herds of vicuna and llamas wandering about. There were dirt roads; but, of course, no piped water, electricity or gas. The hotel where we stayed had solar heating, which was sufficient to heat the water and produce electricity for lighting but certainly not for central heating. The nights were bitterly cold and I slept in my underclothes with my pyjamas on top, having stolen a couple of blankets from the unoccupied bed in the room. However, once the sun had been up for about half an hour it was necessary to put on a panama hat.

The object of being there was to look at the condors which nested towards the bottom of the canyon. We drove to a point where we could watch. As the air warmed up, these great birds simply stretched their wings and were carried up by the hot thermals until they were clear of the canyon and they then beat their enormous wings and set off for the day's work. It was a truly awe-inspiring sight.

Shortly after the end of the Falklands War there was a meeting of the Council of the International Bar Association in Oslo. It was necessary to decide where the next meeting of the congress, i.e. the meeting which the whole organisation would attend, should be held. I received a letter from the President of the Buenos Aires Bar Association in which he said that they wished to hold it in Buenos Aires but realised that because of the Falklands War, if I objected they would probably fail. Therefore, he said, he was appealing to me to support them because they regarded it as important in the process of building up their democratic institutions. I telephoned the Foreign Office and I was assured that far from having any objections, they were anxious to get back on terms of normality with the Argentines and would be only too pleased if I supported the suggestion.

Consequently, as soon as the President of the Buenos Aires Bar Association had made his speech on the subject in Oslo, I rose, cited the passage in his letter about building up their democratic institutions and said that we supported it very strongly. As a result of this the suggestion was adopted without any difficulty whatsoever. The moment this happened the two Argentinian representatives came round to where I was seated and wrung me by the hand and clapped me on the back with tears literally streaming down their faces. It was a very moving moment. I was also very impressed when the New Zealand delegate told me afterwards that, of course, if I had opposed the idea they too would have done so. The name of the Chairman of the Buenos Aires Bar Association was Tommy Dabinovic; he had been born in Yugoslavia. He was a very jolly man whom I got to know well and, of course, of all the people present at the congress you can be sure that no one had a better time than I did.

Whenever I worked in the Far East, I would ensure that I had two or three days' rest at a beach resort before returning to England. These beach resorts were very similar to each other and one could have picked one up from, say, Fiji and put it down in Hawaii and one would not notice the difference save for the names of the different bars and restaurants.

On one occasion after I had visited Celia I decided to stop off at an allegedly four-star hotel, which had been recommended to me by the travel agent, on a Venezuelan island just off the shore from Caracas. I duly arrived at this place and my first impression was extremely unsatisfactory in that I needed to change some American dollars into Venezuelan money in order to pay the taxi driver and on proffering a $20 bill and asking for $10 and the rest in Venezuelan money I was told that I could only be given the whole sum in Venezuelan money. I then went up to my bedroom, where I found that there was no plug in the washbasin and there were little square patches on walls which obviously indicated that at some stage there had been some piece of apparatus there but when it was removed no attempt had been made to paint over the ugly square. I went down and had a rather grisly dinner in the dining room and went to bed, having decided that I would not stay for one night longer.

In the morning I asked the telephonist to get me the head office of the Venezuelan airline so that I could change my flight times but after about half an hour the operator said that it was impossible to get through. 'Well, get me my travel agent in London,' I said, and this she duly did, and I was able to arrange a new itinerary. Quite amazing, that one could get through to London but not the short distance to the airline's headquarters in Venezuela.

I duly went to the airport and paid the tax one had to pay on leaving the country and made the short internal flight to Caracas. The domestic terminal was about eight hundred yards from the international terminal and there were no taxis, and the buses between them were purely theoretical. Therefore, I had to stagger through the midday sun with my suitcase and arrived at the international terminal in no good humour. My mood was not improved when I saw that there was one very long queue consisting of over one hundred people queuing to go past the only immigration officer on duty. I joined this queue and in due course reached him, at which he said that I had not paid my exit tax; but I had, I said. He refused to accept this and told me to go off and pay, pointing vaguely towards where I had come from.

Obviously, one cannot take an argument like that any further and I went off and found on the way two police officers, one of whom spoke English, and asked where I could buy this necessary document. I also indicated how angry I was about what had happened. 'Oh, you should talk to this gentleman,' said the police officer, pointing out a man in grey trousers and a white shirt and he beckoned him over. The man asked to see my papers, which I gave him. 'Follow me,' he said, and led me past the very long queue, we squeezed past where the immigration officer was talking to another person and when we got the other side he said, 'that will be $60.' Of course, it was pointless to argue if I wanted to catch my aeroplane. Indeed, I have a feeling that if I had declined I would have ended up in some Venezuelan prison. Consequently, I paid over the $60 meekly, this being the only occasion upon which I have ever been asked for or paid a bribe. Needless to say, I formed the most unfavourable view of Venezuela and have not the slightest intention of ever going there again.

* * *

In 1987 when the last child had left home, it was obvious that it was absurd to go on living in a house which had four floors and which, if used as such, had seven bedrooms. Therefore, we decided to move and I asked Joan to find us a nice large comfortable flat. My sole stipulation was that I must have my own parking space. Afterwards, Joan said that she felt like someone instructed to find a parking slot with flat attached. However, she achieved this objective and we ended up in a very pleasant flat in a purpose-built Victorian block consisting of four bedrooms, two bathrooms, etc., all of the rooms save the smallest bedroom being nice and large. It is also on the top floor and served by a lift. As I said to Joan before we decided to make our move, somewhat prophetically, 'Our legs aren't going to get any better as we get older.' Of course, another advantage of living in a block of flats is that one has twenty-four-hour porterage, and if one is out, deliveries can be left with the porters. Altogether, it has worked out very well.

In 1989 I ceased to be Chairman of the Criminal Injuries Compensation Board. The whole scheme was about to be altered, in my view not for the better, and after thirteen years, during which I think it had been forgotten that I was still there, since thirteen years is a very long time, I was told that I was to be replaced by someone else. I was awarded a knighthood in the New Year's Honours, which was quite jolly. The main advantage of it in my eyes is that quite apart from good tables in restaurants and being sometimes upgraded in aeroplanes and hotels, people seldom patronise you after you have been knighted. This has always seemed to me to be a splendid advantage and one for which I have been grateful ever since. (It says a very great deal of the extent to which our children keep up with affairs that none of them noticed that my name had appeared in the New Year's Honours List. Lucy only found out when a friend of hers mentioned it to her.) I confess that I was not sorry to leave the Board; I think that there is an optimum time to stay in any job and for some time I had been conscious of the fact that I had gone past it.

Automatically, I was sent a letter from the College of Arms asking me to go down and sign a book. I suspect that this practice was invented by the college solely in order to seek to persuade people to obtain coats of arms. I knew Garter King of Arms very slightly and felt able to say to him, 'But what would I do with it? It would look very odd on the side of my Volvo and we no longer have barouches. Furthermore, if I put it on my bedroom slippers that would be even worse.' He could see at once that I was not a person to whom he would be able to sell a coat of arms. However, they had the last laugh, because when I was made Treasurer of Lincoln's Inn, I realised that I had to get one because it is the custom to put them up in the Great Hall and also in a window in the chapel. In fact, I had got a coat of arms on a bit of cardboard which I think had been written upon by my grandmother, Margaret Mordaunt. Obviously, York Herald, who was looking after my case, did not think much of this but was too polite to say so in set terms. He said to me, 'Of course, we would have to establish your right to bear these arms.' I said to him, 'That sounds as if we all have to go trawling through parish records and suchlike and it seems to me that it might be quite an expensive operation.' 'Possibly,' he said. Consequently, I immediately said to him, 'Don't bother about that. Start from scratch but make me a coat of arms as close to this as is permissible.' I explained to him that the name Ogden derived from Oakdene, a vale of oaks, and therefore that accounted for the acorns and oak leaves on the coat of arms which I had shown to him, and I asked that what he was to produce would reflect this.

In due course he produced quite a jolly little affair which was innocuous. There then came the question of a motto. There were two mottos knocking about in my family: '*Semper fidelis*' and '*Honor deo*'. Both of them seemed to me very unexciting and I decided that I would use neither of them. Fortunately, Edward's wife Rachel had read classics at Cambridge and furthermore her mother was even more of a classicist than she was. Indeed, when I first met her mother I overheard her saying something about teaching and asked her what she taught, to which she replied, 'Latin and Greek to the Jesuits,' which put me in my place properly. Between them they produced a very respectable motto from Statius: '*Agit ut potest optime*', which, being roughly translated, means 'Do your best', which indeed has always been my motto.

* * *

Frank Zappa and The Mothers of Invention were a well-known pop group. They hired the Albert Hall to give a performance. The Albert Hall is a very remarkable place in that it was founded shortly after the Great Exhibition in memory of Prince Albert, Queen Victoria's Consort. Unlike most organisations, it is not controlled by things such as articles and memoranda of association but by a series of statutes. Why this should be so, baffles my comprehension. The ownership is vested in debenture holders, each of whom owns seats or a box which they are able to let out for performances; usually these are let out by the Albert Hall acting as agents for the debenture holders. At this time the President of the Royal Albert Hall, as I ought to call it, was Luigi Gluckstein, QC, who was a Bencher of my Inn. Indeed, at the relevant time he was Treasurer; at that stage I was not even a Bencher. Someone must have recommended me to Luigi and he instructed me in the litigation which ensued.

Of course, as one can imagine, many of the Albert Hall debenture holders are a very stuffy lot and when they discovered a few days before the performance was due to begin that some of the lyrics were not what they would wish, they locked out Frank Zappa and The Mothers of Invention, who promptly sued them for breach of contract.

We had two defences. First, that the lyrics were such that they were indecent and we ought not to be obliged to permit them to take place in our hallowed hall. Second, that there was a term in the agreement which enabled us to cancel. Unfortunately, doubtless having been drafted by distinguished lawyers, this clause was not clear. Most of the trial was taken up by discussion of the lyrics. The Trial Judge, Mocatta, was a very distinguished commercial judge; and Luigi was not a practising QC but a very prominent businessman.

My opponent, Alan Campbell, was a man who had had a very distinguished war, having been a prisoner of war in Colditz. In spite of all of this, he was surprisingly unworldly. In his opening speech he read out the lyrics to the judge, and one which sticks in my recollection is what he described as a young girl in her early twenties regretting the fact that she had never received an offer of marriage. His principal witness was George Melly, who was a very distinguished critic in that field of music. He was not prepared to lie, and when I cross-examined him as to the true nature of the lyrics he readily agreed with what I said. Thus, the lyric to which I have already referred meant something rather different from what Alan had thought that it meant. It referred to a young lady who was repining about the fact that no gentleman had ever proposed sexual intercourse to her. When George Melly agreed that this was so, Alan said to me *sotto voce*, 'Oh dear, I did get that rather wrong, didn't I?' The whole of my cross-examination of George Melly proceeded along similar lines, with Mocatta looking more and more distressed as the true nature of the lyrics was unfolded to his innocent gaze.

Unfortunately, Luigi insisted on giving evidence, although there was no relevant evidence that he could give at all. Nevertheless, as I have said, he was a QC and Treasurer of my Inn while I was not even a Bencher. Obviously, in the circumstances, I had no option but to agree to his giving evidence, and he arranged for his wife to come and listen to him doing so, a course of conduct which I thought was most imprudent because one never knew what might eventuate. Because Mocatta and Gluckstein knew each other very well as prominent Jews, Mocatta, even if he had thought it, was not prepared to say that everything that Gluckstein was giving evidence about was wholly irrelevant, and he just sat there. Fortunately, an aura of respectability was cast over my calling Gluckstein when Alan proceeded to cross-examine him about this wholly irrelevant evidence. The whole thing was utterly bizarre.

The case ended by Alan Mocatta deciding that the Albert Hall won on the basis of the narrow point of construction of the terms of the contract, and he added that, in the circumstances, he did not think it was desirable for a Queen's Bench judge to venture upon any observations concerning 'the other part of the case'. Thus, we had a glorious victory although I think that Frank Zappa and The Mothers of Invention never paid the costs of the action and, indeed, I am not sure that any energetic steps were entered into to get them to do so, bearing in mind that Frank Zappa was based in the United States and was probably not even a party to the contract, besides not being a party to the litigation.

* * *

In April 1991, having attained the age of sixty-five, I received a letter from the Department of Social Security awarding me an old age pension. This was gratifyingly higher than I had anticipated, the reason being that in addition to the basic old age pension, one receives a pension based upon further compulsory contributions paid after 1978, depending upon one's level of earnings. However, in December 1992 the DSS wrote to me saying that my contributions had been inaccurately calculated and that the pension awarded was too much, and that while I was not required to repay the amount which I had been overpaid, I would now be awarded less. Helpfully, the letter was headed 'A reduction in your widow's benefit'.

As a result of this weird communication I wrote to the DSS asking for details of the revised assessment and the original calculation and why the original calculation had been wrong. I continued to write follow-up letters, my first having been acknowledged, but failed to receive any substantive answer. The matter having drifted along in what I regarded as a lethargic fashion, I wrote in August 1993 saying that if by the end of October I had not received a substantive answer I would ask my Member of Parliament to refer the matter to the Parliamentary Ombudsman. I received no answer to that communication and so in due course I asked my Member to do that, and he did. He also wrote to the DSS direct and received a reply saying that as my papers had been destroyed in 1993 they could not tell whether a reply had been sent to my earlier correspondence, adding that if I forwarded details of the questions which I 'claimed were unanswered' they would pursue the matter further. As the Ombudsman subsequently pointed out, this was not a form of words which he would have regarded as likely to satisfy an inquirer.

As a result of the Ombudsman's enquiries, he discovered that because of the lethargy on the Department's part, as he put it, for almost three years I had been receiving barely half my full additional pension entitlement and my eventual entitlement was only established when my liability for the tax years ending 1990/1991 was finally calculated in July 1994. In the course of his adjudication the Ombudsman caused attention to be drawn to the DSS's letter to the Member of Parliament saying that two letters of mine had been destroyed. The Ombudsman said, 'That was not true. The DSS papers which I obtained before starting my investigation in December

1993 contained both of those letters. I strongly criticise DSS for misinforming the Member in what I regard as offensive terms', i.e. the observation that if I forwarded details of the questions which I 'claimed were unanswered' they would pursue the matter further.

In short, the Ombudsman criticised the department for lethargy and ineptitude and, in respect of the alleged destruction of the letters, which was not true, it was an allegation which, at best, was one of the grossest incompetence if not barefaced lying. I promptly received sums of money for the arrears of payment together with interest which the Ombudsman said he regarded as 'a satisfactory outcome to a justified complaint'.

Two thoughts occur to me. First, it had never occurred to me that the original calculation might be wrong. But for the letter telling me that they had been paying me too much, doubtless I would still be receiving a pension which would have been very much less than that to which I am entitled. Second, if I had been a person who simply accepted letters from Government departments, I would not have written making the enquiry which I did or pursued it as far as the Ombudsman. I shudder to think, therefore, how many people there must be in the country who are in happy ignorance of the fact that they are being paid less than they should be. What solution there might be to this problem I cannot think, because it would be impracticable for financial reasons to have every single pension double-checked.

I suppose, in justice, I should add that throughout much of this time not only had I my earnings as a self-employed person, but also I was being paid from four different Government sources – namely, first in respect of my membership of the Criminal Injuries Compensation Board, second, in my capacity as Chairman of the Board, third, in my capacity as Assessor of Compensation in miscarriages of justice cases and fourth when sitting as a part-time High Court judge – which must have complicated things. Nevertheless, none of this excuses the appalling conduct of the Ministry. I should add that I received a personal letter of apology from the Permanent Under Secretary of the Department, to which I was able to reply, with complete honesty that having myself had a part-time job running a Government department, I knew how easily these things could happen.

* * *

It was at about this time that I had a somewhat humorous run-in with the Superintendent of the Royal Parks. Living a few hundred yards away from Kensington Gardens, I often used to walk there, and, in particular, at weekends and bank holidays I noticed that the dustbins were so full of refuse that it was impossible to put more in and that people who had tried to do so had merely left what they were trying to deposit around the dustbin, thereby causing the most frightful appearance to that area. When I wrote to the Superintendent pointing this out and suggesting that more frequent collections should be made, particularly on bank holidays and at the weekends, I got a letter saying, in effect, that this was far too expensive and could not possibly be done. Immediately, I wrote to the relevant Minister and received, almost by return of post, a letter saying that that was wholly unacceptable and he would see that something was done about it forthwith, which he did. As a result, the clearing of dustbins in Kensington Gardens, and I assume the other Royal Parks, was gratifyingly improved and I had no further cause for complaint on that score.

14

BUMAPUTRA BANK

In about 1987 a message came from Hong Kong asking if Michael Ogden, alternatively Michael Wright or else Graeme Hamilton, could do a case which might last at least a year. Wright and I were unable to do so because of previous commitments but Graeme took it on and continued to do it for the next seven years, involving appearances in two trials. At the end of this time he was thoroughly fed up and wanted to get rid of it and so I agreed to take over.

George Tan was an illegal immigrant in Hong Kong who had amassed a large fortune. He was acting on behalf of a Malaysian bank which lost money and he was accused, together with others, of attempting to defraud. The amounts involved were enormous, running to tens of millions of pounds in a number of different transactions. The defence alleged that the Malaysian Government's policy was not to trade with China but dealings by some officials took place using George's company as a blind. Those Malaysian officials were not prepared to admit that they knew anything at all about the transactions involved; hence the prosecution.

The first trial was a lengthy one and involved the accountants Price Waterhouse amongst others but it came to a standstill at the end of the close of the prosecution's case when the judge, Dennis Barker, dismissed all the charges against everyone.

Then the prosecution embarked upon another case against George and others, and this too lasted for some time until it was discovered that the Trial Judge held a substantial block of shares in one of the companies involved. Not surprisingly, since the company had gone into liquidation years earlier, he had forgotten that he had owned them. Of course, the case came to a grinding standstill.

In no way deterred, the Hong Kong Government embarked upon a third case. Graeme started this case but handed it over to me. There were a large number of counts of conspiracy to defraud and also some counts of bribery. I never had to consider the bribery cases because all the evidence relating to them would have been given in Hong Kong at a later stage. I was concerned to cross-examine prosecution witnesses who were giving evidence on commission in Kuala Lumpur. This was a very unsatisfactory arrangement because the intention was that their evidence should simply be read out to the jury in Hong Kong. What made it worse was the fact that the prosecution refused to apply for leave to film the witnesses when they gave evidence. This would have been a ground for appeal. There were a great many unnecessary witnesses whose evidence took a great deal of time, but they were followed by some people who really mattered. Amongst others, I had to cross-examine several very important officials.

In each case I was attempting to demonstrate that they knew perfectly well what was going on. This required a very great deal of preparation. It was one of those cross-examinations which depended entirely upon the documents and would go something like this: 'Please look at volume 8 page 21, now look at volume 103, page 80. What do you say about that...? 'Ah, in that case look at volume 73 page 29..' and so it went on in each case for five days. It was extremely hard work so far as preparation was concerned but quite fun to actually conduct the cross-examinations, which, in many instances, went very successfully. By the time I had conducted all these cross-examinations the conspiracy charges were effectively destroyed.

All of this lasted between the spring of 1993 and early 1996. I would spend one month preparing in England, followed by a month conducting these cross-examinations in Kuala Lumpur. Joan was able to come with me quite often and we stayed in a luxurious suite in a very good hotel. Also, the fees were extremely satisfactory, which was a gratifying circumstance. This meant that I did not appear at all in an English court between 1993 and 1996 except for half a day when I appeared before the Divisional Court in a vain attempt to overturn the suspension of a solicitor who had behaved badly and had been suspended from practice for three years. As I have said, most of the time I spent in Kuala

Lumpur, but it also necessitated visits to Hong Kong for odd days, which was agreeable.

The Malaysian judge was very pleasant and we got on well, and my opponents were no problem. At the end of all of this it was necessary to go before the judge in Hong Kong in order to attempt to get the trial stopped. There were three possible grounds, first George's health, second the incredible delay and third the fact that the prosecution's refusal to have the evidence videoed made the trial unfair. As to George's health, he undoubtedly had a bad heart condition. I brought over from London one of the best heart specialists in the country.

Fortunately for George's health, the consultant I had brought from London was able to prescribe medicine which improved his condition very greatly. Unfortunately, it ruined any chance that I might have had of having the trial stayed on the ground of his health. So too, although the delay had been appalling, I was unable to point to any prejudice to George as a result, and quite rightly the judge rejected both these grounds. This left the prosecution's refusal to have the evidence videotaped. Right at the beginning of the case the judge had announced that there were only two points in the case, namely health and delay, and when I came to address him on the subject of video, he simply crossed his arms and gave every appearance of intending not to pay any regard to what I said on this topic at all. From a very early stage in the application, it was quite obvious to me and the rest of my team that there was not the slightest possibility that the judge would grant a stay. In due course he refused it.

Alas, at this time my leg and back started playing up and it was a convenient moment to hand over the case to Tony Scrivener to conduct the actual trial. The last thing that I did before relinquishing the case was to advise that an application should be made to the judge that he should withdraw from the trial on the ground that he had exhibited such pro-prosecution bias that George would not get a fair trial. This was certainly not something that I had ever done before, nor had I ever heard of it being done. It was a very extreme step to take. I duly swore an affidavit reciting all of this and Tony made the necessary application to the judge, who rejected it, making complimentary remarks about me and very disparaging remarks about Tony. As a result, I obtained the consent of the Bar Council to write a letter to the

South China Morning Post pointing out that he had complimented me and disparaged Tony, but that it was in fact I who had advised that the application should be made. Furthermore, I swore a second affidavit based on what happened during the application made by Tony, which in fact never had to be used.

At this stage the judge had revoked George's bail. It must be remembered that he had been on bail for something like ten years and had attended two trials. It was an extraordinary step for the judge to have taken, which he did on the ground that he thought that there was a risk that George might not turn up for trial. George took the view that if he pleaded guilty to something he might well be released not much later than the date upon which the trial would have finished, and he asked Tony to see whether anything could be done in this regard.

By this time the prosecution must have been very demoralised. Assuming that they had read the transcripts of the proceedings in Malaysia, they must have realised that I had completely wrecked all the conspiracy counts. I have no idea what the strength of the bribery offences were because I never had cause to look at them. In addition, throughout this time there had been continuous complaints in the Executive Council in Hong Kong about the length of time that this trial was taking and the enormous cost to Government of it.

In the event, Tony managed to do a splendid deal for George. He pleaded guilty to two conspiracy counts, of which, in my view, he was certainly not guilty, and the prosecution dropped all the other charges against him. So anxious was the prosecution to dispose of the case that these pleas were tendered and accepted upon the basis that it was not an intent to defraud but an intent to deceive. The fact that intent to deceive can amount to attempt to defraud was the result of what, in my view, was a ridiculous decision in the House of Lords some years previously. However, of course, it made a great deal of difference when it came to sentencing. The prosecution had never been able to point to the absence of a single dollar which could be said to have been stolen, and therefore in no way had George profited personally from what he pleaded guilty to. Credit also had to be given for the fact that George had no previous convictions and was therefore a man of good character, and for the fact that he had pleaded guilty, thereby saving a great deal of time and money. All of which factors required the judge to reduce whatever sentence he would otherwise have felt able to pass.

George was sentenced to only three years' imprisonment, whereas the maximum was seven years, and, as he had anticipated, he was released from prison shortly after the time when the trial would have finished, having spent the entire period in the prison hospital, where he was treated with deep respect by the prison officers.

Having duly passed sentence, the judge asked the prosecution whether there was an application for costs and was told that there was no such application, this having been part of the overall deal. The result was extremely satisfactory.

This case was the most complex which I ever did, in that I had 350 arch lever files in my room in chambers, my solicitor had over 2,000 files in her office in Hong Kong and we had a duplicate set of many of the files in a small warehouse in Kuala Lumpur. However, it was very interesting and, quite apart from the satisfactory result, it meant that I earned a very great deal of money; indeed, in each of those three years I earned more than in any other year at the Bar.

This case was the only one in the course of which my junior was murdered. He was Australian and a local Hong Kong QC. He had had a row with his wife, who had left him and gone back to Australia. Not unnaturally, this left him very depressed and, since he was also very overworked, he thought that he would take a short holiday in Macau.

At that time Macau was a Portuguese possession and was the centre of gambling. It contained one enormous hotel which consisted of five gaming floors one above the other each being about seventy-five yards across. As if this was not enough, there was a small children's gaming room just off the ground floor where there were many fruit machines and suchlike attractions. Round the edges of the gaming rooms were the hotel bedrooms. Joan and I were taken there once by Ronnie Arculli – he was given four tickets on the hydrofoil and two bedrooms, all free. It was an extraordinary place. The rest of Macau was rather peaceful and almost rural and a great change from central Hong Kong. I understand that these days it is a rather dangerous place because of the gangs who are fighting turf wars over gambling.

My junior, having gone to Macau, proceeded to fall in love

with a Russian prostitute. At that time as now, the world appeared to be populated by Russian prostitutes and it seemed to me that they were the main export from Russia. The luckless QC proceeded to go with the girl to Vladivostok in order to 'purchase' her from her 'owners'. He went with her to visit a friend of hers, who was a heroin addict, who had also invited two men, who were dangerous criminals. The QC went into the kitchen with the two men, where he was shot, for what reason is unknown, but was presumably part of a failed attempt to get the money off him. The two men went back to the two women, where they tortured the girl for the same purpose, in the course of which she was accidentally killed by strangulation. The two men were subsequently killed in an unrelated incident. What had happened only became known when the heroin addict confessed it to the police on her deathbed. Thus, all five people concerned ended up dead.

Of course, this caused a sensation in Hong Kong, not least because, judging from a photograph, the prostitute did not look very attractive. Obviously, it caused problems for us, but, fortunately, my junior played only a small part in the case, limited to applications, etc. in Hong Kong. My solicitor, who was extremely competent and hard-working, in effect played the part of junior as well as solicitor. How I would have coped with what was a most complex case and had the most documents which I ever handled without her I hate to think.

I must add that I rather liked George Tan, whom I was convinced had done nothing dishonest or contrary to the best interests of the Malaysians who had employed him.

The Sea Fish Licence Tribunal was a useful example of bungle and wasted time. In early 1993 before the Tan case. I was telephoned by the Ministry of Agriculture, Fisheries and Food and asked if I would be interested in being President of this tribunal, which was to establish fishing quotas for all UK fishing boats in the event of disputes. I said that I would and was asked to telephone a circuit judge to find out more about it. When I telephoned him, he said, 'Oh! You're one of the candidates?' I telephoned MAFF, incandescent with rage, saying that I was certainly not a 'candidate' and they should have told me that this was the suggestion. Of course, I was at once offered the job. All the legislation was enacted and I spent time and trouble helping to select a suitable Scots vice-president, and chairmen and members for panels and procedures. The National Union of Seamen, in my view unwisely, then persuaded a judge to refer the validity of the legislation to the European Court; as it had no fast-track procedure, this meant deferring implementation for some years. Consequently, I said that I was not prepared to continue on this basis and the scheme was abandoned, probably to the detriment of fishermen, because the basic problem of over-fishing remained unresolved for some time and was ended by the EU in a manner which I suspect was worse than it would have been had the Government's scheme not been scuppered.

Of course, when I started at the Bar, computers did not exist, and fees were kept in little fee books, one for each barrister, which were kept up rather erratically by the Senior Clerk, fee notes being despatched spasmodically and often not followed up properly. As a result of all of this, we lost a great deal of money in those days. This was compounded by the fact that some less than honest solicitors deliberately withheld payment to counsel, using the interest on the unpaid fees to run their offices. Of course, once computers arrived on the scene all of this rapidly changed and we got paid with promptitude. Indeed, when I retired, the only outstanding fees related to a case which I had done the month before and were paid a month later. There had been one advantage to successful barristers in former days in that upon retirement, which included being put on the Bench, the barrister was able to take away tax-free all his outstanding fees. Once this loophole was closed, any possible merit in the old method vanished overnight.

Another remarkable change was the invention of the fax machine. Initially this started off as a device called telex, which was a very inferior kind of fax, but was useful for the few years before fax arrived. I well remember my feeling of intense satisfaction when a set of instructions arrived from Singapore in my chambers in London at a time when I was in the cottage in Suffolk. Chambers faxed the instructions up to me, I wrote an opinion in manuscript and faxed it back to London, where it was typed up and despatched to Singapore so that the lawyer who had sent me the instructions received my opinion on the following morning. Doubtless, to-day it would be seen as unremarkable.

One of the rather unpleasant things about travel in former days was jet-lag. This meant that one's brains felt like scrambled eggs and, as I have mentioned, I always refused to do any work at my destination until twenty-four clear hours after my arrival. However, that too, changed. Dioralyte, which for some strange reason is not well known as an antidote to jet-lag, was invented in order to provide rehydration for babies and young children who had been suffering from diarrhoea. Jet-lag is a result of dehydration from being stuck up in a tin box at thirty-five thousand feet in a confined space, accentuated by consumption of alcohol. All this changed once Dioralyte came on the market and could be purchased at Boots over the counter without a prescription. I remember on one occasion I finished a case in Manchester on a Friday morning, travelled back by train to London on Friday afternoon, flew to Hong Kong on Saturday morning, arriving on Sunday morning. I appeared in court on Monday morning in Hong Kong and then went to Kuala Lumpur, where I appeared in court on Wednesday. None of this would have been possible before Dioralyte.

I sat as a part-time judge for thirty-three years, the last nineteen of them as a Deputy High Court judge. During this time I was successfully appealed on only four occasions. The first was an appeal against sentence, the second was a case which went up to the House of Lords, the third was a case in which the relevant authority had not been cited to me and the fourth I can remember nothing about at all. However, there should really be added another case, about which I told the Malaysian judges when I was asked by the Chief Justice to give them a talk at their annual seminar in 1996 in Sarawak.

It was a point of construction, that is, deciding what a document meant. This sounds silly, and arises very seldom. On this occasion, it occurred because one of the parties had chosen to try to amalgamate two documents. This is more difficult than it might appear because if you put two documents together, you may find that clause such-and-such in document 1 conflicts with clause so-and-so in document 2, and thus it was in this case. Of course, none of these cases get to trial unless the decision rests on a knife edge. This was typical of its kind and with great difficulty I came to the conclusion which I duly delivered in court. Almost immediately afterwards, I concluded that my decision was wrong. There was nothing I could do about it and I said to myself, 'Well, that is what the Court of Appeal is for, to put judges right when they get it wrong. However,' I said, looking hard at the Chief Justice, who was sitting in the front row, 'then I thought to myself, but supposing the Court of Appeal gets it wrong and thinks that I am right?' The audience seemed to think this quite funny. However, the reality was even funnier. The case did go to the Court of Appeal, which decided that I was right but for the wrong reason. It did not end there. A few days later the QC who appeared for the successful party said to me that he thought that I was right for the reason which I gave, which I had concluded was wrong. After all that, it is a great pity that it did not go to the House of Lords, which would be able to determine which of these various views was correct – that is, if they did not think of another one for themselves.

The last case which I did before I retired was in the Court of Appeal in Trinidad. In order to be able to appear, I had to be admitted to the local Bar. My opponent moved my admission, which, of course, the Court of Appeal granted; the President went on to make a fulsome address to me, saying that he had heard that I was going to retire but he did hope that I would continue to write my books, and he ended up by wishing me success in my case. Of course, I had to respond to this and said that it was very good of him to say what he had, but I should point out that it was my opponent who had just moved my admission, and so possibly I ought not to say anything about his good wishes for my success. However, I said nothing about something which was much funnier, namely, that I had never written a book in my entire career. Later, I realised that he had mixed me up with a well-known academic called Fred Odgers.

I was due to become Treasurer of Lincoln's Inn in January 1998 but I had not intended to go on practising seriously after the conclusion of the George Tan case, which went on for much longer than I had expected. Meanwhile, between finishing Tan and my case in Trinidad in March 1997 I had really been pottering along doing nothing very much except sitting as a Deputy High Court judge. When I reached the age of seventy in 1996, I was informed by the Lord Chancellor's Office that there was now a new policy whereby Deputy High Court judges would not be allowed to go on beyond that age. This was a nuisance. I telephoned the Department and said that the only reason that I wanted to go on sitting was because I did not want to get out of touch by retiring before I became Treasurer. The person to whom I spoke was very sympathetic and said would I mind being a Deputy Official Referee, i.e. trying buildings cases. Since I had done a number of those during my career, I was quite happy to do this, and for a few months I continued to sit in that capacity.

However, theoretically one was only able to do that if one was a practising barrister. When I mentioned to my accountant that I intended to potter along from the 5 April 1997 to 1 January 1998 he had a severe attack of anxiety and pointed out that because of a change in the tax legislation the transitional provisions relating to the self-employed would mean that if I chose to do that I would have to pay a very large sum of money in additional tax to the Inland Revenue because of the large sums which I had earned during the Tan case. The figure which he mentioned was so large that I spent only a split second in deciding to retire very promptly on 5 April 1997 and fortunately he was able to get the Revenue to agree that, although technically I would remain as a practising barrister, they would not regard me as such provided I did nothing of that kind and only sat as a judge. It was very sensible of the Inland Revenue to agree to this because it meant I paid tax on my earnings as a judge, whereas had they refused to allow me to do it, I would not have earned anything and they would not have received any tax. Nevertheless, the Inland Revenue is not always very sensible and I was quite pleased when they agreed to do this. As a result I continued for a few months sitting in this capacity and this filled in the gap between my retirement and becoming Treasurer of the Inn.

In 1993, shortly after the George Tan case had begun, Malcolm Carver, the Under Treasurer of Lincoln's Inn, told me that it was my turn to join the Cursus, that is, the holders of offices, the top one of which was Treasurer of the Inn. In those days it was strictly a matter of Buggins' turn and apparently I had reached the point at which I was Buggins in that no one senior to me was eligible because of having passed the age limit. I had no wish to undertake this task and told Malcolm so, and thought that was the end of it. However, Lord Oliver, who was then Treasurer of the Inn, seized my arm in a steely grip, dragged me in to the Treasurer's room and stuck the list of Benchers in front of my nose saying, 'Michael, if you don't agree to take it on the next seven eligible Benchers are all judges.' The word 'duty' did not have to be uttered since it was being made obvious to me that it was expected that I would undertake the task as a matter of duty.

As I have said, at that time there were five steps in the Cursus, the first one of which was Master of the Walks, i.e. in charge of the Garden Committee. I knew nothing of gardening and left it all to the members of the committee and merely sat benignly at the top of the table while they discussed these all-important questions. I should add that one of the reforms which I achieved when I became Treasurer was to reduce the five offices to three by combining four of them into two offices. It seemed to me quite ludicrous that one should have to hold one of these offices for a total of five years and it was certainly something which did not apply in any of the other Inns. Of course, while I was conducting George's case I was so frequently out of the country that I was very often not able to preside at the various committee meetings which my various offices required me to do. However, no one seemed to worry about that and in due course in January 1998 I became Treasurer.

Despite having been press-ganged into this job, obviously, I did it to the best of my ability. It was plain to me that there were a number of reforms which needed to be undertaken, but, predictably, these proposals all met with fierce opposition from some of the more elderly Benchers. Without going into boring details, by the end of my year in office I had achieved all of them save one, namely that Buggins' turn should no longer apply to Treasurer. (However, I succeeded in getting that through in the following year when I had become Past Treasurer, because the committee I had set up to consider it reported in favour.)

There was a great deal of work involved in being Treasurer. Once upon a time it had been largely a formal affair requiring the

Treasurer to make speeches on social occasions. This was a part I really did not care for, and indeed I had to attend a very large number of social functions during the year. The really hard work did not come amiss because in effect one was in the job of chairman of a public company for a year, the Under Treasurer being the senior executive. I was very fortunate in the Treasurers of the other Inns. I had known all of them since my earliest days at the Bar and got on well with them, and with the Chairman of the Bar, who was married to someone in our chambers. Indeed, at the first meeting of the Council of the Inns of Court, which was the governing body of the profession in the sense that it was where the four Inns and the Bar Council met monthly in order to determine common positions about various problems, at the first meeting after I had been kissed by the Chairman of the Bar, the first woman to hold the job, and also by the female Treasurer of another Inn, the Under Treasurer said that he was sure that it was going to be a good year because he was confident that no previous Treasurer had ever been kissed by two members of COIC!

I was very fortunate in the Under Treasurer. Malcolm Carver had retired six months before I took on the job and David Hills had taken over from him. The selection committee, of which I was a member, was itself a daunting process. We had over three hundred and fifty applications, mainly from Service people varying in rank from Major General and Air Vice Marshal down to Major. Of course, a great many were weeded out immediately, but that left us with about forty who were serious candidates. Eventually we reduced these to a short list of five and David was unanimously chosen. Fortunately, he picked up the job very quickly and we got on well together.

A great deal of the work involved students. I found this particularly tiring. At a dinner for students, of which there were many up and down the country as well as in the Inn, always they would ask the same questions. The fact that they were intelligent questions didn't make them any the less boring if one had been asked them many times before. Before I became Treasurer I had decided that the Common Law Bar was insufficiently represented in the Inn, and particularly those who came from the provinces. I set about altering this and I visited no less than eight provincial cities where, in addition to dining with local members of the Bar who belonged to the Inn, I harangued law students at the local universities. This was very interesting. I took with me the Under Treasurer, the Deputy Under Treasurer responsible for education, a member of the Bar representation committee, namely a young man who was not a QC, and sat at a table together with one or more members of the local Bar who were members of the Inn. Invariably, I started with a very short speech of about five minutes discouraging people who were not outstandingly clever from attempting to go into commercial or chancery chambers and the like since their prospects of being accepted were very small and they would reduce their chance of getting in to common law chambers. After that we had a question-and-answer session which never lasted for less than an hour and always came to an end because of want of time. One hour is a very long time indeed for a question-and-answer session and indicates how very useful they were.

In due course this paid off in a remarkable way so far as recruitment were concerned. We found that all sorts of people from all over the country were joining the Inn, obviously because we had taken the trouble to go and talk to them, and of course I had ended with a small speech indicating that they should come and have a look at all of the Inns but I had no doubt that they would find ours was by far and away the best. I think that they felt that they had found people who were interested in them and prepared to put themselves out, and all knew in particular the Deputy Under Treasurer responsible for education. Our recruitment figures increased by an enormous amount and in the year after I had finished we recruited more people than two other Inns together.

It would be tiresome to go through the events which occurred during my year as Treasurer; suffice it to say that it was so busy that it could easily have been turned into a full-time job. It also put a great strain upon my liver and my waistline. Fortunately, we got through the year without any terrible catastrophe and afterwards a number of people were kind enough to tell me how well they thought that I had done the job.

After my year of office I became Past Treasurer – a post which required little, if any, work, save to attend Council meetings and sit on the Treasurer's right and be prepared to take over from him should he fall ill. Fortunately, this did not happen during his year of office but, unfortunately, during the subsequent year when he was Past Treasurer he died. Consequently, I had to spend a further six months in the job of Past Treasurer.

The year 1998 also saw the culmination of my efforts relating to actuarial tables for use in personal injury and fatal accident cases. Although in 1995 the Civil Evidence Act had contained provision that the tables could be produced and without any proof of their correctness be used in evidence, courts were very reluctant to use them. However, in July 1998 a case finally reached the House of Lords which overturned a ridiculous decision of the Court of Appeal and ordered that all courts were to use the Ogden Tables in personal injury and fatal accident cases. This was followed by my being elected an Honorary Fellow of the Institute of Actuaries. I regarded it as a great honour to be elected a member of another profession.

This was in marked contrast to the Institute of Chartered Accountants, which had asked me to be Chairman of their Disciplinary Appeal Committee for five years. Although paid, it was in the nature of *pro bono publico* work. In the course of it, I persuaded them to re-draft the Rules, which were in a mess, and I arranged for Sir George Engle, a former First Parliamentary Counsel, to do it. At the end of my stint, I did not even receive a letter of thanks.

At this point, being seventy-two, it seemed respectable to retire completely, which I did.

EPILOGUE

While it would be dishonest to suggest that I enjoyed every minute of my time at the Bar, it is fair to say that I enjoyed nearly all of it. Certainly, it was the right career for me. It would have had to have been a very tolerant employer who would have put up with me. What made things more fun for me was that, unlike most barristers, who spend their entire professional career in court and usually only in one area, e.g. London or the North Eastern Circuit, chance led me to do other things as well. Very few people had the opportunity to do work in the Far East over a period of years, which was not only most interesting but also very remunerative. Furthermore, barristers seldom run anything, and it was extremely interesting to be put in charge of the Criminal Injuries Compensation Board, which, although very small, was in fact a Government department, and for a barrister to run a Government department part-time was great fun. Altogether, I regarded my career as very satisfactory and most enjoyable.

Although I have said little about my family, it made a great difference that we were a happy family and I am very grateful to all of them, particularly Joan.

APPENDIX

LETTER TO THE LORD CHIEF JUSTICE

How I came to write this letter I cannot remember. I suspect that I had complained to him and was asked to put it in writing. I have not kept the answer, which I would have expected to be an acknowledgement of receipt without comment.

I have printed it, with one small omission, because it is interesting twenty years later to see the extent to which my complaints and suggestions have been met; in my view, not much about crime, but most in civil cases.

14 September 1981

Dear Chief Justice,

Speeding up Trials

Crime

In most cases there should be no need for an opening speech for the prosecution. They have no opening speeches in Scotland in criminal cases. My Scots friends concede that this is unsatisfactory in frauds and other complex cases. But in simple cases (?90%) there seems no reason why the victim should not be put straight into the box to give evidence. If the Judges said that opening speeches should be made only in Class I cases or by leave of the Judge, this ought to work. One could always try it out in some pilot Courts.

Pre-trial reviews are of value only if all parties are represented by Counsel instructed to appear at trial and if two

Counsel are instructed, that the Leader is present. A substitute or second Counsel never feels that he has authority to do anything worthwhile and in the case of a substitute cannot be expected to know as much about the case as Counsel holding the brief, who, in such a case, is likely to have had a Conference. It is very difficult to ensure that all the right people are present, especially if the Court is out of London (or, I suppose, other large cities). When prosecuting, I have resorted to asking taxing officers whether, if I assemble all Counsel in my room in Chambers, he will allow a fee equivalent to that allowed on a pre-trial review. This has invariably been agreed to and all such meetings have achieved as much as any pre-trial review could do and, usually, more, because every one attends and, in the privacy of one's own room, one can persuade people not to be silly. This is more difficult outside or inside a Court. Furthermore, when it comes to agreeing bundles of documents, this requires space and time. I know that other Silks adopt this practice and I think that it should be more widely adopted.

When I sit on the Criminal Injuries Compensation Board, I read summings-up in cases in which there have been acquittals. Unfortunately it is often possible to guess that this happened, at least partly, because the summing-up was too long and muddled. Obviously one gets this in cases in which there are convictions but it has certainly struck me very forcibly when I try to guess why a patently guilty man was acquitted. (I should add in passing that recurrent use of the phrase 'Now, Members of the Jury...' has a positively soporific effect on me, especially since shorthand writers take it as a signal to start a new paragraph.) If people who have difficulty in giving succinct directions concerning the law involved could be encouraged to write them down during closing speeches and then to read them out without elaboration, which is often what causes the trouble, a lot of difficulties could be avoided.

It is generally regarded as 'safe', so far as being appealed is concerned, simply to read out most of what all the more important witnesses have said. I do not believe that this helps a Jury in a simple case as much as simply reading the parts of the evidence that really matter. There is usually ample time to mark such passages during closing speeches.

It is apparent that in many places inadequate attention is paid to selecting the right Judge for a particular case. A Judge who is excellent when trying cases other than complex frauds may be less satisfactory when trying such frauds, sometimes with catastrophic results when called upon to do so. The reverse is also true. This would seem to be a problem which should be resolved by Presiding Judges of Circuits.

I say nothing about over-indicting, eliminating 'fringe' people as defendants, prosecuting in trivial cases, failing to accept reasonable pleas because the Police want their pound of flesh, dispensing with unnecessary witnesses and documents, failing to agree documents and evidence and prolix speeches because the problems are well-known to you and there is nothing that I can usefully say.

There are two aspects concerning fees which are important. First, I consider it unfortunate that the most important considerations in the eyes of taxing officers when deciding upon a brief fee are the number of pages of depositions and exhibits, the number of witnesses and the length of time that a Barrister says that it has taken to prepare for trial. Of course, I do not say that these factors are not important but they are adhered to too slavishly, especially the alleged length of time to prepare for trial. It is a state of affairs which favours the lazy, the slow, and the inept and penalises those who work quickly and competently. The other side of the coin is that derisory fees continue to be paid for pre-trial advices, consultations, etc., especially consultations held in Prisons. For obvious reasons, such pre-trial work should be encouraged; at present, it is positively discouraged. Again, it is competence and integrity which is penalised.

Second, I regard it as unfortunate that fees paid to Silks should be lower than in all other types of work with which I am familiar. Since I was responsible for fee negotiations on behalf of the Bar Council from 1970 to 1972 and have a widely based practice, I have a fair idea of levels of fees generally.

The result of this is that competent Silks with mixed practices avoid, or their Clerks do it, criminal cases in preference for civil. This is particularly important so far as long, complex frauds are concerned. Outside London most Silks have mixed practices. The consequences are obvious.

Civil Actions

The bulk of the work being personal injury work, it is here that one can achieve most. In spite of predictions to the contrary, the requirement that experts' reports be exchanged before trial works well. I would like to see it extended to witnesses' proofs of evidence. I consider that this would also lead to more settlements. I would couple this with abolition of examination in chief in such cases and go straight to cross examination. This would be similar to the Chancery practice of cross examination on the Affidavits. I would add to this abolition of opening speeches, coupled with split trials in all such cases, unless the parties agree otherwise, e.g. because doctors have to be called; the issue of damages would be tried immediately after the issue of liability.

We have evolved this system on the Criminal Injuries Compensation Board. We have read all the papers. We know the Applicant's story. We start with cross-examination of the Applicant. We consider that it works well. Since I appreciate that my proposals would be regarded by some as revolutionary and impracticable, I would add that anyone who wants to watch proceedings conducted by the Board has only to ask me. Most of our cases are very simple but some are as complex as any personal injury case and we get through them far quicker than any Court; this applies to both liability and quantum but is particularly obvious in the latter.

If not all of the above suggestions are acceptable, I hope that some may be.

Again, judgments in simple cases are often too long. In the past, judgments on Circuit tended to be shorter than those in London. I do not now go on Circuit very often but I get the impression that this is no longer the case. If shorter judgments in simple cases could be encouraged by the Court of Appeal and reinforced by the Court of Appeal itself setting the example, I am sure that a great deal of time could be saved.

Generally

None of the above would require legislation; some would require amendments of the R.S.C.*

While there are a number of alterations requiring legislation which I would like to see, there is one only which I consider I should mention here.

It has always been an acceptable ground for imposing a lesser penalty in criminal cases that the Defendant has pleaded guilty, thereby saving public time and money and not putting prosecution witnesses to varying degrees of inconvenience or embarrassment. It used to be a useful point to be put to a Defendant by his Counsel. I have a feeling that it is less so today. I get the impression that fewer Judges say so when sentencing people who have pleaded guilty and that some Defendants feel that some of those that do say so have paid only lip service to the principle.

I would like to see a statutory percentage reduction in sentence provided for in such cases.

Although so far as I know no one has ever criticised the principle, I recognise that to enshrine it in a Statute would provoke an outburst of complaint. I consider that this is something to be borne with fortitude in the knowledge that it will save time and money both in the Courts and in the Prisons.

Of course this could not apply in the case of indeterminate sentences, e.g. Borstal. However, I consider that the aim could be achieved in such cases by instructing Borstal authorities, etc., to act in a way which would make it apparent that a plea of guilty would result in less time in custody.

There is one 'P.R.' suggestion which I would like to make about the application of the proviso. I get the impression that there is a lack of understanding at the Bar about the general considerations applying to the subject, certainly among younger barristers. I think that it would help if it could be said fairly forcefully in some case that will get into *The Times*' Law Reports that the proviso will be applied unless there is a real risk that injustice might have occurred.

*Rules of the Supreme Court.

Personally I would advocate application of the proviso more frequently than has been the case in recent years. It may be said that there are miscarriages of justice as it is and that a tougher line would add to them. I do not believe that this would be so. I act as Assessor for the Home Secretary in all cases in England and Wales in which he decides that compensation should be paid for wrongful imprisonment: I cannot recollect any such case in which the nature of the application of the proviso played any part.

I do not mind who sees this document, if you consider it worth some-one else seeing it. However, since it seemed to me to be a useless venture unless I was prepared to be utterly frank and outspoken. I would be grateful if any distribution could be on a basis of confidentiality.

Yours sincerely

(Michael Ogden)